GOING
WIRELESS

GOING WIRELESS

Transform Your Business

with Mobile Technology

JACLYN EASTON

HarperBusiness
An Imprint of HarperCollins*Publishers*

HarperCollins books may be purchased for educational, business, or sales
promotional use. For information please write: Special Markets Department,
HarperCollins Publishers, Inc., 10 East 53rd Street,
New York, NY 10022.

FIRST EDITION

Designed by JoAnne Metsch

Printed on acid-free paper

Library of Congress Cataloging-in-Publication Data

Easton, Jaclyn, 1961–
Going wireless : transform your business with mobile technology / Jaclyn Easton.
p. cm.
ISBN 0-06-621336-3
1. Electronic commerce.   2. Cellular telephones.   3. Internet.   4. Wireless
communication systems.   5. Information technology.   I. Title.

HF5548.32 .E1882 2002
658'.05467—dc21
2001039686

02 03 04 05 06 \RRD 10 9 8 7 6 5 4 3 2 1

*This book is dedicated to the loving memory of my
technologically challenged very dear friend, Judith Rosenthal,
who would have been incredibly flattered . . .
and completely bewildered.*

Acknowledgments

To all the agents of the Leigh Speakers Bureau, particularly Danny Stern, Wes Neff, and Michael J. Humphrey, for being gems in a business where such jewels are rare.

To my mother and father, Nina Lamb and Jac Holzman, who have been truly wonderful parents in the most unusual of ways. I love both you very much.

To my remarkable friends: Robert Casady, Jeannine "JP" Parker, Leah Gentry, Sara Davidson, Paige Grant, Adora English and David Avalos, Ramey Warren Black, Mike Greenly, Bob and Kathy Levitan, Luanne O'Loughlin, and Bobbie Rose. Special thanks to Steve Wolk for the guidance.

To Jack Chipman and Carrie Wolf Carlisi with everlasting gratitude for decades of best-friendship.

To my grandmother Iris Merrrick whose lessons taught were realized upon her death. And to Evelyn Sumida for her legacy of love and understanding.

To the restorative powers of Maria Abreu, M.D., "St. Barbara" Voight, M.M. "Matt" Van Benschoten, Steven Jarsky, Patrick Butcher, and Feline G. Butcher.

To my sages: Kate O'Sullivan, Fredric Lehrman, and Jeanne Holbrook.

To my brothers, Adam Holzman and Marin Sander-Holzman, my sister-in-law Jane Getter, and my sweet nephew Russell Getter Holzman; my aunts, Joyce Benioff, Kathryn Gelbman, and Susan "Me'irah" Iliinsky. My cousins (who I adore but rarely get to see): Sarah Gelbman, Matthew Gelbman, Noah Iliinsky, and Alex Iliinsky. Love always to Stepdad Kirk Lamb.

To the following HarperCollins people: David Conti, Knox Huston, Amanda Maciel, Erin Richnow, Diane Aronson. Extra kudos to Lisa Berkowitz and Kate Kazeniac.

I'd like to single out the following media relations executives who were particualry responsive to my endless and in-depth requests: Kathie Lee Anderson, Tom Potts, Melanie Morrison Stone, Bridget Fulton-Cook, Michelle R. Greene, Karen Logsdon, Ross Perich, Sabrina Chambosse, Thayer Scott, Marci Gottlieb and Harley Elizabeth Ungar.

Long overdue thanks to Scott Turow.

And finally profound gratitude to the Siddha Yoga Meditation lineage.

Contents

GOING
WIRELESS

Introduction:

Your Wireless Future

Wireless is a huge whale floating just beneath the surface.
All people are seeing is the tail fluke. But one day it's going to breach,
and everyone is going to be surprised at the size of it.

—David Hughes, 1970s computer maven

THIS IS NOT a book about technology.

It's a book about empowerment. It's a book about liberation. It's a book about the information revolution we were promised in 1994 when the Internet pledged access to data for all.

But what was positioned as a revolution felt more like servitude. In exchange for access to these silos of information was the need to be strapped to a computer and a wired phone line. Consequently, as we became more dependent on this seductive conduit of communication, we also became more bound to the technology providing it, thus tethering ourselves to monitors, keyboards, and dial tones.

Something was missing. Ah, right. Our independence.

At the risk of sounding like a Chinese proverb, a map does you no good if it sits on your desk while you are lost 10 miles away. That's precisely the solution that mobile technology provides.

Wireless is salvation in two words. Anytime. Anywhere.

So if it sounds like hype, I understand. The speculation is sky-rise high, and as *Fast Company* senior editor George Anders once wrote, "Mention the words *wireless Internet* . . . and it's as if you shouted, 'Free beer' at a fraternity party."

The reality is that wireless is not the next technology gold rush. It's a quiet transformation that has been progressing for years, because, as you will learn in a moment, it's not just about cell phones and Palm-Pilots. There's much, much more to it.

DISPELLING THE INTERNATIONAL MYTH

Before I can tell you about the wonderful wireless world ahead of us, it's important to respond to the most popular belief about mobile technology in other parts of the world.

By now you've been told that the rest of the universe is wirelessly way ahead of the United States. In fact, if you believe the insane headlines about how far behind we are compared to Europe and Asia, you might actually think that the folks in the Netherlands have surgically attached their cell phones to their bodies and that the Japanese are molecularly beaming pizza to themselves using their iMode handsets.

(While these examples are obviously nonsense, what is true, however, is that the Bishops Conference did order all mobile phone transmitters dangling from church tower masts in Italy be removed.)

You see, it's not that the rest of the world is so far ahead wirelessly, it is that the people in these regions use their cell phones a lot more than we do. In many of these countries cell phones are equal to or less expensive than landlines (keep in mind, too, that less than 50 percent of the world's households have any type of phone service), and because prepaid service is the norm outside the United States, anyone can get a mobile phone without credit checks or service contracts.

But the biggest slice of the pie is that there was agreement on a standard of how the phones would work. By doing this, Europeans could roam from country to country and stay connected. Many in the United States can't traverse their own city without losing a conversation.

This was possible because Europeans agreed early on to a standard called GSM (global system for mobile) communications for network compatibility. In addition to a universal standard, there is another nifty feature of GSM that lets users send text messages to one another over their mobile phones.

It is called SMS (short message service), and it works by letting users type a few sentences on their cell phone's keypad (cumbersome, redefined). The message then instantly appears on the handset of the recipient. If you have ever used AOL Instant Messaging, Yahoo! Messenger, or ICQ on your desktop computer, you've had a similar experience, only in this case it is happening through cell phones.

What's so appealing about SMS messages is that they are incredibly quick to send as well as cheap, a fraction of the cost of a phone call.

The only limitation is that these quickie missives are limited to 160 characters or less.

Now here's where it gets interesting. Even though SMS works like the messaging systems we are accustomed to accessing via the Web, SMS actually has nothing to do with the Internet. What happens is that these 160-character packets of information ride alongside voice data on the same pipe. You could think of the voice data like a car driving down the highway and the SMS message hopping on the tailgate. This is another myth exploded because the Europeans' use is basically voice cellular, not wireless, Internet access.

Now, Japan is different because they are using the wireless Internet. It's the style in usage that is different. European users are more plugged in to communicating via voice and SMS, while the Japanese system is far more sophisticated and, interestingly, despite the additional power to communicate, much more of a source of entertainment.

These iMode devices are sleek, with vivid LCD displays that can download images as fast as any standard wired connections in U.S. homes. Appropriately, given the smallness of the units, the Japanese use them to chat, play, and read the news. Just about everything but commerce . . . for now.

While the Japanese amuse themselves on their train commutes with their iMode technology, Americans are behind the wheel, talking instead of tapping. In other words, our cultures are both equally dependent but using the devices in different ways. This, however, should not distract from the iMode's overwhelming popularity. Compare the 10 years it took AOL to reach 20 million subscribers to the less than 24 months in which iMode accomplished the same.

The biggest difference, however, between the United States and Japan is how the users were first introduced to the Internet. Most Americans sat in front of big, comfy desktop systems with large monitors and full-size keyboards. Now when they see a four-line monochrome display on a cell handset you can register the disappointment, and this is part of the reason that the wireless Web is gaining ground more slowly in the United States than expected. Keep in mind, however, that attractive interfaces have historically lagged behind the technology, so this also is a soon-to-be-moot point.

That said, for people living in Japan, where home connections are scarce, their first experience of iMode is just like our first experience of the desktop Internet. It is inspiring as you consider the phenomenal communications and data opportunities available.

Speaking of home connnections, another reason for the perception that we are behind is that our landlines are comparatively quite good.

Even though our infrastructure is far from perfect, it remains one of the best in the world. Our challenge now is that the increase in competition and a continuing lack of standards are delaying wireless's ultimate potential, though it continues to progress steadily.

On a final note to eliminate the misnomer about the United States being "behind" the rest of the world, let me add that statistically the United States has more mobile phone users than any other country in the world, with over 100 million (we began in 1978 with 2,000). Japan is second at about 55 percent of the U.S. numbers.

People love to quote statistics about the Finns because of their 65 percent cell phone penetration, but Finland has only about 6 million residents. These numbers hardly represent any significant dynamics.

So, given all of the above, here's the first note you want to highlight: Nothing in wireless is what it seems.

THE BIG SECRET ABOUT WIRELESS

The phrase *wireless* generally conjures one of two images: a cell phone or a personal digital assistant (PDA) such as a PalmPilot. The reality is that half the wireless installations in business will come from technology you've never heard of.

Have you ever waved a Speedpass wand to buy gas at a Mobil station? That's wireless. Did you ever rent a car with a global positioning system (GPS) giving you directions as you drove? Did you know that the clothing manufacturers are now sewing wireless technology into garments to track the item through both the supply chain and the retail chain?

Wireless not only picks up where the wired Internet left off by being able to "take it with you," it is also the bridge to pervasive computing, which is about computers being in everything and all those things being connected to the Net.

For example, these days most high-end machinery is being equipped with diagnostic chips that can remotely, using cellular-enabled chipsets, contact a service center when repairs are required—all without human intervention.

When you hear of these examples, you realize that we are being distracted by the hype of wireless and mass consumers. The less obvious but more valuable nugget is in the metamorphosis of business processes from which companies are saving astronomical sums and finding themselves ridiculously competitive. This isn't conjecture. This is fact. And you are about to read dozens of success stories to show you how to do this, too. What you will see is that wireless is infiltrating every business in the American economy.

What makes Internet-enabled cell phones important with respect to the wireless future is their ability to solve the fiscal problem of equipping all employees with a laptop so they can stay in touch when out of the office. Now the problem is solved because of the economics of mobile devices, meaning that every employee, from executives to delivery drivers, can remain in the corporate loop.

The other motivation benefit is that wireless Internet connectivity extends the value of the original technology investment. This is particularly true for intranets. Now, for just a few hundred dollars per employee, a company can get a few hundred percent more use from their back-end technology because it is being accessed so much more. Remember, no matter how current or powerful the computer is on the employee's desktop, the moment the employee steps away, it has no value.

WHAT THIS BOOK IS ABOUT

All of this brings us to the structure of what you are about to read. There are two ways to examine wireless. The first section is about wireless "externally," using it to service customers and clients, whether the paradigm is retailing or business-to-business sales. There is where you learn about how m-commerce shines and customer service gets redefined.

Appropriately, this is followed by a corresponding section on the practical business solutions wireless is supplying today "internally." Perhaps the best part is that you'll not only learn exactly which business applications are saving the most money and adding the most productivity, but in place of superfluous prediction, you'll be reading stories of wireless successes that prove it.

Finally, I'd like to backtrack to the opening quote about how wireless is like a submerged whale and associate it with a thought from computer pioneer Alan Kay so that you have an idea of how this all fits together.

Kay believes that world-changing inventions, such as wireless, begin disguised as an improvement on old things. He says, "After 50 years the computer is still masquerading as better paper, but now we are transitioning into what computers and networks are really all about: entirely new ways to communicate, do business, organize politically, think, and live."

Now consider how wireless Internet access is masquerading as a clunky interface with comparatively slow connections. For this reason,

it is an inferior way to access the Internet, similar to the computer act-
ing like "better paper." As interface issues resolve, I guarantee you wireless will become the preferred method of Internet access and hence a
world-changing invention.

It's an easy assumption. Wireless gives the Internet everything we
have now plus an entirely new functionality (for example two-way
color video cell phones), in addition to the anytime, anywhere, advantage; both of which are extraordinarily beneficial to business and mass
consumers.

We need to remember that the Internet began as a computer-to-
computer communication only. Now with wireless it is becoming an
intermediary among dozens of different types of mobile technologies,
whether communicating from handheld to handheld, car to GPS satellite, or magic payment wands waved in front of gas pumps.

The result is that this will give us thousands of points of connectivity.
And when we are a thousand times more connected, we are thousand
times more effective.

Section 1

■

USING M-COMMERCE

TO OWN YOUR

CUSTOMERS AND

CLIENTS

Using M-Commerce to Own Your Customers and Clients

I BELIEVE ALL PROFESSIONALS have a universal goal: to make the most amount of money for the least amount of work.

There's a caveat here, because "least amount of work" is not an ethical issue. It's about doing what you love most, because doing what you love is not work. So the goal, then, is to eliminate the mundane and have fun.

Wireless can do that.

Promises, promises. Perhaps. But I pride myself on underpromising and overdelivering, which means you should prepare yourself for some well-appreciated surprises—strategies that use mobile technology to easily acquire more customers and irresistibly educate them about what you offer. It's also about providing a level of service you never could before.

One of wireless's secrets is its uncanny ability to let you connect with new customers and clients with a refreshing depth that results in bonds that would normally take years—but is accomplished in months. Even more important, customers will demand the attention as they become more active in their buying decisions and therefore are going to want more options.

In practical terms, this means that to compete, you'll be beaming them, ringing them, and messaging them constantly, and they will love it and in fact have specifically asked you to do it. This will make more sense to you shortly.

Naturally, wireless technology is about not just facilitating field sales, but also radically improving retailing. Whether it's eliminating checkout lines (no joke), providing a way for your customers to pay for goods in two seconds or less, or even allowing them access to a database of inventory so they can determine not only if you have the product they want, but how much is on hand and in which area of the store they can find it. How would that improve your employees' performance when they are not being distracted constantly by distressed customers?

Wireless will also have an equally substantial effect on Internet commerce. In fact, remember when it was just e-commerce? Well, you are about to meet its siblings, m-, l-, and v-. With the aid of wireless you'll be making sales mobilely (m-commerce), sometimes even based on location (l-commerce), or by having your customer interface with your automation in a natural speaking voice (v-commerce), all because of the advances gained from mobile devices and their high-value proposition of anytime, anywhere, Internet access.

The overall benefit may best be described by Gartner Group analyst Bob Egan, who declares that "wireless is the growth hormone for e-commerce."

This is how. . . .

1

Defining the M-Commerce Opportunity

"IT'S GOING TO be the most fantastic thing the time-starved world has ever seen."

Hyperbole? Not to Jeff Bezos, Amazon.com's chief executive, who voiced this statement. In fact, he'll take his prognostication a step further by declaring that by 2010, *100 percent* of his company's transactions will take place wirelessly.

Amazon.com boarded the mobile bandwagon in late 1999, about the same time as rival barnesandnoble.com. While the mobile wing of bn.com has been quoted as saying that sales are exceeding their projections, no one is yet discussing actual metrics—the who, what, where, why, and how, including specific revenue figures. Nonetheless, we are starting to get hints, and some of the behavior is a little surprising.

For example, Amazon.com's biggest sellers via wireless connectivity are not books, but music—the pop and R&B genres, to be exact. And, yes, people have purchased large-screen TVs and equally expensive digital camcorders while on the go. Fittingly, Amazon.com's "Amazon Anywhere" platform is delivering on the anywhere part with purchases from dozens of countries, including Peru, Algeria, and Malaysia.

So what does this data tell us? That mobile commerce (m-commerce) may be about commerce on the go, but how it is adapted, who adapts it, and exactly how it fits into a bigger commerce picture remains a mystery.

As you can see already, defining the term *m-commerce* is equally mystifying, as we consider the various models that fit under the mobile commerce banner.

The first one up is most associated with the phrase. It's transactional mobile commerce, meaning you will buy a thing or service entirely through a wireless device. Because of the screen and speed limitations

of the mobile units being used to transact, in most cases you will sign
up using a traditional interface—big monitor and keyboard—to prepare
an account for use on the go. The information supplied includes your
preferred delivery address for goods and the credit card you want to
use so that it takes a minimal amount of time. Amazon.com's 1-Click is
a perfect example. Also, look for electronic wallets to be used across a
bevy of commerce sites that offer this simplicity.

Building on this m-commerce model, we will see mobile fulfillment as
part of the transactional process. You can buy a movie ticket, and a bar
code representing the paper ticket would be downloaded to your device
and scanned as you enter the theater. A similar scenario holds true for
entertainment. You'll buy a book, a song, or a game and it will download automatically to your wireless device. Amazon.com, for example, is
already set up on their main site for the downloading of e-books and
music, so expect them to be one of the first in wireless as well.

ADULT ENTERTAINMENT SETS THE TREND, AGAIN

However, if we are being candid, the unspoken forerunner in the arena
of full-circle m-commerce experiences—purchase and fulfillment—is
adult entertainment, which has a history of legitimizing technology dating back to the introduction of the VCR in 1970s and 1980s and business
models such as renting entertainment.

In the online world, we saw Web sites for adults perfecting technologies that would mainstream later, such as real-time credit processing,
live Web video, and advanced advertising techniques like those annoying pop-up boxes.

Now add to the technology picture the fact that adult-only entertainment is one of e-commerce's biggest success stories (over $1 billion
annually), and you see how quickly wireless is being adapted.

Why is this? Not only is there high demand for the content, but the people who consume it are indicative of the first-phase, m-commerce users:
young men who are early technology adopters. When they were the first
users of the Net, the most popular phrase submitted for searches was
"sex." Now that the genders and ages have balanced in online usage, "sex"
places a mere third on the Internet search top 10, the first being "travel."

When you consider the degree to which wireless devices offer privacy
and discretion that is not possible with laptops and desktops, you have
a better understanding of how even more explosive adult entertainment
can be in mobile, once the technologies to support it are perfected.

In the meantime, the choice of sites is proliferating. The world's first adult entertainment portal for PDAs was SinPalm.com, a free site supported by advertising that allows users to download risqué stories and photographs to their handheld devices. Kathryn Hudson, co-founder of the site with her husband, explains that SinPalm.com is cherished by executives who read the stories during unbearably boring meetings. It helps them take "their focus off of work and their hectic lives," says Hudson.

On the other end of the adult spectrum, the Hudsons have launched an industry first, a dating service for handhelds called PocketPersonals.com, whose slogan is "Love is in the air—everywhere."

While the Hudsons adult business ventures are entrepreneurial, the biggest producers of adult entertainment are also tuning in to the wireless wavelength. *Penthouse* magazine, for example, offers centerfold photos for downloading to handheld devices. The decision to repurpose their content was an easy one for the magazine. "There is a huge demand," a *Penthouse* spokesperson confesses. "People are saying that now they can take *Penthouse* to the beach. Yes, I know they've always been able to take *Penthouse* to the beach, but this way it is a lot more discreet."

BETTING ON M-COMMERCE

Content complementary with these adult offerings is wireless gambling. If discretion and privacy are the benefits of wireless to "red light" content, then the watchword for mobile wagering is "convenience."

Anyone in Germany can easily play lotto with their cell phones. Eurobet, one of the world's largest Internet sports betting emporiums, offers mobile gambling with exceptional precision and sophistication. You can wager on just about any sport, including the Super Bowl, with a few taps on your wirelessly connected portable device.

The advantages are summed up perfectly by Mark Balestra of eGamingWire.com: "If you thought it was impressive that you could place a wager via the Internet on a sporting event from the comfort of your home, wait until you place a wager from a seat in the venue where the event is taking place." He also points out that the three largest sports bookmakers (Coral's Eurobet, William Hill, and Ladrokes) have all launched mobile initiatives that allow betting from virtually any wireless device.

Before we see wireless gambling with any velocity, the legal issues must be cleared. This is another case in which the legalities of the wired Internet have followed the mobile one. The issue of which laws govern, the state where the gambling is being processed (where the Web site operates) or if the government from where the bets are originating prevails. If, when the legalities are resolved, we must adhere to the laws of the state in which the gambling site does business, then look to the cellular carriers to be providing the push for mobile wagering. Again, using the wired Net as precedent, most wireless experts agree that incremental billing—paying for each minute that you use your mobile phone—will, in the area of stiff competition, eventually yield to some form of a flat rate. Though the carriers may deny this now, recall the mid-1990s, when America Online's Steve Case swore that under no circumstance would AOL ever offer a single monthly fee.

For this reason, operators are going to have to make up for their huge dip in profits, and since gambling is one of the many ways to do that, it is therefore predicted as one of m-commerce's highest revenue generators.

Despite the predictable allure and profitability of mobile wagering and adult entertainment, one question remains unanswered: When will this happen? It's an educational process, but look for the big leap at the point that people think of their cell phone as a device capable of more than making calls, or are highly motivated for the content or services that are available exclusively for handhelds. Then factor in spiffier devices (larger displays in color) and faster connectivity, and the convergence will most certainly hasten the inevitable m-commerce explosion.

PAY AND PICK UP

While people associate m-commerce with being online for both shopping and purchasing, we will find that in reality the model we use most will be closer to a "click-and-mortar" paradigm, where wireless devices lead to an offline sale either through information supplied wirelessly or by processing payment for an order that will be fulfilled offline.

A perfect example (ironically) comes from a chain of 1950s-style diners specializing in burgers and fries, who are blending wireless technology with their retro decor. The restaurant is called Johnny Rockets, and they have 150 outlets in 28 states and 8 countries.

Using the mobile commerce gateway go2 (discussed in detail on page 25), customers can find a Johnny Rockets, place their order, and even pay for it, all from their wireless device. The benefits are equally enormous for both the customer and the restaurant chain. Logging on to Johnny Rockets's wireless interface means they are ordering from a current menu with current prices. Cross-sells are included. Order only a burger—heaven forbid—and a screen suggesting fries or a drink is displayed (see accompanying figures).

Payment information is handled ahead of time when the customer registers on the go2 site, so in the wireless environment the customer needs only to tap once to confirm the credit card in use. The prepayment feature is a must for restaurants that need a guarantee to eliminate the risk of an orphaned order.

After the order is submitted, a confirmation code is supplied that is used to validate the pickup. The entire order process takes less than a minute, and repeat customers who set up a standard order can complete the process in mere seconds. Speed is one of the motivating factors for regular Johnny Rockets customers—that and ease, such as not having to stand in line to pay and the opportunity to avoid the kinds of miscommunications that occur when placing an order over a cell phone.

Johnny Rockets is by definition a "casual dining chain," but wireless gives them such an advantage timewise that they can be competitive with the fast-food franchises. The even better news is that the cost to compete is less than what you might think. According to go2, integrating with an existing point of sale (POS) system generally runs under $10,000.

GOING ONCE . . .

While on-the-go dining certainly meshes with the two primary benefits of wireless, anytime and anywhere, it is for this reason that auctions, which are defined by urgency and availability, are such a perfect fit with wireless and another example of the empowerment of m-commerce.

eBay and Amazon.com auctions both have wireless initiatives, with eBay's understandably far more robust since it's their core business. eBay's mobile game plan began in late 1999 with a service that alerted customers via their pagers and cell phones when they were outbid. The problem is that while an alert was quickly dispatched, eBay wasn't yet supporting technology to allow alert recipients to respond with a higher bid, which meant they had to scramble to get to a PC. For this reason, the service quickly grew to include virtually all the functionality of what we could think of as "wired eBay" when they debuted "eBay Anywhere."

The Click Sequence to Place a
Johnny Rockets' Order from a Cell Phone

Main Menu
>1. Order Now
2. Menu Info
3. Location
4. About

Go   Cancel

Beginning the ordering process.

Order Now
>1. Hamburgers
2. Sandwiches
3. Sides
4. Drinks

Pick   Done

Choose the category.

Hamburgers
>1. Original
2. Double
3. Bacon Swiss
4. Sourdough

Pick   Menu

Choose the type of hamburger.

I want
1.*Cheddar 50¢
2.*No Mayo
3. No Mustard
4. No Pickle

Go   Cancel

Handling the extras.

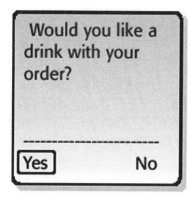

Here's the cross-sell.

Placing your order.

Confirming your order.

Receiving your pickup ID.

Providing wireless connectivity was a great start, but making sure it worked for everyone was just as important. Given the tenacious relationship eBay users have with the service, the person-to-person trading community had to be sure that their wireless course was compatible with all popular wireless devices, which includes a wide-ranging assortment of cell phones and PDAs.

While the Web is renowned for its homogeneity, wireless is equally infamous for its heterogeneity. Virtually every device has a distinct set of characteristics that must be catered to even if it uses the same microbrowser to access the Web. To solve this problem, a company called 2Roam is one of many solution providers who can circumvent wireless deployment disasters by ensuring compatibility between content and the device receiving it, one of m-commerce's biggest early issues.

In the case of eBay, a bidder can use any device that can access the Web wirelessly, and when each one of these mobile units connects to eBay's Web site, the page request goes to 2Roam's servers, which can identify the device and pour the corresponding data into a template that considers the device's screen size and keyboard so that the content has the proper look and accessibility. Even though greater effort has been exerted to ensure that the user's experience is similar from device to device, nuances, such as the number of results listed per screen from a search query, can vary depending on the unit doing the accessing.

Also keep in mind that for the near future, wireless buyers can't see pictures and wireless sellers can't yet upload an item for sale. Despite these not-so-small challenges, Jupiter Media Metrix, a company that analyzes and measures Internet use, has reported that despite the lesser degree of the eBay experience through wireless, users spend the same time with eBay mobilely as they do when in front of their desktops.

PUSHING IT

Yet another leg supporting the m-commerce table is "push m-commerce," where you are notified of pending shipment or information about offline specials. A message may appear on your cell phone from your Internet or neighborhood pharmacy, informing you that your prescription is due for a refill. You can instantly message back a "yes" or "no," and if you are communicating with your local drugstore, you can let them know if you plan to pick up your prescription or have it delivered.

Offline special information can come from the stores you shop the most. The research firm Kelsey Group estimates that by 2005, an extra

$1.5 billion will fall into the hands of local merchants as a result of these types of promotions.

I've heard bookstore owners talking about how they plan to use the service to alert their better customers when authors stop by unexpectedly and autograph their stock. A message would be sent and customers could indicate whether or not they want the item held. Ditto scenarios for retailing of any type where product specials can be previewed for those customers the store cherishes most. This is a multichannel strategy powered by urgency and excitement. Those who integrate wireless in their plans first are, in the opinion of bn.com vice president Robert Albert, the ones who will profit. If, by the middle of the decade, "the only way you are reaching your customers is via the [wired] Internet, you'll be limiting your customer base."

This is precisely the view of Domino's Pizza, who, in an effort to better understand how their customers might use wireless, launched a two-month trial in Las Vegas that they termed "PizzaCast." What they found is that wireless orders mirrored their online orders, especially with respect to size, which were 10 to 15 percent larger than orders phoned into a human. According to a Domino's executive, the reason for this is twofold. First, customers have a menu in front of them, even if it's digital, which can suggest items, especially newer ones that they may not have considered. Second, ordering wirelessly is more relaxed than interacting with a human order taker, because we are self-conscious that someone is waiting and hence we tend to rush the process.

Domino's sees wireless primarily as an additional convenience for their customers in 64 countries and 7,000 stores. And, like bn.com, Domino's is protecting their future by ensuring that their customers can do business with them any way they like. In fact, to make wireless Domino's even easier, during the trial folks went to the Web site to preregister their favorite pizza combinations and nicknamed them, thus reducing the wireless input to an absolute minimum.

The beauty of Domino's trial is how flawlessly their system worked, not just from the customer's viewpoint, but from an internal perspective as well. After an order was placed, the wireless back end was so well integrated, it would automatically pop up on the prep screen of the kitchen of the closest store. Domino's estimates that it costs them 30 to 40 cents per wireless order to process.

BRINGING THE STORE TO THE CUSTOMER

Like Domino's and bn.com, the examples thus far have focused on mobile technology to facilitate an Internet connection between the retailer and the customer. M-commerce, however, has an almost opposite meaning as well by using wireless technology to bring the store to the consumer offline. Here the customer benefits from wireless but does not actually interact with it.

For example, anyone attending the infamous subway series in 2000 may have noticed more than the average number of kiosks to buy World Series–related merchandise. Actually, there were at least 22 more, both inside and outside the stadium, offering Yankee souvenirs, all equipped with mobile units capable of processing credit transactions without having to use the traditional phone "landline" (or electrical outlet) to dial-in for approval.

Instead, the authorizations took place via a cellular connection anchored to each credit approval device. U.S. Wireless Data's Synapse technology was at the core of this merchandising success story. Their solution integrates existing POS systems and escorts the data along the entire wireless approval route, from the time the customer's card is swiped through the final delivery of the authorization code and paper receipt. You may be surprised to learn that the process wirelessly takes only one-third the time, about 5 seconds, versus the landline option, which typically requires 15 to 20 seconds. Because of the "always on" aspect of wireless, time is saved from eliminating the dial-up and log-in procedure required for each transaction. Furthermore, because the data is parsed into packets and sent digitally in separate groupings, it is highly secure.

However cool the technology, it's the customers' experiences that matters most, and these seconds saved mean faster transactions and more customers served in less time—which in the case of the subway series meant, among other things, the sale of more souvenir miniature wooden baseball bats.

While U.S. Wireless Data's technology was installed first and foremost to improve customer service, the venue also decreased their exposure to credit card fraud by being able to verify credit cards in real time. Needless to say, some cardholders were turned away for lack of approval, but the fraudulent buyers did not give up.

A favorite story is relayed by one of U.S. Wireless Data's executives, who recalls how another U.S. Wireless Data client, a traveling entertainment show, used real-time wirefree Internet transaction reporting to observe someone trying to pass a bad card at kiosks all around the arena but kept getting turned down. In the past, the kiosks couldn't approve credit cards at the time of the sale, so this one person, now being observed and turned away, could have represented thousands of dollars lost to fraud. Instead of fiscal heartache, it's now an endearing tale of how wireless beat the bad guy.

While you will read even more about the wonders of wireless credit card authorization beginning on page 73, the point to take away now is how m-commerce allows for instant commerce in ways never before dreamed possible. Without the technology, the concession management company at Yankee Stadium never would have been able to set up 22 additional "stores" on the spot with such ease. Mobile means more than customers being able to buy anywhere with a wireless device. M-commerce is also the engine powering itinerant retailing—bringing the store to the customer.

Stadiums tender another example of m-commerce's forthcoming ubiquitous presence. Manhattan's Madison Square Garden, Boston's Fleet Center, and Tampa Bay's Tropicana Field are just a few arenas that have installed ChoiceSeat's high-tech wireless interactive entertainment system. The system is noted for its relaying of sports-related information, never-ending streams of stats, and live video feeds of up to eight camera angles that attendees can select at whim.

Though the units are being tested first in the high-end ticket areas, the devices attached to the backs of seats are less about spurring sales for the most expensive seats and more about increasing income from the ancillary sale of merchandise and food (fans can order by tapping the units' touch screens) as well as advertisements for items of interest to the sport's fans.

THE JOY OF BAR CODES

Another way in which m-commerce assists with offline purchasing is through price comparison services. One of the most robust is BarPoint, a company that clearly understands the benefits of convenience and comprehensive information when you want it most.

To use BarPoint you simply input the universal product code (UPC) product numbers (the 12 digits under the bar code) into your Internet-enabled device. In return, you get detailed product descriptions, reviews, comparative price information from a variety of online sources, and direct links to purchase. The advantage here is that if you are standing in a store deciding on a new DVD player, you can get instant information, including the best prices online, at that moment, which is the most important because you are in the throes of deciding. Yes, another warm fuzzy for mobile information.

With over 100 million retail items carrying these codes, the uses are endless. And at the point that our wireless devices can read the bar codes (sooner than you think), all you'll need to do is swipe them. Consider the advantages of scanning several of a similar item—blenders, for example—and seeing a side-by-side comparison of the features of each.

Stepping a few more years out, bar code scanning will actually be the conduit to your offline sale as well. Symbol Technologies partnered with the nation's largest shopping mall operator to test "shopping wands" at one of their Atlanta, Georgia–based properties. The "wand" was essentially a bar code scanner attached to a PalmPilot digital assistant. As you worked your way through the mall, you scanned the items you wanted to buy, and when you were done you returned to a central booth and docked your device, where you then paid for all your purchases at once. As if this were already a scene from *Fantasy Island*, let me stoke the image of this shopping oasis with final note about the service. You are also given the option of where you want your purchases delivered (to your home, to your car, or somewhere else).

One of the reasons bar codes make so much sense for wireless is that they streamline the inputting process. The biggest hurdle for m-commerce is the interface. Tiny screens and lilliputian keyboards are encumbering. That's the bad news. The good news is that as the devices improve, so will the ensuing experience.

For the time being, m-commerce is about getting small things to work like big things. A tiny screen is quite viewable when the resolution is high enough, and keyboards don't have to be large to be functional, as we've seen with the pocket e-mail devices. Add speed to the mix of an ergonomically considerate wireless device, and m-commerce will skyrocket. And if the slice is as small as the devices—let's say 1.3 percent of online sales and 0.1 percent of total retail sales—the figure, according to Forrester Research, is still $3.4 billion by 2005.

While it took years for the majority of the population to adapt to electronic commerce, the adaptation has been made. Porting the functionality in new, more useful ways will ultimately light the fuse, at which point m-commerce will explode.

For more photos and direct links to
all the sites featured, go to
www.easton.com.

2

The Location Advantage
(aka L-Commerce)

THE INTERNET HAS failed local commerce.

Think about it. It's easier to buy a Bruce Springsteen CD from Amazon.com in Seattle, Washington, than it is to use the Internet to find a hardware store within a five-mile radius of your home.

The good news is that this conundrum will fade over the next few years as location-based commerce (l-commerce) flows into the mainstream.

Discussed in detail momentarily, l-commerce is the result of a law that requires all cell phones or devices capable of making a cell call (like those PDA–mobile phone combos) to be able to pinpoint a caller within a certain number of feet for the purpose of dispatching emergency services. Because l-commerce is based on where you are using global positioning technology, it is sometimes referred to as "p-commerce," in which the "p" represents "position-based." Regardless of which term is associated with it, the marriage of GPS with the wonders of the wireless Web has brought forth an entirely new commerce model.

Essentially, l-commerce can be classified into three categories. Using a Web-enabled device, consumers now have access to information that 1) leads directly to an offline sale of goods or services, 2) services a customer on the premises of a retailer, or 3) offers a combination of both. Furthermore, because of the GPS functionality of the mobile device being used, it is often called "location-based m-commerce."

GIVING LOCAL BUSINESS A HIGHER PROFILE

In the retail environs, physical stores, especially local ones, can now utilize the wireless Web to increase their revenue, because customers can now find them. The primary source of new business referrals will come from location-based directories.

One with an increasing profile is go2, the first location-based directory strictly for wireless. By using it, consumers can find real-world businesses via their cellular phones, vehicle navigation systems (such as GM's OnStar), PDAs, and any wirelessly enabled portable computer. The system is simple. You enter what you are looking for, and a list of what is closest to you is offered based on where you are. Your request can be generic, such as "Indian restaurant" or "basketball," or specific, such as "Jiffy Lube," "Arby's," or "AMF Bowling Centers."

One of go2's biggest deals is with Coca-Cola. This five-year strategic alliance valued at $30 million now ensures that anyone who just has to have a Coke at this very second can find one. The directory of choices includes fast-food outlets, franchise restaurants, movie theater concessions, gas stations, and convenience stores. Since Coca-Cola is the most ubiquitous beverage on the planet, the difficulty in finding a sales outlet borders on the absurd. For this reason, we have to assume that Coke's move is clearly one of providing a value-added service to their wholesale clients.

Burger King, with over 8,300 restaurants, is another of go2's deals. While Coke is creating a connection between their retail and wholesale customers, Burger King is more interested in a direct connection with their consumers.

A "Burger King" search on go2 will result in a selection of outlets closest to you, based on where you are, along with driving directions, a click-through calling option (handy if you want to call the store directly to be sure they still have the promo toy of the week available), and a list of specials and other promotions. As one Burger King executive noted, "We're eager to give Burger King customers the simplest and most effective way to find us—wirelessly."

Connecting people to their favorite soda and burger costs just a fraction of the $50 billion estimated to be spent in retail establishments from mobile referrals in the United States in 2005, according to the Yankee Group, a technology research firm. Much of this money will be generated by small businesses that want to be found.

The playing field for local establishments is level as long as the potential customer is in geographic range. A search for hardware stores will build a list with the closest ranked first, based largely on Yellow Pages information. Those businesses that desire additional exposure may opt to enhance their listing with ALL CAPS (one of the few options for the small black-and-white screens of cell phones) as well as a click for additional information (store hours, breadth of selection), coupons, and other promotions. Furthermore, go2's system is designed in such a way that businesses can customize and manage their listing in real time. This means that a pet store with an oversupply of flea collars can spotlight a promotion until they're sold out, at which point they can immediately yank that special and replace it with something else.

This is another of the major advantages of l-commerce. Traditional media, such as newspaper, radio, and televison, often require advertising copy weeks ahead of their print or broadcast dates. This is stifling for a business that cannot predict that far ahead where they most need to promote. Furthermore, national chains cannot customize or account for localized pricing and promotions. For example, a nationwide sundries chain is promoting flip-flops and sand toys in their stores near beaches; there is no way to account for this in broad-based advertising. L-commerce allows for a new form of mass personalization.

Two major retail chains are already acknowledging this.

Office Depot, in addition to offering a list of geographically desirable stores based on the location of the user, allows inquiries related to product availability. The customer can order the product on the spot (one way to guarantee a hold) and either pick it up or have it delivered, the latter being a perfect example of a hybrid transaction of m-commerce (purchasing by mobile device) and l-commerce (based on location).

Circuit City, Jiffy Lube, and Autoweb are examples of other retailers with similar l-commerce-based objectives.

Location information doesn't have to be part of a directory service such as go2 or a direct connection to a company's wirelessly enabled Web site, like Office Depot and Circuit City. Another increasingly popular location-based conduit for retail sales is Brandfinder, which is powered by technology from Vicinity Corporation. The company has partnered with cell providers such as AT&T and Nextel as well as companies that give wireless connectivity to PDAs, such as OmniSky. This way, the brands are on the main menus of the default directory provided by these companies, under the category to which they belong, such as "Shopping" or "Restaurants." Starbucks and McDonald's are examples, and a click on either will immediately guide you to the nearest location.

Clearly, most people know where to find either of these megabrands within shouting distances of their home or work. The bigger value of l-commerce lies in travel outside your daily sphere. For example, on the way to a friend's for dinner across town you may decide, at the last moment, to bring flowers. Now you have a data-rich resource to find a florist on your way. In fact, once located, you can even call ahead so the arrangement is waiting for you to pick up the moment you arrive.

THE IMPORTANCE OF BEING ABLE TO SHOW YOU ARE BETTER AND DIFFERENT

While getting a location-centric idea of what's available is already a giant step for mankind, in my opinion the key component that makes l-commerce a quantifiable source of customer acquisition is "differentiation."

In Los Angeles, we have an overgrowth of sushi bars. Sitting at my desk as I type this, I can name four within walking distance of my home (and that doesn't include the two supermarkets in the same circumference that have live sushi makers in-store). Accordingly, a tap on my location-enabled wireless device would show all of these within a one-third-mile radius. So how do I decide?

Restaurants are, by definition, a service, as opposed to a retail operation, where you are holding something in your hand after the sale. The differential in retail will almost always be price and/or availability. The closest store with the item in stock and the cheapest price will usually get the sale.

However, service businesses, such as restaurants, need positioning other than geography. Aware of this issue, the better directories and services are offering unbiased information (non-advertorial) using *Zagat* guides and newspaper reviews. In time, as our mobile devices and the networks they connect to get more sophisticated, audio descriptions and video footage will also enhance the decision-making process. Though it will always be a gamble if you are clueless about any and they all rate about equal, a data-rich description that can, for example, display or describe ambience might be the deciding factor.

If you are in a business that makes you a candidate for these services, I highly suggest you start thinking about how you are better than and different from your closest competition so you are prepared to position yourself well in the location-based wireless universe.

THE OPPORTUNITY FOR RADICAL PROMOTIONS

In addition to geographic sensitivity, customers' inquiries are real time as well, meaning that they are probably looking for the product or service because they want it now. For this reason, l-commerce will give service businesses an advantage they have never had before: the opportunity to move perishable inventory through radical promotions.

A movie theater with a half-empty house can sell the tickets at 25 percent off minutes before showtime. The offer can be preprogrammed into its point-of-sale system. A certain percentage below desirable sales a certain number of minutes before a show will trigger a set of business rules. These rules will not only lower the price, but will immediately update the theater's wireless directory listing and dedicated mobile Web site to reflect the offer.

Bluetooth-enabled devices, a technology that will soon be commonplace on cell phones and PDAs (and discussed in depth on page 124), will automatically display information about a business the moment you and your device come within a 30-foot range of it. This means that at the moment you turn up at one of those movie theater megaplexes with 35 screens, your wireless devices will give you a rundown of what seats are available and at which price, based on supply and demand at that moment. Specials such as "buy a mega-tub of popcorn, get a mini Milk Duds for free" can also be highlighted.

Earlier I spoke of how l-commerce enables physical businesses to service a sale. On that note, let's head back to the theater to see how it works. Let's say you bought your tickets three minutes before showtime, along with the trough-size serving of popcorn, which means the previews are showing as you enter the theater. It is dark as you step in, but your portable device with Bluetooth has a gloriously backlit screen, which at the moment is showing you a seating grid of the theater in which you are standing, highlighting the seats that are empty. No more trolling the aisles in the dark.

JACK NICHOLSON IS AT TABLE 303

While it's easy to navigate your way through a movie theater even without Bluetooth, consider the advantages of location-based information in large venues. Think airports, Disney World, stadiums, and trade shows, and you have a clear picture. The solution is called "sub-geographical navigation," and it was termed by a company called NearSpace. NearSpace are masters of providing interactive custom guides to be used with wireless handheld devices.

What the company learned is that large venues already have much of the data they need (such as detailed maps) to easily port to wireless. NearSpace simply takes this information and repurposes it for wireless devices, along with other intelligence to give the scraps of data a cohesive whole. NearSpace goes far beyond putting a map on a handheld. Instead reams of information are associated with a tap on any specific area of the map.

Let's look at a corporate campus environment as one application. All employees would have an up-to-date high-level geographical representation of the entire campus in addition to views of each building and each of their floors. This means instant and accurate information to mail stops, employee office and cubicle assignments, meeting rooms, and, as GPS integration gets more sophisticated, precise walking directions to any of the above based on where you are.

Similar applications are being used by Stanford Law School and the Forum Shops at Caesars Palace.

One of my favorite applications of NearSpace's technology was a dynamic seating chart they developed for the American Film Institute's salute to Barbra Streisand, a sit-down dinner event for 700 people seated at 100 tables.

The application was developed primarily for the hostesses seating guests, but any of the attendees who had a Palm or Handspring could be beamed the complete application in seconds. This meant they had the complete list of attendees (you could also search by name), which also identified the table at which they were seating and an overview map of all the tables. You could also click on any of the tables in the overview for a complete listing of the people sitting there. (Clint Eastwood was seated next to Dustin Hoffman.) If you wanted to say hi, another tap would give you directions to the table (second tier, front, left).

If you want to impress your friends, you can download the app and the seating chart at *www.easton.com*. I offer this example not only for its entertainment value, but also to show you how useful wirelessly available, location-sensitive data is in even the most mundane of settings, a business banquet.

We will soon see retail stores applying this technology as a service to their customers. Using their wireless device (or one supplied by the store), customers can input what they are looking for and be told if it's in stock and exactly where to find it. For example, walk into a bookstore, input "Going Wireless," and you will be told the aisle number, exact shelf, and how many copies you can expect to find once you get there (hopefully only one because the rest have sold out). This all leads to an important axiom of business: Make it easy to buy, which in this scenario means the quicker you can get your customer to the merchandise, the more you sell.

One of the big questions surrounding l-commerce is how the information is obtained. There are two options. The "pull" scenario occurs when information is specifically requested. This has been featured in the examples given thus far. The flipside is the "push" model, where information is sent to you automatically. Drive past a store that you've indicated as one of your favorites, and your device's location sensitivity may trigger a ring indicating a digital coupon or special offer. As you can imagine, a multitude of privacy issues are raised when a device always knows where you are, and I discuss this in the privacy chapter on page 233. Also consider the fallout from the cacophony of marketing missives. Nonetheless, l-commerce, like all technology that has preceded it, will find a rightful balance. While it's in its nascent stages, expect a honeymoon phase where people sign up for every l-commerce offer made to them, if only for the novelty.

HOW WE GOT LOCATION SENSITIVE

Understanding how we got to this point means tracing the evolution of l-commerce in broad strokes. Its origin can be found in emergency services—911, to be exact, who get as of the very early 2000s a minimum of 70 calls a minute (over 100,000 a day and growing) from cell phones but have no way of knowing where the caller is located. Meanwhile, the caller is unaware of this information anemia. Accustomed to landlines, operators instantly get data about the caller from the billing records that match the number from which 911 was dialed. Because wireless phone callers are mobile, when they have an emergency they have to first tell 911 operators where they are because 911 has no way of knowing.

Sometimes, actually more often than you would imagine, cell callers have no idea of their location, or there's a language barrier, or, even worse, the caller is screaming and crying and unable to speak. Without being able to determine where the person is, the 911 operator is unable to dispatch help. This has resulted in a number of high-profile deaths, such as the case of the Florida woman trapped in her sinking car who reached 911 successfully but was clueless about where she was.

What is saddest about these stories is that users cite access to emergency services as one of the primary reasons they buy a cell phone.

To solve this problem, the government mandated the FCC E911 bill, which requires cell phones to be able to pinpoint a caller within 50 meters (about 164 feet). Interestingly, this would not have been possible before May 2000 because the U.S. government was scrambling part of the signals from global positioning satellites, the core location technology. Once the Clinton Administration began allowing access to complete signals, an accuracy range of 100 meters was narrowed to 10. All it took was the push of one button.

This expansion of signal quality improved every aspect of location-sensitive applications, particularly time-sensitive ones such as those that estimate when something will arrive. One of the most famous is San Francisco's NextBus service, which informs riders, through a choice of wireless devices, exactly when their bus will arrive at their stop.

The information provided is based not on prepublished schedules, but on the precise time a particular bus will show up at a particular stop on a particular day. NextBus uses a combination of wireless technologies to track public transportation while en route in real time. Factoring in the actual position of the vehicles, as well as their intended stops and typical traffic pattern, NextBus can transmit an estimated arrival time with a high degree of accuracy.

In practical terms, this means that if you are in Manhattan, standing at the corner of 45th and 6th and it's 14 degrees out, a couple of clicks on your Web-enabled device will let you know exactly (by minutes and seconds) when your bus will arrive, which may help you decide if you have time to dash into the Starbucks you are standing in front of for a preoffice latte (for which you just received an electronic coupon that expires in 15 minutes).

The precision of location-sensitive information is a boon for businesses for whom pickup or delivery is a core business. By using the same technology and variables applied by NextBus, companies such as Federal Express, Domino's Pizza, or your local dry cleaner could, theoretically, be able to estimate with equal precision when their driver will arrive at your home or office. Even better, this information would available to you on demand via a wireless device so that you can plan accordingly.

TELLME ALL ABOUT IT

Inevitably, the form in which you would receive the estimated arrival time would be text. And that is true for all of the l-commerce applications I've discussed so far. But there is an additional use of l-commerce that dispenses with visuals altogether. It's called Tellme, and it's an extension of l-commerce in that it uses voice commands instead of text and graphics to relay information. For this reason, Tellme and similar services are referred to as voice portals, or "vortals."

A call to 1-800-555-TELL will deliver the expected sports scores, headline news, financial information, and weather, all by voice commands and with remarkable precision. Say "traffic" and it will ask which city. Name a city and in a moment an audio playback will give a complete report. Where Tellme shines is how it goes beyond the obvious and offers depth that overdelivers on its promise.

Sports scores include not only those of the standard NFL, NBA, NHL, and others, but those for soccer, horse racing, and women's college basketball as well. Restaurant listings cover 54 categories that include cafeteria, Ethiopian, and Swiss, all linked to *Zagat* reviews that can be heard on request.

Out-of-the-ordinary depth is complemented by Tellme's unexpected services, many of which focus on connecting you directly to the companies that you need most when mobile. Just say "taxi" and you are connected instantly to a reputable company in the area from which you are calling. Airlines, hotels, and car rental companies are immediately available just by speaking their names ("British Air," "Hilton," or "Hertz"), and if you need to inform anyone of a late arrival (or simply to convey a quick hello), just say "phone booth" and the number you want dialed and you are connected for a free multiminute call to just about anywhere in the United States. In fact, every aspect of Tellme is free.

What Tellme understands is the power of location-based commerce and the huge revenue potential when you connect people with the goods or services they want. Tellme's revenue model has complementary spokes focused on revenue sharing and advertising, along with the use of their toll-free service as a customer acquisition tool for their primary business.

Interestingly, Tellme is a leader in voice commerce, which you will read about next, and building products for companies that want to use their technology to add value to their consumer or business-to-business customers. For this reason, 800-555-TELL is as much about showing off their incredible technology as it is about providing value for the people who might, in the long run, need similar functionality for their business.

No matter what location-specific solution a company incorporates, whether it's a go2 directory listing, a Brandfinder connection, Near-Space guides, or Tellme voice data, l-based technology benefits every type of business, from national franchises to corporate campuses to mom-and-pop businesses.

It's this entirely new customer service, acquisition, and marketing paradigm that will, in the years to come, give the "l" in l-commerce an additional meaning: lucrative.

For the Barbra Streisand salute seating chart and other nifty free software for your handheld, visit *www.easton.com.*

3

The Voice Advantage
(aka V-Commerce)

HERE'S A TRANSCRIPT of a typical inquiry call to United Parcel Service (UPS). See if you can find the twist:

> ATTENDANT: "Thank for calling UPS. . . . Please say your tracking number."
>
> CALLER: "1z 15x 630 01 4011 2820."
>
> ATTENDANT: "Your package was delivered on May 12 at 9:20 A.M. It was received by [spelling] D-e-c-k-e-r at the receiving dock."

So far, this looks like a basic interaction between UPS and a customer in need of a package's shipping status. Correct, except that there was only one human involved in this dialogue: the customer.

Along with the wireless revolution is another technology explosion. It's called "voice commerce," also known as "v-commerce." What makes v-commerce so special is that computers, and the people they are interacting with, can speak naturally. In doing so, technology automates business actions from routine information requests (package tracking) to lengthy and complex product orders.

From the get-go I want to differentiate v-commerce from its detested sibling, "interactive voice response." Interactive voice response systems rely on push button tones and voice prompts. Their one-sided soliloquies sound like this: "Please choose from one of the following 17 options: press 1 for accounting, press 2 for sales, press 3 for accounts payable . . ." I refer to these systems as "voice jail."

Technically speaking, v-commerce is an interactive voice response system, but it uses speech recognition technology that gets around the tedium of "press 1 for accounts payable." As you can see from the UPS example, "speech recognition–enabled interactive voice response" is a natural communication where questions are asked and answered. The result of these interactions ranges from the execution of a sale—literally an order being placed—to the dissemination of sales-related information, such as a shipment's tracking number or a product's availability.

Granted, v-commerce is not a wireless technology, but a discussion of the wireless explosion must include v-commerce because it is being empowered by the worldwide proliferation of cell phones. Cell phones are becoming the most ubiquitous communication device in the world. In other words, without cell phones, v-commerce lacks sparkle. Delete the mobile convenience from v-commerce and you've got a desk phone with a computer nearby, in which case many feel that they might as well use "e-commerce."

As you will soon see, v-commerce goes way beyond natural voice interaction and will actually integrate with your wirefree device. Yes, when the ultimate all-in-one mobile device is eventually invented (I'm tapping my foot with anticipation), you could speak the tracking number in our example above, but the response will appear on the display of your smart device, showing "Delivered on May 12 at 9:20 A.M." along with an image of the actual signature.

Until these smart devices appear, it's cell phones that make v-commerce shine since they are convenient, easy to use, affordable, and, as you will see, surprisingly secure. And they are always with the customer. Better yet, v-commerce allows non–computer owners to take advantage of e-commerce, which, on the flip side, provides a potential tsunami of new customers to businesses that previously could market only to people with Internet access.

Think Amazon.com. Even my 72-year-old neighbor who (I swear) has never sat in front of a computer—but now owns a cell phone—is familiar with Amazon.com. She's just one of the millions. But Amazon.com could never make a profit selling to her. The combination of the costs to staff an inbound call center combined with paper-thin profit margins make traditional inbound phone centers a negative-revenue proposition. Dispense with the humans on the order end and the word *profit* comes into play.

Another advantage of speech recognition–powered v-commerce is that it's much faster than interactive Touch-Tones. Imagine how much time it would take to drill down through a list of voice menus using Touch-Tones to get a roster of Stephen King book titles or the arrival time of a flight from an airline that services over a hundred cities. Today, you call American Airlines and simply speak the flight number and city and the information is dished-up. The whole process requires less than a minute.

Furthermore, the telephone component of v-commerce means that purchasing can happen anytime, anywhere. Although I can't imagine wanting to buy a new refrigerator while walking the dog, v-commerce makes it possible. It's nice to have options.

THE DIFFERENCE BETWEEN V-COMMERCE AND V-BUSINESS

Since v-commerce is a new term, its definitions differ depending on whom you ask. So I'm going to give you mine by drawing an analogy to e-commerce. It is generally accepted that the term *e-commerce* refers to direct buying and selling via the Web, whereas the phrase *e-business* refers to using the Internet to enable commerce. In other words, with e-business the transaction doesn't take place online, but the information that led to the sale came from the Web, or a sale was serviced afterward via the Internet (order tracking, product manuals, warranty information, and so on).

To maintain sanity in the cacophony of buzzwords, let's give v-commerce the same meaning as e-commerce and let's fuse the term *v-business* with the same intention as e-business.

On that note, let's look first at v-commerce, which is direct inbound automated sales by phone. At first glance, this looks like a business paradigm that has existed since the advent of the Spiegel catalog and toll-free numbers. This is true, except that the call center was manned by humans instead of microchips. That's what makes v-commerce so special. It's so cost-effective.

One of the first and most robust v-commerce components was launched by Office Depot.

As forerunners in e-commerce, Office Depot is one of the Internet's first and largest retailing operations on the Web. However, despite their ultrasophisticated Internet presence, many customers either can't or don't want to order online. This means that Office Depot must maintain costly call centers. With a burning desire to reduce the tab for human operators, the company contracted with NetByTel to integrate speech technology so they could start automating routine calls to their centers.

Dialing 888-GO-DEPOT is your best demo. The interaction is what you would imagine, with a request for an item number followed by questions of quantity and size or color, just as though a human were taking the order, with the same access to Office Depot's 50,000-plus items. At the end of the call, a voice shopping cart reiterates the order, which, when it is approved by you, is posted automatically to the Office Depot Web site for tracking and other future reference.

The use of NetByTel's v-commerce system reduces the cost of a call by 87 percent as compared with an order taken by a call center representative. Part of the huge savings is related to the fact that NetByTel offers its services on a pay-per-performance model, taking a fee for each successful v-commerce transaction, which means avoiding any up-front capital. While that alone is enough to endear the company, NetByTel also had the system up and running in one month, handling 250,000 calls at a cost of only 16 information technology management hours. Not surprisingly, they won a Frost & Sullivan award for business development and strategy.

A first look at Office Depot's system would make you think that they are trying to avoid their customers. In fact, they see it as exactly the opposite. "The goal here isn't to lose human contact," states one their executives. "The goal is to provide value-added service."

The value add for the customer as it stands now is being able to avoid on-hold time while waiting for a human. Over time, however, the value proposition will broaden, allowing Office Depot's v-commerce customers to set up repeat orders for even faster ordering, as well as dictate the way in which they want to reference products (example: by name or by UPC code).

While v-commerce is in its infancy, a company like Office Depot can shuttle calls to the automated system with the hope that the novelty and convenience will be enough to engage callers. However, as the technology proliferates, I sense that many companies will have to offer incentives to their customers to use v-commerce systems instead of humans. If there isn't much of a time difference between v-commerce and human commerce (h-commerce?), then why not have the assurance of a live person confirming your order and instantly answering questions?

As you'll recall, after the major airlines began offering online ticket purchasing, they motivated their customers by offering additional frequent flier points for those who skipped the toll-free number and used the Web instead. Watch for similar incentives to develop for v-commerce transactions, such as coupons or flat-rate discounts. The result is a win-win scenario. The customer gets something extra for saving the company money, but the company's incentive is small enough that they still rack up savings.

While Office Depot customers can select between human and machine, some companies choose to have their first level of interaction be completely voice automated. The Home Shopping Network (HSN) was one of them. While they have since completely updated and integrated even more v-commerce applications, this was in part owing to the fact that their first foray was so successful. In fact, they knew instantly that the technology was a perfect fit with their company. What callers appreciated most was the system's security and convenience.

Callers would begin their HSN interaction by saying their home phone number. Using breakthrough speech recognition and voice authentication software from Nuance, the company was able to retrieve the number and its appropriate information from a database. Using the same spoken phone number, the software verified the caller's voice against the stored voiceprint for the household, which was captured when the caller initially enrolled in the system.

The security inherent in Nuance's verifier is highly reliable and thus avoided the need for PINs (personal identification numbers) and cumbersome customer IDs. Prior to implementing the Nuance software, up to 30 percent of HSN's callers hit zero to summon an operator because they couldn't recall their number.

The verification system also assisted with cross-sells because the database was able to differentiate among callers from the same household and offer specials based on gender and buying history. Needless to say, it was valuable to know that Jane was on the phone and not Adam, who probably didn't want a hot pink angora sweater, even if it was 70 percent off. This ability to accurately offer appropriate complementary items increased revenues per call by an average of 10 to 20 percent.

While callers had the option of completing their orders using an automated system, those who chose to place their order with a human had already been verified, thereby saving an operator at least 20 seconds of call time. At that time, HSN estimated their operators were paid an average of 33 cents a minute ($30,000 per year). This translates to a savings of 11 cents a call. Prior to HSN's voice verification system, of the 160,000 calls they receive per day, about 48,000 were from customers who had forgotten their IDs. Thus, HSN was in a position to save as much as $1.9 million annually. By the way, the system successfully identified 95 percent of all callers.

SERVICE BUSINESS USES OF V-COMMERCE

While v-commerce is about transactions through voice-automated systems, usually accessed by wireless phone, we need to note that it's not just about buying "stuff." V-commerce is also about buying time directly, which we usually refer to as services. V-commerce's technology has become reliable and sophisticated enough to be rolled out in an environment fraught with variables, such as appointment scheduling.

Using a natural language interface, callers state their preferred appointment time. If it's available, it's booked; otherwise the system offers alternatives, until the verbal Ping-Pong between caller and automated attendant makes a match. At that point, the master calendar is updated. Clients are then sent an e-mail reminder.

The back end of the system is extraordinarily sophisticated and allows for the programming of intricate business rules, which I discuss in detail in "Appointment Scheduling and Reservations" (page 45). Just for now, I want to show a very simple use of the application in a microbusiness environment to make the point.

Kay Stewart, a San Francisco–based chiropractor, integrated a voice recognition scheduling system after her longtime receptionist left and she had not yet found a replacement. Stewart found herself spending way too much time on the phone and not nearly as much time as she wanted with her patients.

On a lark, Stewart decided to research voice-enabled electronic schedulers as an alternative to hiring a new receptionist. She went with a system designed by Xtime called TIMEngine. She was lucky enough to be a beta-tester; otherwise the system would have cost $36,000, equivalent to two years' pay for a part-time receptionist.

According to Stewart, about 75 percent of her patients use the system, which has freed up considerable time for her on the weekends, when she would have to return calls; in addition, the system provided her peace of mind when she was forced to take a three-week medical leave and didn't have to worry about covering the office.

CALL CENTERS' NEW BEST FRIEND

As defined earlier, the flip side of v-commerce is v-business, where speech recognition is used to facilitate a sale or service after it has been made. This is the area in which voice recognition technology is being applied first, as demonstrated by the earlier UPS example.

In the case of UPS, the cost savings from their v-business initiative for package tracking alone realized a 100 percent return on investment in just 90 days. This makes sense when you consider the 240,000 tracking calls UPS receives each day. One look at that number and you understand how desperately UPS had to eliminate as many human-handled calls as possible.

Your first thought might have been, Why not use voice jail and let people tap in their tracking numbers using tones? While that may work for some carriers, UPS uses alpha-numeric tracking codes (they deliver up to 14 million packages a day, so numeric-only is not an option).

These tracking numbers can also reach up to 18 digits. It's nearly impossible to get "1z 15x 630 01 4011 2820" into the system unless the caller taps the number 9 several times to indicate "x" instead of "9." Since "z" is still not indicated on the call pad of older phones, it too requires additional explanation.

None of this is a problem with the specialized voice recognition system. A customer dials 1-800-PICK-UPS and simply says "one-zee-one-five-x" and so forth. It's even possible to emphasize the letters by saying "s as in Sam" and the system will understand. The technology has been working so well for UPS and their customers that it now handles 120,000 tracking calls a day (1,000 simultaneously), half of the total 240,000 inbound requests. Not only do these automated responses relieve UPS operators of their most mundane calls, it saves customers and the companies they work for anywhere from 60 to 90 seconds on the average package tracking call.

After the über-successful launch of v-business package tracking, UPS expanded their system to include package pickup requests. Here, customers state their phone number, and the natural voice system verifies the address and establishes a pickup time as well as the number of packages. It saves UPS about two minutes per call, as compared with a human-assisted interaction.

According to UPS, customers prefer their v-business system to live agents. Not only is it faster, but one executive admitted that some customers "didn't even realize they were talking to a computer."

This is probably true for many customers contacting Sears, which, like UPS, uses Nuance's technology: when they call a store, they can speak the name of the department or the item they want and are connected to the right people without delay. Sears's system handles more than 200,000 calls daily and also paid for itself in 90 days. Thrilled with its performance, Sears has added multilingual capabilities, starting with Spanish for customers in areas with large Hispanic populations such as Puerto Rico, Florida, and New York. In fact, this newer breed of software is so advanced that it is more easily than ever recognizing different accents and speech patterns (think Boston) with 90 percent accuracy.

TALKING TO THE CUSTOMER
WITHOUT TALKING TO THE CUSTOMER

With success stories like these, corporations with intense call center activity or lots of customer interaction, whether they are consumer driven or business-to-business based, should be on the hunt now for ways to implement v-business options.

One of the clear leaders in this area is Tellme (discussed at length in l-commerce), which is the first, the largest, and the most commercially proven platform ever developed. Tellme is also one of the best-funded new ventures of the early 2000s, with over a quarter billion dollars from premier institutional investors.

As one of the companies responsible for one of the standards behind v-commerce technology, Tellme has 12,000 independent developers building applications for clients with a staggering array of needs and requests. At this point, they believe there isn't anything they can't do.

Their v-business services offer automated outbound customer notifications. One of their services is Tellme Notifier, used by Jiffy Lube to voice alert their customers when it's time for an oil change. The big benefit is that many people give their cell number as their phone contact, which means they often receive the notice when they are in their cars and can verify with the odometer the time for an oil change. The service, called My Jiffy Lube Reminder, is a two-way actionable system. Customers can tell the voice recognition service to either send them a reminder to their e-mail address (which Jiffy Lube has on file) or connect them to their nearest Jiffy Lube center to make an appointment. Furthermore, the system allows Jiffy Lube to make targeted cross-sells at the same time. Given the "mom-like" quality of the female voice representing Jiffy Lube, you might go for the additional purchase opportunity, if only out of guilt.

What's important to note about My Jiffy Lube and related notification services is that they are "opt-in," meaning that customers have specifically approved their participation. The offer is never initiated by the company with the idea that if the customer doesn't like it, he or she can opt-out. We often see this unfortunate scenario on the Web. I call it "involuntary opt-in." These are the aggravating prechecked boxes you run across during a registration or buying session that indicate "Yes, I want to receive your periodic e-mailings." If you miss "de-checking" the box, their spam is on its way. As it stands now, companies are notifying only customers who have agreed to service by supplying the information necessary—cell phone number, e-mail address, and so on—to complete the notification.

The benefit of these notification systems is their cost-effectiveness and improved customer retention. There's a sales philosophy I agree with that states that those companies who get the most time with a customer will get more of that customer's business.

For this reason, I expect to see opt-in notification services being used by large and small businesses, because the technology is so cheap to integrate and the return on investment is so high. Keep in mind, those who start using voice notification systems first are going to have a huge competitive advantage because they are going to get most of the customer's time.

For example, I would advise a brokerage house to offer an end-of-day notification that would call me with a rundown of my complete portfolio. For security purposes, the system would require me to say or input a PIN before the information is relayed. Keep in mind that this works best and is most appropriate for time-sensitive information, like stock info, sports scores, clearance sales, and so forth.

On that note, look to airlines to offer their most coveted passengers personalized alerts to their cell phone that update them on flight information. For example, if a flight is canceled or running extremely late, the airline could proactively call their million-mile flier and offer to rebook on another flight to the same destination so that he or she might get there sooner. Naturally, speech technology would service the entire call. If Airline A offers this service, but not Airline B, and all other elements are equal, which airline would you fly?

AUTOMATING THE MUNDANE

Keep in mind that v-business services don't have to be outbound, like the notifier and alert systems I've just described. They also beautifully handle inbound calls that are routine and time-intensive, such as those regarding price and availability.

Office Depot (using the NetByTel system) offers this service. You are prompted to state the zip code you are calling from, the item number, and the quantity you want. The system announces the price as well as the closest store that has in stock the item you want in the quantity you desire. A v-business system like this can also offer directions to the store, current promotions available at the location, the store's hours, and an option to transfer the call to the physical store, if requested.

Not that this will surprise you, but when a company can quickly and accurate service a customer, they have significantly improved their chances for a sale. In fact, the Kelsey Group did a survey that showed that 25 percent of all directory assistance requests made by a cell phone resulted in a sale. For this reason, voice-enabled search engines, such as BeVOCAL's Business Finder (1-800-4-BVOCAL), which will let you locate any business by name or type based on location, is in a position to be valuable for all types of companies.

IT'S JUST ANOTHER LAYER, REALLY

Before I end this discussion of speech/voice-enabled commerce and services, I think it would be beneficial for you to have a super-brief understanding of how it works. The reason is that v-commerce/v-business is just an extension of a company's existing Web site. The technology is simply another layer of technology that interacts with the Web site, which explains why it's so cheap, so easy, and so quick to integrate.

The two most used technologies in voice commerce are speech/voice recognition, where the words you say are translated to text, and text-to-speech, which is the opposite and converts written words to audible speech.

With these two components in place, it has never been easier to integrate a v-commerce component. It doesn't require separate databases or other information pools. It uses the Web site of the company and various other technologies (too geeky to explore, trust me). Speaking in the broadest terms, what you say is inputted as text (using speech recognition) as though you were actually on the Web site. When a response is generated from the query you spoke, the text-to-speech component speaks the result it is "seeing" from the text that the database delivered. Again, using our UPS package tracking example, the voice recognition software essentially typed the tracking number you spoke into the tracking info box of the Web site (behind the scenes, of course), and when the database gave a result, the text-to-speech component saw it and read it to you ("Delivered on May 12 at 9:20 A.M.").

Because the voice application is plugged in to the Web site and the Web site is either the primary database or is connected to the primary database, when information is updated or a product is added, so is the data relayed to v-commerce customers. If your business has a call center (or could use one), you are a worthy candidate for v-commerce, especially if you are in business-to-business sales, where the profits margins are higher and so are the stakes. Responsiveness and the ability to get accurate information to customers in seconds may be the best and only differentiator between you and your competition.

You already know that in today's economy customers are demanding better service faster and companies are under constant pressure to reduce costs. Live agents are pricey; interactive Touch-Tone systems are senseless. V-commerce technology is the obvious solution.

While v-commerce as I have described it thus far seems like a flawless technology, I'll be happy to remind you that it isn't. It has come incredibly far (and just gets better), but it's not perfect. Call Charles Schwab for a stock quote for Cisco, the networking company, and you might get Sysco, the food distributor, although they've found a workaround along with the ability to make trades or transfer funds using a natural language interface.

Furthermore, background noise and interference from cell phones can cause problems for speech recognition systems, which just goes to prove that the real killer app for wireless might is high-quality voice service.

In the same way that catalogs were beholden to the postal service until the advent of the toll-free phone number, pure-play Internet companies will experience the same liberation, especially those that can't afford to staff a call center. And multichannel companies like Victoria's Secret, with catalogs, retail stores, and a busy, busy Web site, can now add another conduit for sales, using a device that most of their customers own and actually carry with them.

The perspective of Tellme's president is probably closest to reality in predicting the explosive future of v-commerce. "The Internet is man's second most important communications invention," he says. "The first is the phone."

To hear samples of v-commerce experiences visit
www.easton.com.

Appointment Scheduling and
Reservations, Anytime, Anywhere

PERHAPS OUR FIRST glimpse of wireless appointment scheduling may have been by way of cartoon character Jane Jetson. While traveling the galaxies in her hovercraft, she glanced in her rearview mirror and quipped that she was "desperate for a new 'do." A couple of taps on a TV-like screen and the appointment for her new 'do was done.

While the concept seemed miraculous, even far-fetched, when *The Jetsons* premiered in 1962, today we are living the dream. Well, almost. Of course, the real dream is circumventing traffic in personal helicopters at speed limits of 500 miles per hour. Nonetheless, at least we can schedule appointments while stuck in bumper-to-bumper traffic.

Online appointment scheduling is essentially the wireless killer application for service businesses. While the Web has been helpful to service companies by allowing their Web sites to work as digital brochures, the promise of true e-commerce has essentially eluded the service industry. The Web can educate potential customers and thus help acquire new ones; but the actual sale—the appointment—has to be made offline.

It's interesting that the growth of online appointment and reservations technology is occurring just as wireless is becoming commonplace. While there are advantages to clients to schedule via the Web, the person making an appointment still has to be at a computer, which just happens to be next to a phone. For some, at this point it's just as easy to call. It's only when you add the wireless component to the picture that the entire scenario goes from helpful to intensely practical for both the customer and the service business.

Every one of the many benefits of online appointment scheduling for service businesses justifies the decision to offer the option, but collectively the benefits prove that this type of specialized scheduling software is the biggest automation advantage for service businesses since the introduction of computers.

BETTER THAN HUMANS

Steamatic of St. Louis proves this point. One of the nation's largest cleaning and restoration companies, they found that after integrating online appointment scheduling—which is accessible by wireless with Web access—the company's profits increased $105,000 annually on an investment of approximately $1,000 a month.

Steamatic is using technology pioneered by eService Manager, which is by far the most sophisticated and flawless available. Owned by wireless experts Mobile Data Solutions in Canada, eService Manager overcomes the obstacles of online scheduling by allowing for complex and intricate business and pricing rules, which are determined by the service business and integrated by eService.

These rules include not only how long it should take for a service to be performed, but the availability and expertise of the technicians, price quoting (for instance, it's not necessarily double the price for a service if it's being applied to two of something in the same place), and all the other "what if" scenarios. Essentially, eService's scheduling algorithms allow any kind of service with an unlimited number of complex attributes to be accurately scheduled and optimized.

Steamatic's business rules were as complicated as you can imagine for a company that offers both cleaning and restoration services for everything from carpets to furniture to draperies to mattresses. In fact, even a human keenly aware of the nuances of these bookings turned out to be less efficient than the automated system, as proved by the fact that since they integrated eService Manager, the company has been able to schedule many more jobs in one day.

But that's only part of the story. Being able to let clients book appointments 24 hours a day is both a convenience to the customer and a boon for Steamatic, who is getting more bookings because it can schedule appointments during nonbusiness hours. Plus, there were no out-of-pocket expenses because eService Manager is not a piece of hardware or software, but an application that resides on eService's computers and is linked from Steamatic's site. eService costs as little as $99 per month, making it affordable to microbusinesses as well as national chains.

In addition to the advantages for the consumer, the wirefree connectivity component is a huge plus for Steamatic's field service technicians, who, using their wireless devices, can have instant access to their entire day's or week's schedule. They also love the option of being notified of new or changed appointments with complete information, which avoids the time-consuming and job-distracting process of "beep and call-in."

As promised in the v-commerce section, we are going to take an in-depth look at wireless appointment scheduling using speech recognition instead of using the Web on a handheld device.

IT HEARS WHAT YOU'RE SAYING

As compared to Web-based scheduling, voice-enabled appointment making has one primary advantage—it's easy in that it's similar to what we are used to—and one disadvantage—we lose the benefit of seeing an entire week's worth of options at a glance, so the process can take longer.

All in all, though, the back-end technology offers the same sophistication as the Web-enabled option. Systems designed by Xtime, the leader in voice-enabled scheduling systems, has a client that is one of the nation's largest automotive repair chains, with thousands of locations. Consider the implications of the breadth of this business as you learn that the rules engine Xtime designed accommodates several thousand employees' work schedules and skills sets, and each location has the ability to set its own rules on hours, services offered, and resources.

Because of the detail orientation of the system, the info available for analysis gives management feedback they have never had before. They now know everything they want to about their business operations, customer demand, and resource constraints. Managers can measure seasonal and demographic trends, responses to advertising and promotion, and the profitability of each service.

However, this data is only part of the wireless wealth factor. Consider the additional customers they can book by being able to schedule appointments during nonbusiness hours, especially new customers, for whom the lifetime value is $3,600 per, being able to allocate resources more efficiently, and reducing "turn-aways," which, according to one of Xtime's reports, can add $32,400 per location annually.

Last, and far from least, the system can also automatically offer upsells and cross-sells intelligently based on the customer's history and the resources of the location. Incentives can also be included if business is slow.

While the demands of these automotive centers are intricate, it proves that any service business is a candidate for online appointment scheduling and that staking a claim in the e-business landscape by converting Yellow Pages advertising or Web leads into customers with booked appointments is the best use of marketing dollars. Less obvious are the benefits of services such as automatic appointment reminders sent to customers, which increase profitability by decreasing no-shows, the ability to manage workers with different skills sets, and the advantages of being able to schedule equipment required for certain jobs and to maximize the number of appointments that can be accommodated on a tight schedule. Just like the automotive centers, once integrated, some companies are for the first time able to analyze such critical data as appointment summaries by resource, appointment details, service statistic reports, and customer statistic reports.

While all these practical benefits are more than convincing, there's a psychological advantage when a company is willing to reveal its schedule to its clients. You implement a much higher level of customer service when you can say to them, "Choose what works best for you."

REDUCING TRAVEL HASSLES

It's precisely this hospitality advantage that has made wireless for reservations another hot ticket in the world of mobile services. Naturally, the concept is being applied first by travel- and entertainment-related business such as restaurants, hotels, and the airlines.

In fact, virtually every airline is integrating wireless into the entire customer experience. Travelers can check flight schedules, buy their tickets, be notified of flights delays, and check their frequent flier accounts using their wireless devices. Even the check-in system is being automated wirelessly.

This concept was pioneered internationally by Lufthansa and domestically by Alaska Airlines. How it works differs with each airline, but by way of example, with Alaska Airlines you can generate a boarding pass using a wireless device at an airport kiosk, then show your ID along with the pass to the flight attendant as you board.

Sabre Holdings, the leading provider of technology and marketing services for the travel industry, has an alternative system that uses voice authentication in their wireless check-in systems, which allow passengers to avoid memorizing passwords and PINs. As part of a registration procedure, passengers record their voices with the airline by answering questions that are used to establish a biometric voiceprint, another commonplace technology in Jane Jetson's day. Fortunately, the system has a

99.5 percent accuracy rating, enough for the Federal Aviation Administration to authorize it for security clearances. After the passenger has been authenticated using the voice technology, an image of a bar code is transmitted to the traveler's wireless device, and this bar code image is then used as a boarding pass by having passengers wave it in front of a scanner as they board.

Airlines admit that in addition to the cost-saving advantages, these wireless systems were designed to meet the needs of business travelers, who are notorious for doing whatever they can to avoid lines because they are constantly rushing to their flights.

Of course, at the other end of the travel spectrum are accommodations, which can be reserved wirelessly as well. Bass Hotels & Resorts, whose brands include Holiday Inn, Inter-Continental, Crowne Plaza, and Staybridge Suites (for a total of 3,000 hotels in 100 countries), launched one of the industry's most comprehensive wireless initiatives. Working with Air2Web, the Bass Hotels & Resorts wireless reservation system is guaranteed to work with over 260 different devices based on manufacturers' specifications like screen size. The company also has an understanding of the current limitations of most mobile devices and has designed the system that requires the least amount of input. Customers can designate their preferences and credit card numbers on the hotel's secure Web site so that as they make reservations a minimal amount of text is necessary from the mobile device.

Choice Hotels, the second largest hotel franchise in the world, with over half a million beds, have tapped into a portion of a satellite to keep all their properties linked to a central reservations database (connected through the use of compact wireless satellite dishes). The solution makes 100 percent of the room inventory available—a huge benefit to the hotel chain's customers, who now have access to all unoccupied rooms instead of just those each franchisee allotted to the central reservations system. With a few clicks of an Internet-enabled device, travelers can instantly see a roster of every room available in the city of their choice in the price range they've indicated. Over time, as wireless Web devices become more sophisticated, color photos of the rooms will appear onscreen along with a list of hotel amenities.

Room reservations are a perfect fit with the wireless of advantage of "anytime, anywhere." Hotel arrangements have always been made remotely, so booking with a wireless device is only a slight behavioral shift.

One of the biggest advantages of automated Web-enabled appointments and reservations is the quality of the customer interaction and the high quality of the data, something executive management can rely on, whether the company is a multinational corporation such as Choice Hotels or a microbusiness with a handful of employees run by a careful owner.

One of the first small businesses in the country to implement real-time online appointment scheduling was Harry, the owner of a hair salon in Seattle, Washington, who asked to remain anonymous because each time his site is publicized it crashes from an overload of visitors interested in seeing his technology. Because of his online appointment option, which is also accessible from mobile devices, the technology significantly raised his value to his clients, who book haircuts as frequently in the middle of the night and on Sundays as they do during business hours.

Harry's salon is located in downtown Seattle and naturally caters to a lot of dot.commers, especially those who work for *Amazon.com,* who are both impressed by and appreciative of the system. This sentiment is echoed by Harry, who is dealing with health challenges that keep him away from the shop. "I don't have to call the salon anymore," he notes. Theoretically speaking for all executives, he adds, "Now I can watch how my business is doing in real time."

For visual examples of wireless appointments and reservations, visit *www.easton.com.*

5

Making Your Field Service Reps the Happiest in the World

IT'S THE THIRD time today that Bob, a Sears Home Central service technician, is faced with a "not at home" appointment. At least that's what he thought. After knocking repeatedly without an answer, Bob sent a wireless text message to Sears's dispatch. Before rerouting him, dispatch called the customer at whose door Bob was standing and learned that she was home, just hadn't heard the door through her blow dryer. The nearly aborted job was back on track, sparing time and customer goodwill.

Once inside, Bob began servicing a broken dishwasher. It was an older model that had been misidentified by the customer when calling for the repair, and Bob realized that he didn't have the necessary parts on his truck. Again he wired dispatch, alerting them to the situation. He received a text message back that a service tech at a house call two miles away had the parts. He was just leaving and would drop off the parts in less than 10 minutes.

The communications technology Bob uses now, as a senior technician for Sears, is a stark contrast to the pay phones and customer lines he would tie up throughout the day when he first began working with the company. At that time, a missing part would have meant a trip back to headquarters, which in turn postponed the completion of the service call to the following day, which translated to an unhappy customer with an inoperable dishwasher.

Now in the 2000s a quick keyboard tap eliminates layers and years of inefficacies.

Bob is just one of 15,000 Sears Home Central field service technicians, 100 percent of whom are equipped with rugged handheld PCs and an integrated wireless modem that allows instant connection with home base. It's an astonishing feat and one that evolved over several years as devices, networks, and other variables were tested and implemented.

Considering that Sears technicians service 20 percent of all appliances in America—over 12 million customers—their field technicians are some of the most depended upon in the country. It is for this reason that it was important to Sears to have 100 percent wireless coverage for their service technicians, no matter where they provide service. Wirelessly equipping the first 80 percent of their reps was comparatively simple, since the company could use existing cellular and radio networks for coverage. However, Sears needed to resort to satellite technology to equip the remaining 20 percent.

Why the massive effort to get to 100 percent? The efficiency improvements for Sears Home Central service are jaw dropping. Field service reps have gained back at least 30 minutes a day by not having to call for product and stock checks, saved another 50 percent in time spent ordering parts, and added hours in the field because they no longer have to shlep back to the office to complete service bills and other administrative tasks. In addition, service call information is inputted as part of the visit, and because of the electronic entry in the field, there is no need for an input staff at the branch offices.

The Sears Home Central technicians love these advantages and are also grateful for the decrease in aggravation from "not at home" trips. This happens a minimum of 100 times a day in a service district of 100 to 150 technicians. Now dispatchers can instantly redistribute workloads, which is not only a better use of labor, but also promotes goodwill among the technicians, who no longer have to stew because one is working overtime while a coworker is home before sundown.

BIG PAYOFF FOR SMALLER BUSINESSES, TOO

While Sears is a large-scale operation, wireless is also benefiting service field reps associated with smaller operations.

OnSite Maintenance Center is another success story. The company provides services and repair for quick printing machinery. They have a presence in 15 states, and their customers range from Kinko's (over 200 branches) to mom-and-pop quick printers, many of whom are also 24-hour.

OnSite's goal for a wireless platform was simple. They wanted to increase technician productivity by balancing workloads and maximizing each technician's time. What they didn't want was to spend much money, which can run anywhere from $2,000 to $200,000 per seat. For this reason, they implemented the eDispatch solution, whose costs were not only lower, but whose software is adaptable to work with virtually any wireless device. Moreover, a layer of friction was eliminated between OnSite and their customers, since the eDispatch solution allows customers to track the progress of service calls online. OnSite can also monitor works in progress and job requests and balance the loads accordingly.

In addition to the customer service improvements are the equally impressive metrics. With the new wireless system, OnSite reduced their communications costs by 30 percent to only $100 per person per month (which includes the eDispatch fees). Revenue has increased from the three additional service calls the technicians are now making each day, as well as from a 30 percent reduction in redundant information entry and reduced paperwork for the technicians. This latter point is one of the reasons the technicians love the system so much. It nearly eliminates paperwork, the part of the job they like least.

As evidenced by the previous case histories, it's easy to see how field service automation is such a perfect fit with wireless. There are more than 50 million mobile workers in North America. Mobile workers are defined by the research groups as service technicians, utility and government field personnel, transportation workers, and outside sales representatives. Consider the high degree to which organizations depend on these itinerant employees for time-sensitive activities and the benefits that wireless brings in efficiencies, and you see how mobile workers are as productive in the field as they would be in an office.

6

Making Your Sales Force the Most Productive in the World

WE MUST ADMIT there is nothing less appealing than a salesperson updating marketing materials via ballpoint as you are being pitched. It's a common problem. While business in the new economy may be moving at the speed of light, there's still a supply room loaded with 8,000 brochures.

But what if brochures could be eliminated and marketing materials could easily be personalized for each prospect?

This is exactly the solution Lexis-Nexis wanted for its field sales force. Using a package from Mobilize, the entire 400-plus Lexis-Nexis field sales force can create personalized proposals and contracts, which they can then instantly e-mail to the potential customer or print on the spot using wireless infrared technology. The obvious advantage here is the money saved in literature printing, warehousing and shipping costs, and, of course, sales responsiveness. The costs make sense, too. Mobilize charges $10 to $50 per user (depending on the number of applications the client wishes to integrate) plus a build fee that generally runs 40 percent of the contract value.

While Lexis-Nexis had implemented a mobile presentation application, it required downloading large amounts of bandwidth-intensive data over standard modem connections, data that would inevitably get dropped in the process. Using the new solution from Mobilize, the reps automatically receive updates only, which means these small data transmissions can easily be managed using a wireless modem. Furthermore, the information arrives preorganized, filtered, and personalized to the reps' profiles, determined by their customer base.

It is this concept of providing accurate product, pricing, and inventory information that is critical to sales. The automation of a centralized presentation manager also increases selling time. Nothing can cool a hot prospect quicker than an "I'll have to get back to you" response. Not just because they are ready to buy, but also because the statement is indicative of the level of service you can provide. Sales is the one place you want always to appear completely equipped and informed. It may be your best competitive tool and most profitable, since wirelessly automated sales tools can accommodate dynamic pricing as well.

Mobilize, founded in 1995, is one of the leaders of wireless sales force automation, due in part to one of their offerings: Mobilize Presentations software, the package used by Nexis-Lexis. While the increased productivity is incentive enough for a sales-oriented corporation to integrate Mobilize Presentations, businesses in brand-sensitive and compliance-sensitive industries such as finance are integrating the product, not just for sales improvement, but for legal protection as well.

THE COMPLIANCE FACTOR

Fidelity Investments and Oppenheimer Funds are two examples of Mobilize Presentations clients, and the reasons are simple. Since the presentations are controlled by a central database, slides that must be shown to comply with industry regulations are inserted automatically. To make the legal department happy, built-in reporting shows an audit trail of what was presented to whom and when, so corporate liability is limited without hindering mobile sales productivity. Prior to this solution, it was common for finance sales reps to personalize their presentations, inadvertently violating industry regulations in the process.

Since personalization is important, it should be noted that there is a business rules engine that can ask reps for audience demographics so that the points presented match their audiences' interests.

HOW TO SAVE BIG IF YOUR NEEDS ARE LESS INTENSE

If you work with a sales force whose needs are less intense than that required by such a powerful product as Mobilize Presentations, there is an alternative via My Docs Online Enterprise service, which is discussed in detail on page 131. This solution is essentially a wireless extranet that allows anyone in your company to access a central database of files. It's different from the Mobilize product in several ways, but most important, it is cheaper (from a high of $24.95 annually per user to a low of $13.95 depending on the number of users) and the files must be accessed in their entirety (versus just updates), which for big presentations can be time-consuming. However, if your company's sales materials are on the lean side (and your budget is as well), My Docs Online may be your best option.

Just like Mobilize's product, My Docs Online allows a user to send materials via e-mail or fax from any wireless device. This means that if you are late to an important sales meeting but one of your colleagues miraculously made it on time, from where you are you could wirelessly send the presentation (even a PowerPoint) to a fax machine, or e-mail the presentation as a file attachment (or both), so the meeting can start.

MOBILE POWERPOINT

As sales forces adopt wireless technology, many are finding that in addition to the efficiencies of wireless retrieval and deployment of sales materials, they are able to dump their laptops as well, even though their presentations require Microsoft's PowerPoint. Through a marriage of a Pocket PC device—a handheld that runs Windows CE—and a software application called Mobile Playback Option from Presenter, Inc., sales professionals can pitch prospective customers on the fly without having to lug a laptop. One of the primary advantages of Pocket PCs (available from Compaq, Casio, and others) is their bright, colorful displays and large amounts of RAM, which can easily accommodate memory-intensive uses like multislide presentations. What makes this first-to-market product ultraimpressive is that it allows for audio and video to accompany the slides. This way, if a salesperson was unable to make the presentation personally, the prospect could download the presentation to their Pocket PC and watch it at their convenience. Far more conducive than asking a prospect to sit in front of their desktop computer.

Presenter, Inc.'s Mobile Playback has other uses for sales pros. In addition to using it as selling tool, Mobile Playback can train the sales force, allowing them to be educated about their company's latest products and services. Since convening sales forces is always a challenge, this distributed presentation method is instantly embraced, as it allows a sales team to maximize their business hours in front of new clients and can utilize downtime, such as airport waits and time between prospects, for corporate training.

Of course, Mobile Playback makes sense only if using the software for converting PowerPoint for use on a Pocket PC is fast and easy. That it is. All you do is upload your slides to presenter.com, where they get converted and can then be downloaded for personal use or use by clients or colleagues for shared viewing. If you want to add voice narration, all you do is call a number and start speaking. Video integration is handled through their interface as well. Most important, presentations don't have to be truncated for the mobile devices. Standard Pocket PCs can hold up to four hours of audio-based presentations or over one hour of video-based presentations. If the memory of the device exceeds the minimum, eight times these amounts can easily be stored.

While the Pocket PC option is an excellent alternative for distributing sales materials, we all know there is no substitute (and never will be) for a face-to-face meeting. Essentially, then, what this technology adds is another point of contact. In other words, its augments the sales process *at the convenience of the customer.* While a prospect must consciously carry around printed materials for later review, one of the primary benefits of the Pocket PC presentation is that potential clients have the device with them already, which drastically improves the chances that the information will be reviewed at all and that a sale will ensue.

In addition to wireless presentation tools, sales force automation includes the domain of wireless order entry, the benefits of which are numerous: no inputting (therefore no paper processing costs), reduced call center staffing, credit authorization and validation in real time with the customer, application of current pricing, real-time inventory checks and status, and approved configuration or bundles. Furthermore, these systems, such as the one available from Mobilize Commerce, can make upsell and cross-sell recommendations during the order entry process, thus increasing average order size.

SAVING THE SALE

There's no question that the more information your salespeople have, the more they can sell. Since wireless is particularly adept at empowering people with the data they need at the exact moment they need it, it's no surprise that the technology can improve sales and even make one when least expected.

That's the experience of California-based realtor Chris Hailstone. In a story reported in the *Los Angeles Times,* Hailstone talked about the advantages of having access to data while out with clients: "There was one instance where I thought a client was going to make an offer on one of my listings, but while we were at the house, they decided they wanted to see some of the other [homes] I'd shown them on a list."

Because he was expecting the couple to make an offer, he had not made any other appointments for the day. Normally, he would have had to go back to his office to start arranging additional house tours, especially for those properties that don't have lockboxes (which allow agents access without a key). On this particular day, Hailstone was reminded of the value of his wirelessly enabled PDA when he located a listing he thought his clients would like and was able instantly to phone the owner, who was just about to leave but agreed to wait. It was worth it. The couple bought the house on the spot—a listing Hailstone had never even intended to show them.

This story reminds us that it's not just access to data, but real-time access that makes a difference.

This is especially true for door-to-door sales forces, who face challenges particular to their working environment. And these challenges can be frustrating when encountering customer hostility face-to-face.

This was the experience of door-to-door sales crews for the *Atlanta Journal-Constitution* newspaper. Every time a prospect answered, the salesperson was clueless about the needs of the customer standing in front of them because the rep had no idea if the person was a subscriber or not. And if the person was a subscriber, was he or she taking the paper two, three, five, or seven days a week. Furthermore, without this data salespeople were unable to concentrate on their best prospects and at the same time were annoying current subscribers.

While the newspaper knew they had to get their mainframe information into the hands of their salespeople, they had an additional impediment: Their sales force lacked strong technical skills. For the *Atlanta Journal-Constitution,* simplicity was the key. The obvious solution were Palm computing devices.

Developed in only eight weeks, the system allows sales people simply to tap an address from a list displayed on their handheld to know instantly if the household is a current subscriber (and how many days it receives the paper), is a lapsed subscriber, or has never received the paper. Based on the profile of the prospect, the handheld advises the sales rep which promotions to offer and also automatically calculates the applicable sales tax that needs to be added depending on which of the 16 counties the sale is being made in.

Back at the office, managers instantly know everything about the sale—the time it was made, who was visited, and the terms—which allows them to constantly measure and thus evaluate sales performance; this means they can work with their reps at the beginning of a potential slump, not months later when the sales dive has been ongoing but the data wasn't available.

Shortly after the Palm implementation for the *Atlanta Journal-*

Constitution's sales force, the newspaper calculated a 30 percent improvement in productivity.

Sometimes the benefit of the introduction of wireless has as much to do with the size and functionality of the devices as it does with the connectivity. U.S. Surgical, a division of Tyco, which develops and manufactures advanced surgical products and markets them to hospitals throughout the world, were thrilled to move their 400-person sales force to handhelds for reasons having to do with the environment in which they are selling: hospitals.

In most cases, the sales professionals can't bring a laptop into the operating room (it interferes with sensitive hospital equipment), and because it's nearly impossible to secure a safe place to store a laptop at most hospitals, many "disappeared" when they were left unguarded during sales calls.

INCREASING VOLUME, REDUCING COSTS

There's an important adjunct to sales force automation, and that's how wireless is reducing the cost of sales. A typical example is, interestingly, a wireless company that needed to make their tethered sales reps mobile. The company is Arch Wireless, and they specialize in two-way Internet messaging and mobile information. Based in Westborough, Massachusetts, the company generates $1 billion in annual revenues and has more than 200 offices and a 1,600-member sales force.

Arch's goals mirror that of any company of any size that wants to fortify its sales force with a wireless solution. They want to save money, lots of it. And they want to offer the best customer experience possible. The reason the Arch case history is so informative is that they have kept scrupulous records about the performance of their solution.

Arch deployed Mobilize Commerce, which integrated with Arch's order entry, billing, and fulfillment systems and accommodated changes to their back-end information systems that could occur at any time. Just as important, Mobilize Commerce was compatible with Arch's existing two-way pagers, with an option to interface with Palm OS devices whenever Arch was ready.

In terms of savings, the order entry arena is where Arch has seen the biggest windfall. The annual total is over $850,000 in diminished call center costs. Furthermore, with their previous phone-it-in system for orders, 10 percent of sales were rejected by the system, a reject rate that has been whittled down to near zero since the introduction of mobile order entry.

With the mobile solution, all orders are processed in real time, which means the order can be checked against inventory instantly. If inventory is insufficient to fill the order, the rep is alerted and given alternative delivery dates and valid product substitutions that meets the customer's requirements.

Since the order is being inputted in the presence of the customer, the rep can immediately discuss available options so the customer can select an alternative product during the actual order input process. In the past, the rep would not have been informed of the inventory short-age until after he or she left the customer's locale, at which point the salesperson would sheepishly inform the customer—after the sale—that the product would not be available when promised. In some cases, this gave Arch's competitors an advantage, as customers would contact alternative distributors for a product order Arch could not fulfill.

In addition to real-time order confirmations, the improvement in sales dollar volume can be seen in two other areas. The first is the result of the real-time order entry. Since the mobile product is menu-driven, it allows for dynamic real-time upselling and cross-selling, as the system is programmed to prompt the rep with suggestions for add-ons and upgrades as each part of the order is inputted.

The second advantage is that field sales reps can respond to cus-tomer queries wherever they are, since they have instant access to all their customer records via their mobile devices. As one rep put it suc-cinctly, "Telling customers you have to get back to them isn't good enough anymore."

Arch, being sensitive to customer needs and the necessity of provid-ing product as soon as possible, would often carry inventory in field offices so that the company could fill orders overnight. This caused a myriad of problems at the end of each month when their satellite offices had to reconcile their stock.

Typically, this took three days a month for each team of ten sales-people, with an annual cost of $750,000, an expense that has nearly dis-appeared since satellite office administrators no longer have to hunt for missing order information necessary to complete the monthly reconcili-ation.

Now that you understand the implement, let me reveal to you the bottom-line numbers: By automating the order entry process, Arch Wireless now saves over $1.2 million annually with time to payback in under three months.

SALES LEADS THAT CAN FIND YOU ANYWHERE

There's one last aspect of wirefree sales force automation, and frankly, I think it may be the best part: wireless sales lead management. Now that we have wireless technology to facilitate the sales process, how about using it to help generate leads, thus eliminating some of the cost of customer acquisition, the most expensive part of the sales process?

Next time you buy a Lexus, you might note your salesperson carrying a wireless e-mail device or other two-way Internet communicator. While you and your husband are admiring the interior of a new LS series four-door, the sales pro standing just three feet away is servicing his or her next customer.

The lead came from Lexus's Web site, where potential buyers can "Build Your Own Lexus." It's a simple and fun process, which, after asking for your zip code, lets you select the model and all the options you want. When you are done, a summary sheet is generated showing exactly what your dream Lexus looks like, including the model in your selected exterior and interior colors, along with the total MSRP based on the options you selected. At the bottom of the summary are the names of two dealers closest to the zip code you supplied, along with the opportunity to e-mail them.

If you click on the e-mail option, you are asked for your terrestrial coordinates, a text box to relay any questions you have, and the option to be contacted by e-mail or phone. The model configuration that you just designed is attached automatically to your query.

In a few seconds, the request is received by the dealer via Aether Systems' NetSearch merchant notification system. This software peruses the inbound lead and either shuttles it to a manager, who will then pass it along to whomever he considers the best person for the sale, or the software uses its intelligent lead distribution "rules" to decide which sales pro is the best fit with the sale based on individual core competencies.

Moments later, a device capable of sending and receiving e-mail (it can be a cell phone or handheld) receives the missive. At this point, the salesperson can respond immediately with a personal message or use any of his prewritten replies that essentially says he will get back with the customer as soon as possible.

The beauty of this system is that it doesn't end on the ability to respond instantly. Meanwhile, back at the computer systems audit trails are being generated of every inbound request. For example, if a salesperson fails to respond within a pre-set time frame, the manager is notified. This feature not only ensures timely responses, it makes sure that

A Typical Sales Message as It Appears Using
Aether's NetSearch Wireless Sales
Lead Management Solution

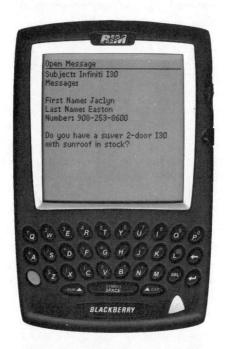

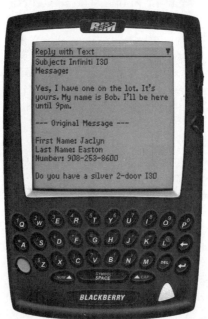

none of the valuable leads get lost. The robust reporting also includes data on every lead, all the wireless activity of a specific salesperson, as well as the opportunity to view the entire history of a particular request, which includes the initial inquiry as well as all subsequent responses.

There is a lot of downtime for salespeople during a sale, especially for large-ticket items like cars, where the buyers often take time just to contemplate the purchase or engage in lengthy discussions about it with family or friends in tow. Now test drives and "one more look around the lot just in case" can be time well spent for sales pros, who can multitask by making connections with other motivated buyers. Keep in mind, too, that the mobile devices work just about anywhere the sales pro's device has coverage, which includes heading into work from home, in a restaurant on a break, or while attending a kid's sporting event during dealership hours. This is a ubiquitous option.

Web sites that include an e-mail link are renowned for their lack of responsiveness. Days or weeks can pass before a query is responded to, if it is answered at all. According to a *Consumer Reports* survey, only 35 percent of potential car buyers got a quote back in less than two days. Therein lies the problem. People don't want to wait two days. They want a response in minutes. If they don't get it, no problem, they go to the competition only a click away.

In defense of the car dealers, Internet inquirers are not nearly as hot as folks standing in the showroom. The level of intention from a pajama-surfing, daydreaming Lexus owner is far less plausible than a sale from the couple in their early forties with pristine credit who just ambled onto the lot. But the fact is the car dealers have gone to the trouble to invest in a Web site, so why not make a comparatively small investment and get the fullest return on investment from the site? While not every e-mail will convert to a sale, those that do will have a shorter cycle because the salesperson was quickly able to establish a dialogue and rapport.

Realizing the value of wireless sales lead management, many automakers are integrating the systems. In addition to Lexus, Hyundai, Infiniti, Nissan, and others are realizing the value. Large automotive dealerships that offer various makes, such as MSN's Carpoint, have integrated the technology into their Dealerpoint network, which is currently licensed to Ford, Honda, Acura, and Isuzu.

While the NetSearch system is worlds better than phone memo slips and time-consuming faxes, there is still room for improvement. I predict we will see systems like this extending further into the business intelligence pool. For example, the lead management system will review the lead and then check inventory against it before passing the message along to the salesperson. It could indicate if there is an exact match and also offer a list of similar vehicles with most but not every option requested ("Sorry, no moonroof"). The software could also search the database of like dealers to see if they have exactly what the prospect is looking for. This information, with the initial inquiry, is then sped along to the rep.

Armed with this high-quality data, the salesman can initiate a much more intelligent response, substituting a lackluster "I'll see what we have and get back to you soon." While the response is timely, it lacks content. Instead, imagine your delight with the following reply: "Yes, we have exactly what you want. I'm staring at it right now. It's gorgeous. When do you want to come in and take a test drive?" The enthusiasm alone is enough to motivate any serious customer to stop everything and get right to the dealership.

Needless to say, auto dealerships are not the only business ripe for wireless sales leads management. While it theoretically applies to any sales environment, it is particularly well suited for high-ticket purchases where the salespeople are difficult to reach while on the job (real estate agents and contractors, for example). The latter group has already contracted with Aether, the folks who make NetSearch, while real estate agents affiliated with Century 21, Coldwell Banker, and ERA also have the service. The idea behind both these applications is that prospects can feel as though they have gotten the same quality of attention and speediness they would have if they were in sitting in the sales professional's office.

COCA-COLA'S "DO-IT-YOURSELF" SOLUTION

Reading these successes may now have you more certain than ever of your desire to enable your sales force, so there are two considerations of which I want you to be aware. The first is that there are numerous companies that are terrific with these installations, and many of them are mentioned here. Any can skillfully make your goals happen. The second thought is that you may actually be better off doing it yourself.

Read this inspirational story of a successful launch from one of the best-known brands in the world: Coca-Cola:

Billy Wang is our focus. He's the business development manager for the Southern California Division of the Coca-Cola Company and the person who wanted to upgrade his sales force from paper to pixels. Apparently, Coke was losing ground to competitors whose sales forces were wirefree and hence more productive and efficient.

Wang is not a technophile, but he is comfortable with gadgets and astutely aware of the benefits of the right device in the right environment. In fact, finding the right device was the easy part. Wang quickly decided on the Compaq iPAQ Pocket PC because of its speed and performance. It was in finding the right software that the tale takes a few turns.

Wang needed to find a program that he could integrate with Coke's existing Web-based SQL Server business applications running on their salespeople's desktops.

Without using any consultants and instead relying on the help of Tim Troglia, the cold drink technology manager for the Southern California Division, the duo began soliciting proposals from companies to build the input forms necessary for the handheld system to work. The proposal prices kept getting higher and higher, and Wang lacked confidence in any of the companies pitching the account. "Not a lot of people know how to do this," he remarked.

Since the companies he was consulting at the time didn't have much more experience than he did, Wang decided to look at some of the off-the-shelf applications in an attempt to write the program himself, even though he was far from being a programmer. Unfortunately, all the software he tried was either too hard to customize or too difficult to use in general. Except one.

The software was from a company named Syware, and the product is called Visual CE. It was actually one of the first programs Wang bought, but the last one he tried. And when he did he was shocked . . . at its simplicity and ease of use. What Wang didn't know at the time was that this program he flippantly bought for a few hundred dollars was currently being used by managers like himself at IBM, Blue Cross and Blue Shield, and Chevron.

Within a week, Wang and Troglia completed their first set of customized forms, which they aptly named Pocket Cold Drink. Needless to say, the pair did make a few calls to Syware's tech support, which is exactly what the company expects. "We target people who are comfortable with computers," says a Syware executive, "but are not necessarily programmers."

While Syware admits that they don't do everything, they are also quick to note that what they do, they do well.

Syware and Coke were a perfect fit. Coke's goal was simple. They wanted to distribute their database on a device that could also accept inputted data and bring it all together in the central database. Of course, once the initial goal was met, Wang and Troglia began adding the features that were important to the salespeople, like the ability to sort prospect addresses by zip code.

The sales force embraced their Pocket PCs and immediately discovered newfound time. One account manager confessed that he spent his Friday afternoons planning for the next week, handwriting prospect information onto paper forms. That process is gone now, and he estimates the new program is saving him over 100 hours a year.

Once Wang's handheld solution was deployed, he quickly noted with pride that he and Troglia were able to get a $500 device to work like a $4,000 PC. "Just in our division you can get an idea of the savings," Wang noted.

A few months after the salespeople began using the "homemade handheld," Wang made an appearance at a national Coca-Cola conference that focused on the sharing of new inventions and ideas. Wang proudly demonstrated the iPAQ running Wang-ware, to which his peers responded, "You did what?"

Apparently, going solo, without a cushion of consultants, didn't fit into the mind-set of what Wang refers to as "our corporate architecture."

But Wang proved that do-it-yourself—even when you don't think you know what to do—may be your best solution.

For a complete list of links
to all the companies mentioned, visit
www.easton.com.

7

The Death of Cash
(and Waiting in Line)

IF WE WERE to date the first wireless payment system, we'd probably be looking at the dawn of civilization. Barter was the trend, and a common dialogue might have begun and ended with, "See those six cattle? I'll trade you for my daughter."

Eventually, the currency concept arrived and involved gold, paper money, checks, and credit cards. All physical. Payment by way of atom. Accordingly, inefficiencies have dogged each system. The weight of gold. The time consumed to write and register a check. The authorization, signature, and paper receipts associated with credit cards. Payment systems have not improved, they've only become more complicated, and no one is getting what they crave most. Customers want convenience. Merchants want efficiency.

While technologically 1997 may be remembered most for the landing of *Pathfinder* on Mars, 20 years from now the most enduring event may be the debut of a little device that in a nanosecond wirelessly paid for goods. It was not issued by a bank or credit card company. It was distributed by an oil corporation.

THE FOB PHENOMENON

It was in 1997 that Mobil introduced Speedpass, a black, 1.5-inch barrel of plastic that weighs a fraction of an ounce. It dangles inconspicuously from a key chain and is generally referred to as a fob. It allowed Mobil's customers to do the impossible—pay for gas in two seconds or less. Customers simply pull up to the pump and wave their fob in front of Mobil's mascot/logo, Pegasus, who lights up, indicating that the customer is approved to start pumping. Payment due is charged automatically to the credit card provided by the customer when he or she signed up.

In only four years, the fobs could be found attached to over 4.5 million key chains, with their popularity developing so rapidly that now ExxonMobil (the result of a merger) estimates 30 million in use by 2006. Their exponential growth has less to do about gas and much to do about other uses, such as paying for convenience store purchases, video rentals, and fast food—routine shopping experiences where time saved is key.

The technology in play here is radio frequency identification (RFID), and the only reason I mention it is to point out that radio waves are transmitting the wallet information, therefore there are no line-of-sight issues. Because transmission is by radio wave, the fob concept is also available in a tag format that is applied to a back or rear window of a vehicle, which means all you have to do is drive up to the pump. No need to remove a key chain from the ignition to wave the fob because the tag is sensed by a nearby reader.

Companies have been eager to sign up for commercial Speedpass accounts because of these semipermanent car tags, which assure companies who own the vehicles that the gas being purchased is for one of theirs. Compare this to the fobs, which can pay for gas for noncompany vehicles as well as a Twinkies, batteries, and other "necessities" available at an ExxonMobil station convenience store.

On a final technical note, whether the data is transmitted from a fob or a car tag, the devices are collectively called "transponders," a combo of *trans*mitter and re*sponder,* both of which they are.

These transponders also come in the form of dashboard mounts or front window tags for use by cities to hasten the toll collection process. The Transportation Corridor of Orange County (TCA) is one of them, with a system called FasTrak. Realizing the potential of the captive prepaid audience, the TCA offered area McDonald's the opportunity to accept payment from transponder devices.

As might be expected, the FasTrak devices saved McDonald's and their customers time. In this case, 15 seconds from the 131-second transaction average to complete an order, including gathering the food order. Even better, however, the average order increased by $2.06, which more than offsets the 25 to 35 cents the fast-food chain pays to the TCA. In addition to the increase in revenue per order (attributable to the credit card psychology of always spending an average of 35 percent more when not using cash), the McDonald's in the TCA grouping noticed that

FasTrak users increased their visits by 17 percent. In other words, they were both spending more and eating at the chain more often.

McDonald's, as well as other fast-food chains such as KFC and Taco Bell, are also beginning to integrate these wireless RFID payment systems in other parts of the country. Some are using ExxonMobil's Speedpass, which justifies the oil companies' predictions of exponential popularity, while others are using a device from 2Scoot that is gaining notoriety, particularly for their deal with Nokia.

Although 2Scoot has a fob device, they have also banded together with the cell phone king to produce SmartCovers, which allow owners of certain models of Nokia phones to use a faceplate that integrates an RFID tag. The faceplates function just like the fobs, meaning that the customer simply waves their phone in front of the reader. The faceplate advantage is a huge convenience, since most cell phone owners always have their cells with them.

2Scoot faceplates and fobs have the same potential for success as ExxonMobil's Speedpass. Their system is open, which means any merchant can accept payment from any 2Scoot transponder. There is no exclusivity, unlike with Speedpass, which works only at ExxonMobil stations and a smattering of non–gas establishments.

In other words, 2Scoot would work at McDonald's, Wendy's, and Burger King, which means they have the same ubiquity potential as Visa or MasterCard, with none of the hassle and huge dose of simplicity. When consumers initiate the service, they can designate which cards they like to use at which establishments: their Shell Oil card at those gas stations, their frequent flier miles branded credit card for all retail purchases, and American Express at restaurants. Highly specific assignments (Visa at Pizza Hut and MasterCard at Barnes & Noble) is also possible.

What's in it for the merchant are cross-branded promotions, a boost in purchase size, smaller checkout lines that move more quickly, and loyalty from customers who clearly prefer the convenience.

The motivation for merchants to install a 2Scoot system is their *return on investment* (note emphasis). According to a study by 2Scoot and verified in the real world by Tricon (the proud parent of Pizza Hut, Taco Bell, and KFC), the use of a transponder, in this case that of 2Scoots, saves each location $200,000. A cash payment requires about 30 seconds, and transponders reduce that to 5 seconds or less. If a credit card is used, it reduces the 70-second process to 5 seconds or less. These reductions convert to a 20 to 25 percent increase in total sales volume during peak hours.

Merchants will pay between $6,500 and $13,000 for the equipment, plus a nominal fee paid to 2Scoot for each transaction. A lease option is also available for as little as a couple hundred dollars, making the transponder affordable to any small business.

By the way, on the off chance you are ever a contestant on *Jeopardy*, you'll want to know that no matter which company brands the transponder (ExxonMobil, 2Scoot, or other company), all are manufactured by Texas Instruments.

PAYMENT VIA PALM, CELL, OR THUMBPRINT

While transponders got the wireless payment revolution under way, they are just one of many wireless payment options surfacing. The next generation is personal digital assistants and cell phones.

VeriFone, the company responsible for most of the country's retail POS terminals (ultrasophisticated cash registers), developed the first system with Palm, Inc., in early 2001. Shoppers simply line up the infrared port (which is on all PDAs, even those not using the Palm operating system), activate their "eWallet," and select the payment method they prefer (credit card, debit card, and so on). After a PIN is tapped to prevent fraud, the information is encrypted and beamed to the POS terminal and the transaction is processed. Though it's a simple procedure, the benefits are endless.

In addition to shortening the time to buy, customers will receive an electronic receipt that can be seamlessly integrated into an expense report (liberation for the business traveler). Moreover, shoppers will be beamed back e-coupons and promotional opportunities for later use, which, because they are stored on the Palm, are never lost and therefore have a much higher probability of being redeemed. Ditto for loyalty programs. Gone are the paper cards for the "buy 10 lattes, get 1 free." Now the cards are digitally punched.

Then there's the synch factor. In time, all the VeriFone POS terminals will connect to the Internet as part of the transaction processing, and as they do, you will have the option of letting your handheld pick up your e-mail or synch your calendar at the same time you are paying for the latest John Grisham novel. (Can you hear my heart beating a little faster?)

The integrating technology is a simple infrared reader that can be attached to most of the existing VeriFone POS terminals. For this reason, such a payment method can be quickly adopted. In fact, expect to see these first on POS systems in travel industries such as hotels, car rental agencies, and airport food concessions.

Further down the wireless payment food chain are cell phones. The technology to make these a predominant payment method simply has not been deployed on any scale and, in my opinion, requires too many chefs in a very small kitchen for it to happen very quickly.

For the sake of description, there are a couple ways cell payments could work. First is that you would call a number that would enable a sale. Marconi Systems offers this with Coca-Cola. Customers using GSM phones, the European standard, dial a phone number, the vending machine's selection lights up, and the Coke machine's soda charge shows up on your next cell phone bill. In Amsterdam, drivers dial a phone number to pay for parking by calling one number when they arrive and another when they depart.

Another possibility is that Bluetooth, a technology that communicates wirelessly with a device in a 30-foot circumference (and is explained in detail on page 124), could activate the phone. The display could give the cell phone payment choices, making it less tedious to interact on the small displays. Since millions more people have cell phones than PDAs, great emphasis will be placed on cell phones as an elegant payment solution. The quickest solution is probably an infrared device, like those used with the Palms. People will use their cell phones for the convenience (no change, but high thirst) or to save time (dial a number, walk through the train station turnstile). Keep in mind that the phones I have just mentioned are not the same instruments most people use today. In fact, it will take until at least 2005 before we start to see a majority of these more sophisticated phones replace the handsets people use now.

Any system that can beam will also let merchants accept payments from checking accounts. The Infrared Data Association is establishing an infrared Financial Messaging protocol that will allow check authorization and the ability to settle transactions without ever having to deal with labor-intensive paper checks.

Cellular carriers love these payment systems because they add revenue to dwindling profits by siphoning off a percentage of the sale, even if you choose to pay via credit card using the phone because the carrier will act as the clearinghouse. (Ah, the advantages of infrastructure.) Banks are wooing the cell carriers for this reason, realizing that they also have the option of offering high-interest payment plans for purchases.

While commerce is not a core competency of cellular phone companies, keep in mind that they have ultimate leverage to guarantee swift payments: the threat of turning off a customer's phone.

WHAT DOES THIS MEAN IN 2010?

By 2010, we could revisit the wireless payment option I've just described, and on the surface, it may all look the same. The difference will lie behind the devices. Instead of having a device specific to a task, like the Speedpass fob for gas purchases, you'll have digital wallet data attached to any device you like and own as many different devices as you want.

For example, fobs are great for people who like "small and inconspicuous." Fobs, however, are completely impractical for businesspeople who receive too many benefits from the electronic receipts available from PDAs and cell phones. But instead of having to choose one over the other, there will be a central wallet that will be activated by the device you choose.

For example, if it's a fast-food purchase, you'll drive through and let the car tag pay for it. Buying a book for company research, you'll use your Palm for the electronic receipt that downloads to your mobile expense report. Out of change and dying for a Dr Pepper, you'll dial the vending machine and pay through your cell phone. The common denominator here is that the payments are all being pulled from the same credit card, debit card, or bank account. The "wallet" would actually have several credit cards, with each card designated for certain types of purchases, as I discussed earlier.

In other words, as with credit cards, there will be two or three dominant wallet companies, and people will subscribe to at least one. Most retail outlets will accept all of them (as long as there aren't too many). Where the credit card companies will fall into the loop is still a question.

Distinguishing will be the trick. All offer convenience to the merchant and the consumer. All offer nifty value adds such as coupons, purchase summaries for the customer, demographics, and buying histories for the merchants. Then there's the added security. Transponders either encrypt data when it is being sent or send a customer ID only, which is matched with payment data on a separate server, or a combo of both, using an authorization number instead of the actual credit card account number. If a transponder, faceplate, or other RFID-type payment is lost or stolen, the same rules for credit card theft or loss apply. The holder is responsible only for the first $50 of fraud, and that applies only if the holder is negligent in reporting the situation. Another motivator for transponder use for consumers and credit card companies is that transponders cannot be cloned, unlike credit cards with their easy-to-copy magnetic strips. With respect to PDAs and cell phones, they encrypt data as it is beamed.

By the way, there is another payment device available now that every person already has and always has with them. A thumb. A retina. A voice. Welcome to the world of biometric payments, where your electronic wallet is associated with your body parts. A reader scans any of the above and identifies you instantly. Once your identity has been established, it is reconciled with your electronic wallet.

The technology is available now, but despite the viability it may be longer than expected before it's commonly rolled out. The gatekeeper is the psychology, both business and personal.

Credit card companies and other organizations that profit from transactions aren't big fans of body-type payments because our parts don't bear logos, and corporations just love to brand. From the consumer viewpoint, thumbprints may still be too intrusive for baby boomers and the older generations, but they have a chance with Generation X and especially Generation Y; in fact, many schools have now replaced lunch cards with fingerprint scanners.

Despite the ease of a thumbprint, retinal scans, and voice recognition, until they can also store receipts and coupons, handheld devices still have a lead.

RETAIL'S NEW KILLER APP

Finally, there is an aspect of wireless payment that is just as liberating as those described so far: wireless credit authorization. This is one of those under-the-radar technologies because it's not very glamorous yet will be almost as liberating as the wireless payments discussed thus far.

Since the advent of the credit card, mobile professionals have never been able to accept plastic payments with confidence because they didn't have a quick way to get an authorization. While plumbers, cleaners, repair personnel, and cabbies could call their overburdened dispatchers, the process took an indeterminate amount of time, which was bothersome to both the employee and the customer. Furthermore, if the credit card number was recited over a radio, there was a huge security breach. Then there are the mobile retailers, which include home "party" sales folks, mall carts, and stadium vendors, who don't even have dispatchers to fall back on.

To grasp the breadth of problems being solved, let me first introduce you to the terminal so you understand how ultraportable these units are. Called the Omni and made by VeriFone, they are only about the size of paperback book. Authorization requires a mere three to seven seconds, which includes encrypting the data and sending it up and back for processing via the internal radio modem. There's a card swipe, large display, and keypad, plus a printer that can dispatch receipts or coupons. The rechargeable batteries last for about 100 transactions. While these specs are nifty, the uses are even niftier.

How do you think service would improve if a salesperson could seamlessly serve the customer by accepting payment on the spot? Customers would never have to wait in line. Instead, as the buyer admires a product deep in the store, at the height of emotion, the sales rep could say, "Hand me your card and in 10 seconds it's yours." At this point, the customer offers a credit, debit, or gift card (the Omni accepts all three), and the payment is processed, complete with receipt, in seconds.

Restaurants have a bonanza opportunity as well. Instead of bringing the check, waiting for the card, coming back to pick up the card, getting it authorized, and then returning to the table for the signature, waitresses would just bring the portable terminals to the table with the tab and authorize the card on the spot. This system could easily turn a table at least 10 minutes more quickly.

Then there's the safety advantage for mobile professionals, who carry much less cash. By way of example, the city of Chicago was so concerned about the security of their taxicab drivers that it drafted regulations requiring the cab companies to install devices to wirelessly process credit and debit card payments. Unfortunately, driving a cab in Chicago is one of the most dangerous jobs in the city due to the volume of armed robberies (since cabbies can end a shift with plenty of cash).

Another example comes from the highly competitive cab market in Caracas, Venezuela, where the Taxco cab company improved its turnover volume by 35 percent in just three months by installing wireless credit authorization. This jump was due partially to the fact that they were the first (and for a while the only) taxicab company that could accept credit and debit payments, a competitive advantage when transporting hordes of business travelers. Furthermore, the terminals include wireless global positioning technology, which allows dispatchers to track the taxi, adding even greater security.

Any business of any size that accepts payment is a candidate for wireless credit authorization terminals. Even a small store can benefit with only one terminal by being able to open a temporary checkout lane for high-volume days or to service a sidewalk sale.

Keep in mind that since these machines have built-in printers, they can also handle receipts, confirmations, and warranties. Couponing is also supported, which means an incentive for another purchase can be issued on the spot, tailored to what was just bought.

Before I start sounding like the Wireless Credit Card Authorization

VeriFone's Omni-Series Wireless Credit Card Authorization in Action

Wireless credit and debit card authorization allows for sales and rental transactions anywhere. The device includes a built-in printer for receipts, coupons, and warranties.

Poster Girl, I'll make the final point that these systems, along with wireless payment, cannot happen fast enough for me and countless other customers for whom service and speed are paramount. In these days of listless salespeople and subpar service, any technology that can get us in and out of a store more quickly with a higher level of service is proof that the retail gods have answered our prayers.

To see photos of all the wireless payment and authorization options discussed, visit *www.easton.com*.

8

The Wonders of Wireless in Inventory and Operations Management

YOU WOULD THINK that a company with a 99.8 percent delivery accuracy rate would be congratulating themselves for such extraordinary performance. Not at McKessonHBOC, a pharmaceutical and medical supplies company. This Fortune 40 corporation was distressed by their 0.2 percent (I repeat: Zero point two percent) daily average, which translates to 50 mistakes a day from their 25,000 deliveries.

The reason for the need for 100 percent is related to cost. Owing to the nature of the goods being delivered, a wrong delivery or failure to obtain a customer signature on a manifest exposes McKessonHBOC to disputes that can easily lead to litigation.

To patch that exasperating 0.2 percent, McKessonHBOC's first line of defense was to ensure that what was being delivered matched what was ordered. To do this, the company had to automate data input from points of delivery all over the country into the company's central order and distribution system. While such data integration was the responsibility of the company, McKessonHBOC had to find a solution that was affordable for their 2,500 delivery people, many of whom are contract drivers from courier companies. Hence, laptops or other expensive technology could not be considered. Fortunately, they are able to do everything they need to with comparably inexpensive handheld devices. Using Symbol handhelds that utilize the Palm operating system, drivers have manifest information from the company's order distribution system at hand, so as they drive their delivery route, the handheld scans each package as it comes off the truck and electronically captures the customer's signature. When the drivers have to deliver to areas outside wireless network coverage, the handheld can store data and run the applications offline.

Since introducing the handheld solution, McKessonHBOC has almost

realized their dream of 100 percent accuracy. While they haven't eliminated all of their point-of-delivery legal claims, these have been
reduced by 50 percent, with another 30 percent in general point-of-
delivery claims. Where McKessonHBOC is 100 percent is in the reduction of their manifest imaging costs, which are now zero.

McKessonHBOC, seeing the big picture, knew that to get the most
from their handheld deployment they had to backtrack right to the customer, where many of the problems begin. By allowing them to input
their orders wirelessly, the company has not only made their customers
more mobile, they have also allowed them to view real-time product
descriptions, prices, and more. Best of all, McKessonHBOC is reducing
errors at the first step in the process.

One of wireless's best attributes is its ability to weave together existing technologies, something McKessonHBOC had to do to automate the
entire process from order through delivery. Wireless integrations are by
nature rather simplistic because it's usually a case of the addition of a
simple technology to an existing setup, rather than the full replacement
of an entire back end.

A CHALLENGE BEYOND A CHICAGO BULL

Another valuable example of the gains wireless offers operations management and inventory can be found at Chicago's United Center. Imagine selling 50,000 to 300,000 items in one venue in just a few hours but
having no accurate, detailed sales report or inventory at the end of the
buying frenzy.

This was a standard occurrence at the venue famous for hosting
games for the Chicago Bulls and Chicago Blackhawks. At each event,
thousands and thousands of fans purchase shirts, posters, hats, leather
jackets, and other souvenirs from any of 12 stands and 2 retail outlets
scattered throughout the complex.

These dispersed vendors did not use POS systems, therefore the only
reliable data was gross sales—certainly the most important figure, but
lacking crucial marketing and inventory data such as specific colors,
sizes, and styles of the items sold. Furthermore, there was no method
for tracking items sold, lost, or missing. Because the back-end
processes were paper based, it was impossible to have an exact
account of the amount of merchandise given to each stand or how to
replenish the right merchandise, forecast which merchandise to stock,
and efficiently and accurately reconcile the inventory to the in-house
accounting systems.

Bismarck Enterprises, the company that manages all merchandise for the United Center (as well as food service, beverage, and culinary operations), sensed that a handheld device and the right software could eliminate their inventory management frustrations. They were right.

The system is called (appropriately) Fandemonium Inventory Management Systems and was developed by Ponvia in four weeks. The devices from Symbol Technologies using the Palm operating system were equipped with bar code scanners to collect point-of-sale information. The handhelds were deployed throughout the venue so that reconciliations could be handled on the spot instead of usurping three days each month to complete.

Now the inventory reconciliation takes place at the end of each event. It's easy to do since the process is completed in only 30 minutes, 100 times faster than their pre-wireless method.

In addition to labor savings, estimated at $100,000 per year, data quality is impeccable. The inventory tracking using the handhelds is an end-to-end solution, beginning at the loading dock when the merchandise data is scanned and synchronized with the purchase order. Only when the two reconcile does the receiving manager sign for and close the purchase order.

Not surprisingly, Ponvia, Symbol, Palm, the United Center, and Oracle won a Moby award for this innovation.

PRICING IT RIGHT

While Chicago's United Center was trying to account for merchandise, Famous Footwear was trying simply to make sure their merchandise was labeled with the right price.

Famous Footwear, the largest brand-name shoe retailer in the nation with over 927 stores in 50 states, was constantly plagued with pricing issues and desperate for a way to speed up price verification, which was currently taking four to six hours per week per store to update. The laborious process produced significant errors, which meant that advertised specials often didn't match the price as marked, or the price marked did not agree with the register at checkout.

These pricing inaccuracies became such a problem that the company believes it was actually losing buyers because of it. Famous Footwear describes their core customers as "price-conscious shoppers, often mothers with young children in tow who have little patience for mistakes." Owing to their customer service initiatives, the lower price was also honored, which meant the stores were often losing revenue on these inaccurately priced items.

Moving from feet to hands, Famous Footwear in just six weeks developed a handheld solution using technologies from Palm, Inc., and Symbol Technologies. This equipment allowed stores to ensure accurate pricing simply by scanning shoe boxes with a handheld and entering the data on its keypad. In the back room (and admittedly this gets kind of geeky), the system connects to a wireless local-area network in each store via radio technology and from that network connects out to Famous Footwear's central computer system, where pricing information is maintained in a central database. In seconds, the handheld's display indicates the correct price and sticker color. The next version of the system will integrate a wireless automatic printer clipped to employee belts for automatic sticker output.

What looks like a price solution is actually indicative of a bigger paradigm shift for Famous Footwear. Giving the store employees wireless real-time access to the enterprise system ultimately allows Famous Footwear to manage their near 1,000 properties as a cohesive unit.

It's precisely these operation and inventory issues with which wireless is such a good fit. The minute you try to find solutions in hardwired lines, you are looking at complicated installations and back-end integrations. On the other hand, with mobile technology you are simply extending the computers that already exist. The United Center is collecting sales information electronically—in other words, "data input"—while Famous Footwear is tapping into their enterprise systems for data to properly service the sale—"data output."

"I'LL TAKE 15,000 PALMPILOTS, PLEASE"

Since mobile technology has established that it can improve every aspect of a retail operation, Sears, a company already ahead of the curve wirelessly (see chapter 5, page 51), ordered up so many customized Palm units that the deployment is considered one of the biggest in history.

The Symbol Technologies tailor-made units can be found in the hands of 15,000 employees in Sears's 860 full-line stores. These devices are equipped with an internal wireless modem card that lets employees automatically tap into their store's wireless local-area network. The store's staff uses them for inventory, price changing, and merchandise pickup, receiving, and replenishment.

Not to be outdone, Kmart signed a $70 million contract with Symbol to install wireless networks in all 2,100 of its stores to support operations such as receiving, inventory, label printing, price checking, and employee communications.

As both the Sears and the Kmart installations prove, retailers are learning how wireless technology can solve so many inefficiencies that these enormous multimillion-dollar contracts to install mobile technology are now common.

NEAR PERFECT INVENTORY

With that in mind, let's focus on specific wireless applications for an even more thorough understanding by showing you how wireless can drastically reduce the cost of accounting for inventory whether it's checking inventory out (as in a sale) or in (as in rental returns).

Let's look first at the technology in play, so that the examples I give you will make even more sense. Retail's new best friend is called RFID, and it's so simple that it takes only a paragraph to describe.

RFID stands for *ra*dio *f*requency *id*entification. While you just read about them in fobs and cell phone faceplates, they also come in the form of a tag that sends out radio waves that can be read as far as 100 feet away and hence don't require line of sight, one of the biggest challenges of bar codes. Up to 50 tags can be read per second, which beats bar codes by a swiftness of 40 times. By the way, if you've ever bought something and the clerk forgot to remove the sensor before you left the store, thus triggering a shrill alarm, you've had a personal experience of how effectively a non-line-of-sight technology like RFID can work.

RFID tags are paper thin and as wide as two matches laid side by side, but despite their size they are incredibly durable. On the other hand, if a bar code is even slightly dinged—in other words, your three-point rim shot with a box of Grape-Nuts scratched the bar code as the cereal bounced into your cart—the info has to be inputted manually by the supermarket checker, and you've had a typical experience of bar code sensitivity.

Given these facts, what is a bar code's big advantage over RFID? Bar codes cost virtually nothing because they are imprinted on the item. Meanwhile, RFID tags cost an average of 30 cents, which means they are still too expensive for that box of cereal. The goal is to get the tags down to a penny a piece, which means that everything in the supermarket will have one. Keeping in mind that 50 items can be read per second translates to a new model for supermarket checkout by the late 2000s: a momentary push of your cart within the zone of a reader.

But the advantages I've described thus far about RFID tags, along with their incredible ability to have information written onto them (I'll come back to this in a minute), are streamlining retail's biggest challenges. In the same way that the Internet offers friction-free communication to anyone, anywhere in the world, RFID is effective in reducing the hoops retail inventory and operational processes have constantly to jump through.

All right, so now let's look at ways this is applied, starting with RFID in outbound sales. The in-a-second grocery checkout I've just described is one example of the RFID ability to hasten the concept of self-checkout. Because these tags can be read collectively and so quickly, a swipe of a credit card is all that is needed to complete the purchase. Furthermore, the tags hold 100 characters of information (bar codes hold only up to 16), so you'd get the same extreme data now available about your purchases down to the origin factory of your jumbo bag of Lay's potato chips.

RFID tags imbedded in products is another path. Let's look at the purchase of a $700 leather jacket. At the point the jacket is purchased, all the receipt information would be written back to the tag. Present day, this means that if the item had to be returned for any reason and there was no paper receipt, as with a gift, the jacket's history is available using an RFID reader. This history prevents a discounted or stolen item from being returned for a full-price refund and allows retailers to ferret out counterfeit merchandise. It has been estimated that minimizing return management fraud can add 0.5 percent to a store's operating margins.

On a similar note, if a barrage of defective merchandise is being returned, it can all be easily traced back to a vendor's build lot.

Rentals are another area where RFID really shines, particularly for video stores with hundreds of tapes moving in and out. The 1,000-store Movie Gallery installed an RFID system using Intellitags made by Intermec, one of the premier RFID companies.

Movie Gallery's primary goal was to improve rental check-ins, and that's exactly what they got. A tape need only be dropped in their return box to be read automatically by an RFID scanner, with all the vital data accurately read and registered back into the store's inventory. Gone are the days where tapes would sit in the return bin for up to a day or more until employees had a few spare hours to manually scan the dozens of inbound tapes. Now they can skip this time-intensive activity and move straight to reshelving, which has the added advantage of turning over the inventory more quickly.

According to Intermec, a similar scenario will be a boon to catalogers, who report that up to 30 percent of the merchandise they sell is returned. The return process, which includes restocking merchandise and crediting the customer's account, can be more costly than the margin potential of the sold merchandise. RFID tags on catalog-sold merchandise could support automated return processing, since the SKU (stock keeping unit) and customer data are already on the tag.

There's also an intelligence aspect of this technology for retailers that can be a big help for estimating inventory. Stores in which clothing can be tried on will install RFID readers in the dressing room doorways, and these readers can identify which items customers are interested in. The data can then be reconciled with sales reports and returns information for a better understanding of what sells, what's returned, and what's being tried on but rarely bought. In due time, it is anticipated that all clothing retailers will install RFID readers in their dressing rooms to monitor the data.

Dressing room visits are a key sales component for the Gap, whose research has shown that 77 percent of people who try on at least one item make a purchase.

"If we get you into the fitting room, we've got you," explained one Gap executive. But "to get you," the Gap has to have the item you want in the size and color you prefer. And that's exactly where RFID technology comes into play.

Using Intermec Intellitags technology, the Gap is hoping for "perpetual inventory." According to the company, with RFID they know exactly when an item is out of stock on the display floor so that it can be replenished, either retrieved from the store's backroom stock or ordered from the distribution center.

Gap's use of wireless technology began as a pilot project in 2000 at the factory level, tagging each item while it was being manufactured. This tag then benefited the supply chain and distribution processes.

Using Intellitags, which will cost about 25 cents per item in due time, the Gap estimates that they have reduced labor costs by 50 percent, since garments can be counted and verified in a box without having to open it. In their Atlanta distribution center, Gap has found that up to 60 tags within a carton can be read while moving along a conveyor at 30 feet per minute, with virtually 100 percent accuracy.

As a last look of the efficiencies wireless offers retail operations, here is a sidebar that tenders an unusual resale scenario.

"WIRELESS RACQUET"

The "store" in this case is Wimbledon, the All England Lawn Tennis Club's annual event. If a spectator leaves the festivities before the day ends, he or she can surrender the ticket for resale, with the proceeds going to charity. Problem was, many of the tourists wanted to keep their prestigious stubs as souvenirs. Wimbledon knew they wanted to maintain the program because they were raising £40,000 per year. They found an elegant solution with wireless.

The technology comes from Symbol and uses bar code scanners and a wireless local-area network, so that the data can be transmitted wirelessly from the exit gate to a resale kiosk in seconds, making the resalable tickets available for immediate resale. Because virtually all the early exiters are happy to comply with the fund-raising program and the resale kiosk gets the information to turn over the ticket inventory so quickly, the program occasionally has days now where there are more resale tickets available than buyers. "This," notes a representative, "is a problem we welcome."

9

Redefining Customer Service

IT'S THE DREAM of every golfer—knowing exact yardage to the pin, pace-of-play monitoring, scoring with a real-time leader board, and being able to place snack bar orders from anywhere on the green.

You can have this experience at any of the golf courses that have installed ProShot Networks golf management system. Majestic at Lake Walden Golf Course in Hartland, Michigan, is one of them. They use the displays to not only provide a screen detailing the layout of each hole, distance to the center of the green, and key hazards, but also to inform players of less infrequent but far more dangerous conditions like tornadoes.

It happened in May 2001, when Majestic's Pro used the text messaging feature to alert the 150 golfers on the course of a pending twister. About 120 of the golfers made it to the clubhouse basement while the balance, too far out to make it on time, took cover on the course before the tornado hit.

The purpose of the ProShot Networks system installation was essentially a form of customer service, by providing players with the maximum amount of information about their game. While golf courses rarely have to compete for business, creating the best experience means higher desirability, hence more prestige, the standard by which many courses are compared.

That's precisely the idea behind using wireless technology to compete on better service. Many times, the basic elements from one service to another may be indistinguishable, so what makes one service better than or different from another can be something as simple as the quality of information the customer has access to.

Information as it is displayed on Proshot's Golf Network's wireless terminals mounted on golf course carts . . . on a day with tornadoes.

MORE SERVICE = MORE SALES

We also know the business dictum that customer service quality can always be equated to sales. The more of one, the more of the other, a fact rerealized by Grenley-Stewart, which outfitted their customers with handheld devices that provide a quality of service that always exceeds customer expectations. By overdelivering on an underpromise, Grenley-Stewart has increased sales by 300 percent.

The company's product is diesel fuel, which they sell on a volume contract basis (which nets their customers a savings of a few cents per gallon). Not a big deal when driving a Volkswagen, but a significant cost consideration when fueling a big rig that gets five miles to the gallon and can easily travel a 1,000 miles in a day. When fuel prices fluctuate as much as 25 cents a gallon, the net cost savings can be substantial.

Grenley-Stewart wanted to solve two big problems associated with their business. The first is that their unattended pumps are in out-of-the-way locales—a necessity to keep their prices low, but a problem for drivers. Second, their prices change every day and can vary from location to location. The company wanted to keep drivers up-to-date on where they could find the best deals at the closest location.

The company's interim solution was to post their prices daily on their Web site. Fleet owners could find the day's bargains and communicate this information to their drivers, but doing this over the phone was time-consuming and inefficient.

Enter wireless. Problem solved. Using software customized for them from AvantGo, the drivers can download pricing information and station locations along with maps to the pumps. Because the interface has a standard Web look, the device is in use from moment one.

As an added incentive to use their services, Grenley-Stewart developed an application for the devices that lets truckers complete their Department of Transportation–required log sheets and submit them electronically over the Grenley-Stewart network.

Owing to the information and service value add, the 300 percent sales increase is not much of a surprise. However, the response from customers was far above what the company could have scripted. Because the wirelessly enabled handhelds provide so much extra value, customers became so eager for Grenley-Stewart's services that salespeople found themselves thinking, "They don't know I'm here to sell them anything."

IF YOU ARE NOT FIRST, YOU HAVE TO BE THE BEST

Schwab didn't have it quite that easy, but their mobile strategy deployment is a success story worth noting because although they were not first to market, when they did enter, they had a much better mousetrap.

The competitive edge is that their PocketBroker mobile solution works on any network and across all devices, including RIM pagers, PDAs, and cell phones of particular carriers such as AT&T and Sprint. It offers all the features you'd want, including equity trading, real-time quotes, account balances and positions, watch lists, alerts (which notify you when your user-select price and volatility parameters are met), and market summary information. And therein lies the difference: Their competition has some of the above, but not all. For example, at the time, Ameritrade customers had access via Sprint PCS and a Palm V or VII, but nothing on a RIM pager, AT&T or Web-enabled phone, or PDA.

From a service standpoint, it's interesting to note that two-thirds of Schwab's customers use the service to access news headlines, quotes, and market alerts, with just one-third actually conducting trades. Schwab is not only their place to trade, it's functioning as a portal as well.

Regardless of what their customers do while online, Schwab has additional motivators for launching such a broad wireless plan. It is assumed that those accessing wireless services are the more affluent. For example, Wells Fargo Bank has noted that their customers who bank online are "wealthier clients, and these clients tend to be more loyal." The same can be extrapolated for Schwab.

Second, the online broker has a crush on the overseas market, where wireless is a key to success (as in such mobility-dominated places as Hong Kong). If Schwab, despite its highly effective branding and reputation, could not offer these client bases a wireless option, they would have to concede these markets to their competitors.

IMPROVING RESPONSIVENESS

While most companies move from a paper-and-phone-based situation to a wireless solution, Country Companies Insurance Group, based in Bloomington, Illinois, were further ahead of the curve. Their field appraisers, who work in 10 different states, were using handheld systems but had to rely on one-time-a-day uploads via a wired modem at their offices. Realizing the advantage of real-time communications, they implemented a wireless strategy primarily to let appraisers transmit claim forms from the field; this significantly increased the level of customer service and saved field appraisers an hour a day, since they no longer had to go to the office to upload or download data or receive assignments.

One of their favorite stories is about a customer whose car was vandalized while its owner attended a White Sox game. The following morning, the customer reported the claim to the Country Companies main number and was assured that an appraiser would make contact later that day.

A short while later, appraiser Ken Smith received the assignment in real time while in his car. Noting that the customer was about three miles away, he immediately headed over to meet with him, inspected the vehicle, wrote the estimate, and issued a draft . . . all by 10:30 A.M.

Progressive Insurance also understands the importance of responsiveness and that their product is service. In 1995, they were the first major auto insurer to launch a Web site and have continued their tradition of using wireless technology to provide better service.

Mobile Progressive allows anyone with the right type of wireless access to log on and find the nearest agent based on zip codes. With a second button press the customer can be connected to a Progressive representative, which can be especially helpful to those customers who have been in an accident.

Understanding the value of servicing customers wirelessly, Progressive is also considering a wireless application that will allow their policy holders to find out how much it will cost to insure a new car they are thinking about . . . while they are on the lot.

To continue the car thread, wirelessly empowering representatives always leads to customer satisfaction and retention, and that was the goal of the Hertz Corporation, which installed a wireless system they refer to as the Gold Electronic Manifest. The system's primary function is to communicate arriving customer information to Gold Booths, which are used by the company's #1 Club loyalty program (composed primarily of Hertz's highest-volume customers).

What was originally a voice radio network and paper manifest system when it started, the Gold Club has evolved into an elegant wireless system used by shuttle drivers and curbside attendants to ensure that their best customers' cars are ready to go and that their names and stall numbers are displayed on the digital sign the moment they deboard the airport courtesy bus.

Instead of waiting in lines to complete routine paperwork, Gold Club members simply look for their name and go directly to their cars, where their keys and rental contract are waiting.

While the latter part of the scenario has existed for years and is known by many, the deployment of wireless technology has allowed Hertz to more consistently deliver on their promise. It would make sense, then, that the Hertz Corporation has won over 74 awards for excellence in just the past five years.

Since responsiveness is the key to a successful restaurant, we are already seeing the technology penetrate the industry to improve efficiency, resulting in not only higher profits, but a much better experience for the customer.

For example, PixelPoint is already deploying an application that lets waiters enter orders via handheld units, which wirelessly transmits those orders to the kitchen. When the order is ready, the server is alerted. These two-way wireless communications drastically reduce the time spent running back and forth to the kitchen, which yields not only a higher level of attention to the customer, but the shortest wait possible for an order, both critical elements in determining service quality.

USING GPS TO IMPRESS

Wireless customer service also translates to newfound autonomy, which basically means being able to do your job with a minimum of customer interaction and, by doing so, giving your customers higher-quality service.

This is what Ron Leffler, a Chicago-based limousine driver, discovered after he installed a CoPilot by TravRoute. The program incorporates a voice guidance system that literally tells Ron when it's time to "make a right." The CoPilot has actually turned into a marketing advantage for the entrepreneur. He no longer has to rely on his airport pickup passengers for directions to their homes. Now he says that they can relax or do business on their cell phones and laptops without having to be concerned with giving directions, a fact that has improved his customer repeats.

Another CoPilot customer, home inspector Jim Oler, was stunned at the level of appreciation shown by his customers thanks to his GPS device, which he says far exceeded his expectations and saves him at least two hours a day.

He initially bought the unit to guide him more easily to addresses, especially those in rural areas. The added bonus was that the CoPilot system has a route-planning feature that orders his trips by efficiency, including the approximate travel time required, which allows Oler to plan his day with precision. Oler says that he's proud to be known by his customers as "the home inspector who shows up on time and doesn't even ask for directions."

This leads to one of the most important points you should glean from this chapter and this section. It's not a question of "if" you will have a wireless component that helps you serve your customers. It's only a question of "when." Since it is inevitable, do it now and gain the competitive advantage of differentiating yourself.

While Ron the limo driver uses GPS so that his clients don't have to be responsible for navigating him, how long do you think it will be before his competition installs these devices, which cost only a few hundred dollars each?

UPS is typical of a company that understands the need to be competitive and that using wireless technology to keep their customers informed is their best offense. With an international presence in more than 200 countries and a payroll 340,000 employees long, UPS has held the top spot by being able to predict what their customers want and delivering it, literally and figuratively.

"These days, the information that goes along with each package we ship has become as important as the package itself," remarked one UPS executive.

On an average day, UPS delivers almost 14 million packages, of which customers track 3 million (23 percent) via the UPS Web site. The problem was, UPS research showed that customers want to track packages while out of the office as conveniently as when they have desktop access or a place to plug in their laptops. Likewise, they didn't want to bother phoning a UPS call center.

Tracking packages was not the only information they wanted "anytime, anywhere." UPS research revealed that also important was the ability to compare shipping costs among services such as next-day, one-day, two-day, three-day, and ground; to know the exact in-transit time; and to find the nearest drop-off location.

At the same time, UPS also understood the importance of their entire customer base having access, which meant info for everyone regardless of platform. Contracting with Air2Web, UPS commissioned a solution that would satisfy 94 percent of wireless users (via any existing device—pagers, cell phones, PDAs, RIMs, SMS—that can accept e-mail or accommodate text messaging).

Since virtually all UPS customers have at least one of the above, their wireless service was enormously popular. Even before they issued a press release or began advertising the new service, thousands of customers had signed up.

SURVEYING FOR BETTER SERVICE

When your customers spend up to $5.6 million for your product, you have to be on top of your service, but the best way to do that isn't always apparent at first.

Flexjet sells fractional ownership of corporate jets, where even the cheapest option is close to half a million dollars. While Flexjet is wholly responsible for most of the experience their clients have with their aircraft, they do contract out a few of their services, including catering.

Because Flexjet's customers are often entertaining their most important clients, no detail is too small. A Flexjet executive explains that their customers "want to make sure the caviar is cold, the Champagne is from the right region, the wine is from the right year."

In the past, if sturgeon had been substituted for beluga or there was some other catastrophe, this information would have been included in the trip report that was phoned into Flexjet's headquarters and left on voice mail after each and every trip. With this system, it took up to a couple weeks for all the information to be transcribed, inputted, analyzed, and then acted on, in part owing to the volume of messages, up to three a day for each of their 110 aircraft. While this procedure worked, it lacked the essential timeliness necessary for any customer service initiative to make sense.

Realizing this, one of the company's senior executives spoke out at a meeting; holding up a Palm VII, he asked if there was any way they could "use this thing to solve the problem?" Actually, there was, and a proposal budgeting a comparatively meager $50,000 for programming and equipping each jet with a specially programmed Palm VII became a reality a short time later.

Now, before a plane lands, a flight attendant offers the Palm to the client, who taps his way through the survey, which is then augmented by cabin attendant and pilot responses to questions about their specific areas as well. As soon as the plane lands, the antenna on the device is flipped and the data is sent by e-mail via wireless connectivity to corporate headquarters (and because it is sent via e-mail, it avoids all those messy firewall issues because they are not tapping directly into the database). Once the e-mail is received, the data is integrated into the back-end databases, where it can be analyzed every 24 hours—extremely important, since the company outsources to different companies at different airports and could never have resolved a problem so quickly before.

Flexjet's billionaire clients all expect a high level of service, and it is the responsibility of the company to meet this expectation. But the corporate leaders are on the ground, not in the air, and their only guarantee of happy high-value passengers is timely intelligence in the event of an irregularity. But as we can see from this scenario, no solution other than wireless could have elegantly solved the problem faster or less expensively.

For this reason, I'd like to use Flexjet as an example for virtually any business that interacts directly with customers, clients, or patients. Handhelds may be the best intelligence tool ever invented and should be anchored to the counter or place people stop at the end of a visit so that these folks can rate their experience. Implementing such an initiative costs a few hundred dollars at the most, and that includes the survey software (suggestions can be found at *www.easton.com*). There is absolutely no excuse not to implement such a tool.

Keep in mind that the surveys are anonymous, yet each record is time and date stamped so if complaints are consistent to a certain day or shift, it becomes easy to pinpoint the problem. Feedback is easy to glean from the reports, which can be generated as frequently as you like.

It will be interesting to watch this trend as it develops, especially as corporate America and politics begin using mobile wireless surveying. In fact, voter opinion polls, which can be conducted during speeches, debates, and other political events, may very likely be handled just this way for the 2004 election.

REVAMPING AN INDUSTRY

To understand the far-reaching benefits wireless technology is contributing to businesses whose core service is service, no better example exists than medicine.

While it is believed that better service means more business, this is not necessarily true for medicine, because the trade is being so badly hammered by HMOs and unreasonable insurers.

Ironically, the HMOs and insurance companies are responsible for making physicians technologically more fit. While doctors are notorious for offices that limp behind technology (they were some of the last to install fax machines, and many still use manual bookkeeping systems), HMOs and insurers are demanding they get digital by instituting policies to eliminate all paper in the next few years. Ironically, it may be medicine, with the help of wireless, that will become one of the first truly paperless industries.

Furthermore, from a behavioral perspective, the mobility of wireless makes for a perfect fit. Doctors bounce from patient to patient in their office exam rooms and local hospitals, which means they are rarely within feet of the information they need most: patient histories, lab reports, prescription logs, and drug interaction databases. While this scenario probably reminds you of most mobile workers, keep in mind that medicine as a service business is currently under pressure, being accused of defaulting on the "service" element. Moving doctors into the handheld arena is a simple task. It is estimated that 20 percent of them already carry mobile devices and that this has saved thousands of lives.

A typical example is a patient of Dr. David Jarvis who would have been dead within minutes had the doctor not consulted his heldheld (loaded with ePocrates) the night before preparing to dispense a drug to a patient whose brain was hemorrhaging. Had he used the standard procedure medication, the patient would have died, since there is a violent interaction between that commonly used drug and another that the patient was already taking. Disaster was averted when Jarvis double-checked for interactions on his Palm while standing in the center of an Appleton, Wisconsin, intensive care unit.

Another favorite technology aiding doctor and patient is PocketScript, which is a speech-driven prescription writer. The physician simply speaks both the patient's name and the prescription into a handheld device such as a Pocket PC that has a built-in microphone. PocketScript's speech-driven interface matches the request with the patient's records on file. In about a second, the record is returned to the device along with the viability of the prescription (meaning whether or not the insurer will cover it), at the same time providing potential drug interactions based on the patient's current medications.

At this point, the doctor indicates the dispensing instructions (how many pills, how many times a day) with a few screen taps before wirelessly sending it via e-mail or fax to the patient's preferred pharmacy.

PocketScript was developed for doctors because it was noted they are naturally used to dictating information or writing. In other words, they are not typists. Furthermore, doctors are already anchored with beepers, mini tape recorders, cell phones, and PDAs. Adding functionality to an existing technology they already carry with them made sense.

Nonetheless, dozens of wireless prescription devices are flooding the medical market, all of which eliminate the biggest problems of handwritten prescriptions: illegibility, adverse interactions because the doctor didn't check or was not informed by the patient of other medications (this alone either kills or injures 2.2 million patients per year), and viability (whether or not the drug is covered by the patient's insurer). In fact, it is estimated that 30 percent of the 3 billion prescriptions written each year have to be rechecked because either the doctor's writing couldn't be read or the medication was not in the insurer's formulary.

While the service scenarios I've tendered thus far focus on the patient coming to the physician, wireless will allow health care professionals to better attend to the patient where service is needed. Although there is always the possibility that house calls could come back into vogue (we can always wish), there are other medical situations where mobile can speed the service process for customers. Hearing aid fittings are one such example.

Audiologists can now fit hearing aids using the Express Fit system, which runs on a Palm handheld and was enabled by technology from Aether. This mobile device allows extremely precise fittings because it give audiologists a graphic of an equalizer (similar to the one on your home stereo). In the past, the patient's fitting would have used immobile equipment that could customize only with yes-or-no functionality that eliminated any nuanced adjustments.

Conversely, the software outfitted on the Palm goes through an algorithmic process to match the diagnosis with a prescriptive fit for the patient. Not only is the fitting now far more precise, the handheld is reducing the time of the fitting by 75 percent.

Afterward, the parameters of the custom adjustments are uploaded to a central database, where they can be retrieved by any audiologist in the country, thus allowing patients to be served no matter where they are, a service particularly loved by snowbirds, who travel to Florida each winter.

Perhaps best of all, mobile technology lets audiologists travel to the patient, which allows them to adjust hearing aids in the patient's primary environment, a tweaking that guarantees maximum performance.

A favorite example comes from a customer of a Sonic Natura hearing aid who complained that he heard well everywhere except in his car. This immediately prompted a Palm-equipped audiologist to suggest they take a drive while he made the patient's adjustments.

Despite the advantages, there is one bad combination of doctors and wireless, and that is in the operating room. The following story was reported by Reuters on April 18, 2001, from Hong Kong and the headline read DOCS BANNED FROM USING PHONES DURING SURGERY. Apparently, a surgeon was in the operating room discussing a new car purchase for 14 minutes on a cell phone while in the process of removing a polyp. Because of his multitasking, he allegedly punctured the patient's colon, thus causing life-threatening complications. Fortunately, the Hong Kong government responded to the incident by banning wireless phones from the operating theater (though, to the outrage of citizens, the government did not reprimand the physician because it could not be absolutely proven that his lack of attentiveness was the cause).

For survey software recommendations and other wireless customer service options, visit *www.easton.com.*

10

Wireless Reinvents Marketing

IT WAS THE most successful wireless campaign ever. Cellular phone displays across the capital city of Manila read "military needs 2 c 1 million critical mass. pls join. pass on."

This, however, was not for a product. It was a crusade to oust a politician, Joseph Estrada, president of the Philippines, and according to the text messages this was exactly what would happen if the military saw at least 1 million people show up in the street to protest him.

It worked.

The conduit was short message service (SMS), which allows cell phone users to send communications to each other that are up to 160 characters. It's much like Instant Messaging on America Online, Yahoo! messenger, ICQ, and others. SMS is quicker than e-mail because the missives don't have to be retrieved or opened. The text is displayed instantly on the recipient's cell phone display.

The messages are cheap to send, much less than a call, and can be forwarded as easily as e-mail. Because of this ease, one message can reach thousands in minutes, moving exponentially, as these anti-Estrada communications proved.

To understand the popularity of SMS in Manila, just glance at the stats. In a typical day, 720,000 subscribers send 18 million SMS messages. That's an average of 25 per day per person. Manila is typical of most of populations in Asia and all of Europe, for whom wireless has deeply penetrated. It's also indicative of a wave yet to crest in the United States.

Manila's protest-via-handset was effective because it used the most productive advertising strategy yet discovered, word of mouth. Now match this with a technology that can deliver the testimonial to anyone, anyplace, anytime, and you've discovered the ultimate success formula.

So I told you that story to tell you this one:

Around the time Estrada was being catapulted out of his party, January 2001, an important wireless marketing test was winding up in Boulder, Colorado. The company behind the initiative was SkyGo, which, not surprisingly, is in the wireless advertising business. Contrary to many of these sponsored field tests, I believe SkyGo's was nonpartisan and their data is candid and valuable.

That said, you should know that the 1,000 participants (400 mobile professionals, 200 college students, and 400 users who matched a national cell user profile) were given the wireless phones, worth about $125, and that AT&T provided the cell service for free for the entire four months of the trial. For this reason, the value in the information gleaned from the trial is not necessarily what worked, but what didn't work. If the participants are getting it all for free and not using some part of it, that part must really not be a good fit. Or is it?

Before I reveal the results, let me first introduce the metrics so you have a context. During the 120 days, 500,000 ads were issued for 550 unique advertising campaigns from 50 advertisers. Many of them were national brands such as Procter & Gamble, Kinko's, Subway, and Visa. The balance were for local Boulder businesses. Users received an average of three to six messages a day, all of which they signed up for (called "opt-in") and none of which they were obligated to open, read, or act on. Participants willingly supplied plenty of information about personal interests so that some of the ads could be targeted to their tastes.

TYPES OF ADS AND THEIR CALLS TO ACTION

There were five types of ads and four calls to action:

SKYGO'S WIRELESS MARKETING STRATEGIES

TYPE OF AD	DESCRIPTION	EXAMPLE
Interactive Branding	Messages employing two-way communication to engage the customer in trivia, instant surveys, games, and polls to foster brand awareness.	Subway showed a list of their most popular sandwiches and asked, "Which is your favorite Subway?" After submitting a response, respondents were given a digital coupon for a free bowl of soup with a sandwich purchase.

TYPE OF AD	DESCRIPTION	EXAMPLE
Sales Alerts	Time-sensitive updates providing information on sales and special offers targeted to consumer interests and demographics.	ESPN reminded their fans of a "Fantasy Basketball" sale that ended on November 10.
Coupons	Alerts that provide a coupon that could be saved and later redeemed at the brick-and-mortar facility.	KFC offered a special meal deal that could be saved and later presented at the store. The coupon expired in a few days.
Incentive Ads	Messages that offer a gift or promotion with purchase. Buy "A" and get a free "B."	CompUSA offered a deal that gave a free Case Logic case with the purchase of a Sony handheld.
Audio Ads	Messages that contain links to audio samples, recorded information, interviews, and music selections.	Boulder Theater announced an appearance by the Squirrel Nut Zippers that had a "listen" option.

SKYGO'S TRIAL "CALL TO ACTION" OPTIONS

CALL TO ACTION	DESCRIPTION
Click-to-Buy	Alerts contain a "Buy Me" option that can be activated with one click owing to a preregistered electronic wallet that contains all credit card and shipping info.
Click-to-E-Mail	One button press alerts the advertiser to send additional information to the e-mail address supplied during registration.
Click-to-Visit-Site	Instantly takes the consumer to the mobile version of the advertiser Web site for additional information.
Click-to-Call	A single keypad press activates a connection to the advertiser, so that the consumer can get additional information or buy the product.

The aforementioned companies used an assortment of these strategies and even combined them. For example, Kinko's asked a multiple-choice trivia question, "How did Kinko's get its name?," which is an interactive branding strategy, but also included an incentive coupon for free prints, which was presented after the answer was submitted and tendered whether or not the correct answer (the founder's nickname) was selected.

WHAT WORKS. WHAT DOESN'T.

Kinko's strategy was one of the most successful, with their interactive trivia ads attracting an astounding 52 percent click-through rate (a "click-through" means the recipient pushed a button to see more). Other types of ads that scored well were those that surveyed users ("Which do you like best?"), registration for newsletters, or opportunities to receive more information via users' e-mail accounts.

Comparatively, the lowest performer was the "Click-to-Call" option, which lets users, by pressing one button, get a direct, traditional cell call connection to the advertiser. The response rate was a meager 0.7 percent. This is surprising when you consider how much business is conducted in a day by phone. Does this then mean that directly connecting a voice call to the advertising is a wash?

Hardly. An example of a retailer who used this featured was KFC. When was the last time you called KFC to order ahead? Seems unlikely when the time to call and place the order far exceeds the seconds shaved on the pickup. I actually think this may turn out to be one of the hottest uses of the medium, if, and only if, the advertiser's offer matches the call to action. What does work in this scenario? You'll find out in a minute.

Before we go there, I want to be sure you are aware of what else made the "doesn't work well" list. They were offers that were not targeted to specific interests as well as ads that did nothing but tout a product.

Even those schemes that belonged to the high-click-through club eventually dropped over time, which was expected by SkyGo's president, who said, "We had a feeling that the [initial high] numbers would not sustain as the novelty of the medium wore off."

Therein lies the jewel. We may not have a complete picture of the depth and breadth of the effectiveness of wireless, but we do know this: Those who explore the medium first will be those with the biggest payoff. Capitalize on the novelty.

The National Hockey League's Carolina Hurricanes were a big winner for being first. They got a 15 percent click-to-call response (ding, ding) on an offer for unsold seats at a discount. By pressing a single button, the respondents were instantly connected to a Hurricanes customer service representative to purchase tickets.

The NHL team were part of another worthwhile advertising study conducted by WindWire, a provider of wireless advertising services, whose trial, conducted about the same time with 14 advertisers and 2 million impressions, had results as upbeat as SkyGo's.

The bottom line of both studies is that consumers are open to mobile advertising as long as the ads are opt-in, are precisely targeted (Subway eaters, Hurricanes fans), and include incentives or coupons. For these reasons, both trials found that some mobile users prefer an ad environment and would prefer having a reduction in cell costs in exchange for ad-supported service. There is our next big clue about the future of wireless marketing. If the consumer is paying for the privilege of viewing ads, it's a tough sell, no matter how targeted. But swap ads for free time and it's on to the bonus round.

WHAT ABOUT PDAS?

Since both the SkyGo and WindWire studies were based on cell phones, it's helpful to look at other devices—PDAs, specifically—for additional feedback on the effectiveness of mobile marketing, because the environments are considerably different.

There are two services, which have since branched out to other types of mobile devices but were the first to be enormously successful in the PDA content arena, and for that reason they are an excellent study of wireless marketing in a much more conducive setting: larger screens (some even in color), greater ease inputting response information, and targeting that doesn't require the user to fill out extensive surveys or to specifically "opt-in" since the users are not paying for content or airtime.

The first is AvantGo, which offers over 400 "channels of content" in over a dozen categories ranging from business to sports to entertainment. The content is a mixture of brand names—Bloomberg, the Sporting News, and Rolling Stone—and niche content—the Law Making Portal, Hand Held Crime Mysteries, and the Snow Board Network. (Interestingly, you will learn throughout this book that AvantGo's core business is actually enterprise applications.)

Next is Vindigo, whose location-sensitive software and comprehensive guide allow users to find local restaurants, movies, shops, bars, and clubs, along with directions on how to get there in New York, Chicago,

Los Angeles, and 17 other cities across the country. Vindigo is so adored that it has been documented because some folks who tried it once on someone else's device immediately purchased a PDA just for the free service.

The CPM (cost per thousand impressions) on AvantGo averages $55, while Vindigo ranges from $40 to $65, which is up to six times more expensive than standard Internet banners ads, which in most cases are also four times larger.

Why, then, can wireless charge so much more? Their content integration is more highly targeted, since location sensitivity is a great niche maker. Next, users are more affluent and better educated. In fact, according to Forrester Research, most Palm/Handspring/Windows CE users are professionals with college degrees and incomes exceeding $75,000. Last, factor in the big clincher—tap-through rates. On the Net, click-throughs run an average of 0.5 percent, but with wireless the rate jumps—easily up to 6 percent and therefore up to 12 times more successful. By delivering 12 times more customers, these services can charge up to 12 times more.

In all fairness, though, we should note that in 1996, when banner ads were just beginning to mature, their click-through rates averaged 2 percent. Many analysts believe that over time, the wireless numbers will drop, too. But I don't. Here's why.

Vindigo has created an advertising environment that is unlike any other available to local businesses or national businesses with a local presence. While they point out that the focus is on location-sensitive marketing missives, they were the first to understand that the real dough is in "context-sensitive" messages. While location information is part of the mix, they are equally interested in what the consumer is looking for.

Let's use a search for a restaurant as an example. Say you're in Los Angeles but are across town from Beverly Hills, where you plan to meet a friend for dinner who also has a craving for Chinese. Using your Vindigo-fortified PDA, you indicate the part of Beverly Hills where you would prefer to dine by designating the cross streets, followed by a tap on "Chinese." While the results list will begin with the restaurants closest to where you want to be, it will also show at the bottom of the screen "You are not far from [insert advertiser's name]. Tap here for details." If you indeed "tap through," you are whisked to a screen with a comprehensive description of the advertised restaurant.

In another demonstration of Vindigo's smarts, the company capitalizes not only on the context of the search, but on the context of the device performing the search as well. Check this out.

NBC wanted to make sure that their midseason replacement game

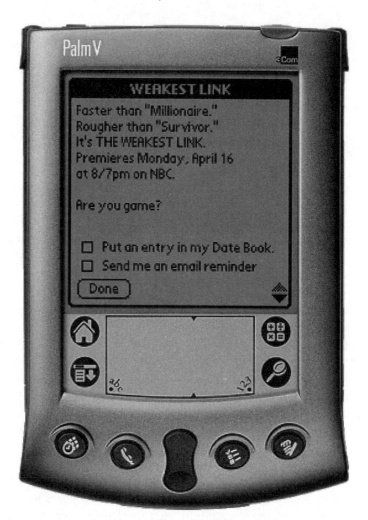

Vindigo's brilliant use of a handheld's functionality. An ad's
call to action includes the option to insert the event into the
mobile device's date book.

show, *The Weakest Link,* would get the buzz they felt it merited. Realizing the ultradesirable demographic of Vindigo's users, they initiated a
simple campaign. The text ad read:

Faster than *Millionaire.*
Rougher than *Survivor.*
It's the WEAKEST LINK.
Premieres Monday, April 16
at 8/7pm on NBC.

Now here's where Vindigo's brilliance lies, in their two calls to action:

❏ Put an entry in my Date Book.
❏ Send me an email reminder.

By utilizing the PDA's date book function, Vindigo weaved the ad into the respondent's life, as an appointment!

7:00am	Breakfast with Bob
2:00pm	Sales meeting
8:00pm	Watch *The Weakest Link* on NBC

While Vindigo's unique selling proposition is excellent targeting for local businesses and integration with the device accessing the service, AvantGo offers a significantly larger user base of techies with high household incomes. Their reach is broader, which is perfect for companies wishing a larger pool of this desirable demographic.

Enter CompUSA, which premiered their first national wireless coupon on AvantGo. The deal was for 10 percent off PDA and cell phone accessories at any of the 224 CompUSA stores throughout the country. The coupon was completely electronic and redeemed by showing the mobile device's screen, which had an image of a bar code the cashier then scanned.

The results were impressive. The opportunity to digitally clip the coupon was displayed 7 million times, which 18,000 did. Of those 18,000, 5 percent exercised the offer. Compare that to the 0.5 percent for traditional paper coupons.

While these successes are focused on traditional ads on AvantGo's consumer service, there is another avenue that the mobile content giant can offer that few can: ads as content, or what we might think of as advertorials.

Admittedly, banners—specifically graphical advertisements—don't work well on mobile devices, especially cell phones, if they can be displayed at all. Furthermore, because of a device's ability to offer location- or time-sensitive data, in order for the ads to be productive they must complement the user's experience, not interfere with it.

For example, weather reports, stock quotes, and sports scores will be "sponsored" rather than displayed with a text banner at the bottom of the screen.

Another approach is for companies to offer content on the service. Bigger brands such as Intel and American Express have information channels through AvantGo that contain worthwhile content, but whose goal is either to upsell to more services (Amex) or to extend their relationship with the customer (Intel). *Note:* Any company can offer an AvantGo channel for a nominal fee.

COMPANIES AS CONTENT AND PROGRAM PROVIDERS

What AvantGo shows us is that people want information to be portable. It is this model that I believe will be one of the primary wireless marketing winners: companies supplying valuable content to their customers. In addition to being a boon for niche information, handhelds are a haven for heavily niched software programs that could be of great value to a corporation's customers.

The reality is that these applications are a snap to program because the device's operating systems are so simple. Furthermore, the units have storage galore, and these applications that I am referring to in many cases could easily be less than 50K. For perspective, what's 50K in a device that (at a minimum) accommodates 8,000K (8 MB). We now live in a world where we can always have with us data that has meaning. The smart marketers will capitalize on this.

Here's my point by way of example. A couple years ago, the American Film Institute issued their "100 Greatest Films of All Time" list. This is information a film lover may want to have when renting movies. (Who can remember all 100?) This is exactly the type of content I would recommend that Blockbuster license cheaply and then put their name on an opening splash screen, offer as a free download, and beam to customers as they enter the store. An alcohol company like Seagram's could offer a "Portable Bartender"—a database of drink mixes. Select from a list of cocktails or enter the ingredients you have on hand by tapping on a drop-down list and a menu of alcohol recipes is offered.

Procter & Gamble, whose consumer goods marketing is so often astute that it's breathtaking, saw the value in mobile long before it was trendy. In October 1999, they launched a portable version of their popular "Tide Detergent Stain Detective" for PalmPilots and any device, such as Handsprings, that uses the Palm operating system.

The application has been available since 1996, when they launched the site, and their mobile version is just as complete, which is meaningful when you consider that the ultracomprehensive list of 29 stain types includes not only the standard blood, ink, and lipstick, but skunk, Silly Putty, "oily road water," and "tree sap—pine pitch." After identifying the culprit, you indicate the type of fabric and color, at which point the Tide Detective presents a step-by-step remedy.

Of course, P&G realized that stains rarely occur within feet of Web access and that an anytime, anywhere, application was a perfect fit, which is why they refer to the program as "fabric care gone mobile."

They average 2,500 downloads a month. The program is completely free but must be registered seven days after the download. Registration data includes name, e-mail address, gender, and age and a survey about your laundry needs. According to a Procter & Gamble representative, this data "allows us to interact on a one-to-one basis with the consumer. We can follow up with improvements and product information and learn about how the application is working from those using the application." (A direct link to the Tide Stain Detective download is available at *www.easton.com*.)

The Tide application is a perfect example of the types of useful programs and data you can offer your customers. In fact, a plethora of free, public domain content can be made available for mobile devices and branded by your company.

You can also find value in timely content for customers. The concept of providing high-value information for customers was established when the Web came to full maturity in the late 1990s. The wireless revolution has ways of capitalizing on the trend and in doing so establishing even more robust relationships with customers.

As part of the fallout from the dot.flop phenomenon of 2000, many advertiser-supported content sites went under, thus giving service-oriented organization a void they could fill. And in many ways, wireless is the best conduit.

For example, CLSA, the emerging markets arm of Credit Lyonnais, began offering access to their coveted investment news and reports on emerging markets in Asia, Europe, and Latin America directly to the mobile devices of CLSA clients around the world, via a wireless connection (or offline synch via PC if wireless connectivity is unavailable).

The goal of the initiative was to have the company's research be accessible to clients anytime they are away from their PC, commonplace for the high-level executives and other VIPs who comprise their client base. While the PC was an interim solution pre-wireless, the handheld technology is a much more sensible solution, since it allows their itinerant clientele to interact with CLSA when they are away from their PCs, especially when they are traveling.

Because of the always on, anytime, anywhere, aspect of wireless, the CLSA mobile service lets their clients act on research recommendations wherever they are, thus further endearing CLSA clients to their service.

THIS APPLIES TO B2B AS WELL

While my analysis has focused on consumer customers, keep in mind that every discussion applies to B2B as well. What I want you to get out of the mass-consumer angle is the need to port the playfulness we find in consumer wireless marketing to your business-to-business goals.

For example, everyone loves games. Who cares if you are in the lug nut business—create a strategy game or adapt one in the public domain, such as backgammon, and use lug nuts instead of tiles. What consumer marketing constantly reminds us is that there is no better way to build relationships with your customers than by entertaining them.

There's an additional advantage to handheld devices, and that is ease of distributing your programs. With a few exceptions, virtually any program or data on a heldheld can be beamed to anyone else. Now combine the ease of beaming with itinerant points of distribution, such as eye-level billboards or kiosks at trade shows, where passersby can instantly download your promotional programs, whether they be games (trivia or strategy featuring the advertiser), information (store finders or city guides that exceptionally highlight the sponsor), or, as the technology improves, audio- and video-enabled promotions such as complete interactive tours of your product, even complete multimedia catalogs.

Once these highly effective portable programs have been developed, B2B organizations must be sure that their sales forces are constantly offering to beam the company's exclusive applications to their clients. Promotional goodies such as baseball caps, T-shirts, and coffee mugs are fine, but give your clients a clever, useful program that entertains or makes some aspect of their lives easier and you have built a much stronger relationship than you could ever achieve with traditional freebies.

In other words, beam, beam, beam.

You should also know that business-to-business sales are expected to become as desirable a market as consumer-based sales, and if we are using the Internet as the precedent, it will be even hotter. However, since it is more nascent than consumer avenues, a few assumptions have to be made.

The first is that the biggest conduit to mobile workforces may actually be via the companies they work for, especially those wishing to subsidize their mobile IT expenses, who may actually allow some context-, location-, and time-sensitive ads to be presented to their personnel. In fact, it is predicted that the cell carriers or mobile handset makers will sell their devices and services at a discount to large corporations and include a pre-set advertising package with it.

For example, imagine that a conglomerate of white-collar workers, an IBM-type company with most employees in either sales or service, might approve advertising of products that might increase sales, improve management techniques, or upgrade customer service.

Yet another angle might be that an organization with thousands of delivery drivers might allow a fast-food chain to offer an incentive coupon with an ad pointing them to the nearest franchise 10 minutes before their scheduled break.

To date, wireless marketing has already benefited many business-to-business campaigns, such as the Intraware experience with AvantGo. Intraware sells software that optimizes IT installations and therefore wanted to reach AvantGo's IT management audience—those folks who subscribed to the AvantGo's technology channel. The mix of text and graphics stated, "Find Out Where IT Pros Go." If the recipient clicked through, additional information was sent via e-mail.

Over 20,000 clicked; hence 20,259 e-mails were sent, of which 4,941 clicked through, accessed the e-mails, visited the Intraware site, and registered as an Intraware member. That's a 25 percent conversion rate.

In the past, Intraware spent $50 to acquire a new member. Advertising on AvantGo ran under $15 per acquisition, which included the cost of the free T-shirt that was offered as an incentive.

TIME SENSITIVITY

While many wireless content companies offer coupons, PlanetHopper is capitalizing on wireless's unique ability to give customers what they want while they are on the go and the businesses that want them an efficient way to reach them . . . in a hurry.

What they offer is "capacity management" for entertainment-based businesses such as restaurants, movie theaters, and clubs. The coupons are sent as SMS-type messages to cell phones and PDAs, but only to those who have specifically requested that they be targeted. The ads are sent when the venue realizes that their "inventory is about to expire."

What makes PlanetHopper's offer different is that their coupons are short-lived and are meant to do one thing and one thing only: attract customers to establishments where the seats—whether in a theater or on a stool at a bar—may otherwise go unused.

General Cinema Theaters is one of their clients who can issue alerts to those out and about (or at home with their cell phones on) when sales for a particular show are slow by broadcasting an enticement of either a cash incentive (a percentage off the ticket price) or a free concession item to motivate attendance up to minutes before the screening.

While the basic model of time-sensitive couponing via wireless is a perfect fit with the medium, it will win over audiences only if the recipients can dictate the offers they receive with relentless precision.

For example, I would be interested only in last-minute movie offers for "chick flicks" (think *Erin Brockovich* or *Fried Green Tomatoes*) or anything starring Harrison Ford or Tom Hanks. That's it. Buzz me even once with an Adam Sandler release and you've lost a subscriber.

Doing this will require in-depth categories (such as Tellme's 54 types of restaurants) or keywords (Hanks, Harrison). But it can be done. And when it's executed properly, with the control in the hands of the subscriber, PlanetHopper's model is a win-win because they offer seats to those most likely to fill them . . . even at the last minute.

TAILORING OFFERS TO LOCATION

Although we looked at l-commerce previously, there are a few marketing models I purposely saved for a deeper discussion until we had a broader understanding of the advantages of wireless marketing.

While Vindigo is certainly a good example of location-sensitive incentives based on context, next-generation devices will integrate GPS technology and beget a new type of wireless marketing that can target based on the recipient's precise geographic location. Furthermore, instead of the offers being deliberately accessed (called "pull"), like Vindigo's model, they may be transmitted in a broadcast model (called "push").

Here's how it works. Let's say you elect to receive unsolicited ads as long as they match the criteria you specify. With this in place, you might find your GPS-enabled cell phone or PDA ringing with offers based on your preference. A plain and simple example would occur if you were within walking distance of a pizza chain that was offering a special. Since you had previously indicated a desire to receive pizza deals, an incentive would be sent to your phone when you were in geographic range, with the hope that you will act on the offer.

Because the technology is nowhere near reaching critical mass, interim solutions will come into play, such as the beaming of coupons (described earlier) to potential customers when they enter venues such as large malls and amusement parks.

What is fascinating about location-based technology is how certain types will begin to surface and the average citizen will have no idea that technology is tailoring the message. New York taxicab tops are one such example. The digitial displays will announce headlines, sports scores, and stock quotes along with ads that change based on the cab's location by using a satellite-based tracking system.

While the cabs are certainly geographically centric, one company has honed location sensitivity to the Point-of-Selection, a term they have trademarked. The company is Klever-Kart, and their goal is to use wireless to allows retailers, vendors, and shoppers to communicate during the shopping experience. Their first foray is attaching wirelessly empowered display devices to supermarket cart handles. These units' screens rotate various views. One is a store directory, which the grocers love because it gets their customers to what they want and cuts down on employee distractions. The balance of the screen views rotate various products in what Klever-Kart refers to as BrandKasting, advertisements for national products such as Tropicana Pure Premium Orange Juice as well as regional items such as Egglands Best Eggs. Mega-brands from consumer goods companies such as Nabisco, Pillsbury, Hormel, and over 30 others dominate the displays.

What makes the combination of BrandKasting and Point-of-Selection so powerful is that the ads are displayed when the customer is within 10 feet of the item. As shoppers traverse the aisles, faint chimes alert them to the proximity of the item being featured on the screen. Furthermore, full-color shelf signs aid in locating the product. When the cart is in between product destinations, the screen rotates scrolling ads of all the Klever-Kart sponsors for additional reinforcement.

The concept is by definition permission based because the units are added only to about half the carts in a typical supermarket; therefore a shopper has ample opportunity to choose a nonbeeping basket.

Ralphs, a major supermarket chain in California, is typical of a Klever-Kart customer. The average store has about 15,000 to 20,000 shoppers per week, of whom 75 percent are exposed to the ads. During their trial, the average improvement in sales across all categories was 46.8 percent. According to Klever-Kart, no in-store marketing strategy has even come close to results of this quality. Now keep in mind that the carts are not notices of sales or specials offers. No discounting was involved at all, which makes the boost even more mesmerizing.

Even more spectacular may be the budget-conscious pricing of the ads. Programs run in 28-day cycles at a cost of $75 per store per item advertised. In one case history involving ice-cream toppings, for only $75 for 28 days, Klever-Kart was able to increase sales from 2.5 cases per store per week to 14.9 cases.

Supermarkets are just a start for Klever-Kart. Next up are pharmacies, sporting goods centers, consumer electronics outlets, hardware stores, and automotive parts centers. The wireless technology is simple. Infrared signals keep track of where the carts are in the store, and local-area networks using radio frequencies broadcast the advertising data to the carts. Because Klever-Kart uses a central database, the ads can be pulled instantly (in cases of, let's say, product tainting) or products can be added instantly. In time, as the novelty of the carts wears off, Klever-Kart plans to add headlines news, sports, and weather reports to keep interest high.

Klever-Kart considers the product a benefit to all. Retailers love it because the cart displays are free, it ups the value of an order, they get a percentage of the advertising revenue generated by each cart, and the store directory improves employee productivity. More important, however, Klever-Kart's use of wireless location-sensitive technology is empowering a new promotional paradigm: micro-marketing.

HOW WIRELESS IS COMPLETELY DIFFERENT

Speaking candidly, the execution of wireless marketing can't always be compared to the forerunning Internet. The fact is that mobile technology devices are highly personal. In general, the closer the device transmitting the ad is to your body, the more intrusive it is considered.

It's precisely this personalization that appeals to consumer conglomerates, which to a large degree have ignored Internet advertising, deciding instead to use their Web sites to facilitate brand loyalty.

Nestlé Rowntree, the United Kingdom's number two confectionary brand after Cadbury, used to rely on television advertising. But speaking at a television conference in Madrid, the marketing director made a bold announcement, that the company was turning its back on TV ads in favor of other new media forays, such as Kit Kat interactive games, available via mobile phones. Understanding the power in being first in the new medium, the executive stated, "There are 40 million mobile phone users in the United Kingdom with whom Nestlé Rowntree must build a relationship."

While some corporations may choose to wait and see what the mobile medium produces, Nestlé Rowntree is capitalizing on the possibilities inherent in this new interactive platform that is packed with mass-market potential.

In fact, one could make the argument that wireless is the perfect marketing environment. Wireless is often referred to as "pervasive," meaning it is everywhere. The back-end technology can instantly and inexpensively be installed anywhere; handheld devices give marketers timely access to niche collections of potential customers, in addition to the fact that the devices are almost always with us and are scarcely ever shared.

Although this may be true, to ensure the greatest success, you have to couple the benefits of wireless's pervasiveness with this one time-tested truth of advertising: don't let your competitors get there first.

To see many more photos of wireless marketing opportunities featured, visit *www.easton.com.*

Section 2

▪

THE WIRELESS

WORKFORCE:

CONNECTING THE

ENTERPRISE

The Wireless Workforce:
Connecting the Enterprise

YOU ARE ABOUT to meet a nun whose convent is probably more technically advanced than your company. What she understood, years before wireless was widely implemented, was the importance of connecting an enterprise, whether it's a multinational conglomerate, a neighborhood business, or, in this case, a convent. Empowerment, and the inevitable success that follows, flows from workers saturated with information available to them anytime they want it, anywhere they need it.

While the promise of wireless in the corporation centers on cost savings and productivity, the real value is in connecting people. We all know that when people are connected, they truly become a team; and as a team, they can dream bigger and execute more meaningfully than any individual.

The ideas in the preceding chapter focused on how wireless benefits customer relationships. This, however, is essentially a one-to-one environment, whether it is speeding up the payment process or responding in seconds to a prospect's question. This section is the flip side. It's about wireless behind the scenes, where the return on a mobile investment can easily exceed 1,000 percent; where payback times are months, not years; and where operating costs are decreased by double-digit percentages. What you are about to read will astonish you. The money saved and the time recaptured are at times jaw dropping. Because the numbers are genuine, consider it additional proof of how wireless almost always overdelivers on its promise.

Last, while this section focuses on the applications of a wide range of wireless technologies, you will see that one of the most liberating for the corporate world are Palm-type devices. Whether it is a Handspring, Windows CE unit, or a Palm itself, the idea of being able effortlessly to carry an ultraportable device costing as little as a hundred dollars, with much of the functionality of a $3,000 laptop, is the realization of an enterprise fantasy. While the Internet improved internal processes, it also meant being a slave to wired connections. Step away from your desk, and you were out of the corporate loop. The tether has now been severed.

What's even more interesting is how handhelds in the workplace go far, far beyond calendaring, to-do lists, and e-mail. You will see how they are also used for business intelligence, competitive reconnaissance, wireless document transmission from anywhere to anyone, and dozens of other applications. All of which goes to show that the 2000s may well be remembered for a new corporate term: handsizing.

Meet Your New Network

"THIS IS DEFINITELY cutting-edge technology, and we've had it for two years. Others are just beginning to use it," notes Sister Deborah Marie Butcher, OP, Dominican Sisters of Mission San Jose.

The technology she's referring to is a wireless local-area network, the installation of which she supervised at her convent in Fremont, California, in 1999, years ahead of the curve. Today, you'll find the nuns there roaming the convent campus with laptops in tow, checking their e-mail via Internet connectivity from their wireless hub installed in the church's bell tower.

It all began when the desire for a traditional network was deemed near impossible by the Diocesan telecommunications department. The campus was too big, the walls were too thick, and because of the age of the buildings, there was no conduit for wiring. As one network expert noted, "You couldn't put a line in there to save your life."

In just four days, the wireless installation was complete, and the nuns were thrilled to have anytime, anywhere, access, especially to the Internet, where they communicate with others in their order, particularly in Europe. Given this fact, it would make sense that the sisters' next addition to their wireless network will be videoconferencing.

The convent installation is just one example of how wireless allows a network to exist where a wired one is near impossible, such as across large corporate campuses, warehouses, and older buildings wrought with thick walls and asbestos.

Then there are the guided missile destroyers.

If one wants proof that wireless LANs (local-area networks) benefit any environment, then meet the USS *McFaul,* which at the time it was commissioned was regarded as the most powerful surface combatant vessel ever put to sea. Despite its prowess in combat, what the *McFaul* couldn't do was keep the crew on board apprised of mission-critical information efficiently, despite the on-board data networks, high-speed satellite communications, and top-of-the-line PCs.

Since keeping a ship operational is akin to running a business, a wireless network installation made the most sense to keep the 330 crew members communicating. Using a combination of Aether software and Palm devices, the ship's Microsoft Exchange–based intranet data is available to anyone with an issued handheld unit. All data is traded via infrared ports scattered throughout the ship in key locations, such as berthing spaces and mess decks. As long as the Palm is within a meter of a port, it can exchange information. The crew can also beam data directly to one another.

With the wireless network in place, sailors and officers can now coordinate their schedules, checklists, and databases, in addition to reviewing imperative technical information about the ship's equipment. And, of course, they can send and receive e-mail. Not only does information flow freely, thus keeping everyone who needs to be in the know up-to-date, the handhelds also decongest the line of people waiting to use the ship's desktop computers.

The *McFaul*'s captain was somewhat hesitant about the wireless network at first. "We were still in the pad-and-pencil days, and it always seemed to be adequate," he notes, adding that the other key benefit of the installation is that "we no longer have sheets of paper being blown overboard." More important, however, is how the wireless network contributes to the mission of the USS *McFaul*. As one officer affirms, "These devices definitely contribute to combat readiness."

While the USS *McFaul* is a less-than-traditional installation, it reminds us of the need for all the members of an organization to have friction-free access to company data, access that sometimes can be achieved efficiently only through wireless connectivity.

THE ITINERANT OFFICE

There are other scenarios where wireless is the only viable option. Imagine, for example, if your company physically moved often—not every few years, but literally every day. Now consider the challenges of a hardwired network, and question the payoff when you factor in the labor expense of daily wiring.

This, however, is exactly the challenge the Dave Matthews Band faces while touring. Despite the fact that the group has few Top 40 hits, they are one of the top-10-grossing concert acts annually. In other words, the

Dave Matthews Band is a powerful, multimillion-dollar corporation with communication needs as robust as those of any company based in a skyscraper.

The band's "rolling office" began as a wired network, which was sufficient for the smaller venues they were playing at the time. As the group's star rose, so did the cabling required for the massive stadiums they were filling. As much as 4,800 feet of cable was common, with about 2,200 feet of that dropped on the floor. More cabling also meant more labor and a corollary increase in the time required for the network's daily rise and disassembly.

To make the network mobile, and hence far more manageable, the band's full-time information technology manager launched a wireless backbone based on one of Lucent Technologies' product lines. With access points positioned near the stages, dressing rooms, crew rooms, and accounting, production, and management information systems (MIS) offices at each show, all key personnel and band members could connect to the Dave Matthews Band intranet, in addition to high-speed Internet connectivity, which they usually get from tapping into an arena's T1 or T3. If the venue doesn't have a broadband connection they can tap into, the group orders a satellite hookup for their Internet access.

Granted, convents, missile destroyers, and rock tours are in a different sphere from corporate life, but that's exactly the point. These situations are far more treacherous and thus confirm the flexibility and usefulness of wireless technology. If it can work for the Dave Matthews Band, which is setting up and tearing down its network daily, imagine how well it will work in a company with far less lofty objectives. We must also bear in mind that these are scenarios where the networks could only be wirelessly deployed. Unlike the Dominican Sisters of Mission San Jose, most companies have a choice between a wired and a wireless network.

DECIDING BETWEEN STRUNG AND UNSTRUNG

What inevitably hastens the decision between the two is that in the year 2000, wireless networks became faster to construct and cheaper to operate. These are also the primary reasons they are becoming so popular.

It was the cost difference compared to wired that kept many companies waiting to deploy wireless networks. Forerunners that went wireless before it was cost-effective usually did so because there was a quantifiable return on investment, such as in an extraordinarily spacious work environment, where the improvement in efficiency more than justified the expense.

One such example is Boeing, for which a wireless installation was basically the only option at their 16 million-square-foot modification center in Wichita, Kansas. This is where they convert 747 passenger aircraft into cargo planes (in addition to performing maintenance on the world's most famous 747, Air Force One).

During the refurbishing process, the planes are surrounded by scaffolding so that the technicians and engineers can tear out the old electrical system and install the new one, which comprises miles of cables and connectors.

Being able to access schematics, blueprints, and other analytical materials that reside in mainframes in Wichita and Seattle was imperative but at one time unavailable to technicians dangling from planks in the belly of the aircraft.

Before the installation of a wireless local-area network (also called a WLAN), an engineer would have to climb down from the scaffolding and walk to the nearest PC, where he would inevitably wait in line to print out the information he needed or order a part.

In an effort to find a solution, Boeing attempted to wire the hangar so that their team had computer access at the same points in the aircraft where they were wiring. Boeing's pre-wireless solution was to snake a coaxial data line 65 feet from the ceiling of the hangar to connect to the PCs. But the cable soon proved unreliable, provided little mobility because it hung from the same place, and, according to a Boeing project manager, "eventually broke." It was at this point that Boeing realized that "instant information to the point of activity is paramount to getting the job done accurately and on time."

AND THEY'RE CHEAPER, TOO

While Boeing could easily justify the expense of a wireless network (and, at the time, much slower data rates) in exchange for added productivity and accuracy, corporate IT managers pre-2000 couldn't rationalize the technology for corporate offices when the wired networks were cheaper and faster.

Then the day arrived when networks sped up and prices fell. Here's how it happened.

The hottest brands in the wireless LAN field are Lucent, which has won awards for its Orinoco line, and Cisco, which, when it purchased

Aironet, triggered an economies-of-scale effect that caused prices for building a wireless LAN to plummet by more than 50 percent. Where at one time it cost $250 to port a wired network and $650 to port a wireless one, now they were about equivalent in cost. However, when you factor in the installation costs for a wired LAN, the wireless version can often be less expensive.

For example, in 2001 the typical price of a wireless LAN network interface card (NIC) was around $200, with some as low as $99; while a (wired) Ethernet LAN NIC costs about $50. However, the latter still required installation of an Ethernet tap, wall plate, and Category 5 cabling, which can cost $200 per tap for labor and materials.

Now that the costs were equal to or even less than a wired network, the next advantage to be considered by IT managers was the flexibility of installations. Wireless LANs are considered a boon for companies with employees who need to be continuously connected no matter where they are in the building. With a wLAN, the staff can work in a conference room or a colleague's office with the same access as if they were at their desks and plugged into their Ethernet connection.

HOW IT WORKS

Despite the miraculous way wireless LANs work, the technology is extremely simple. The information is passed back and forth through radio signals. The signals transmit on average 300 feet, and as far as 1,000 feet with certain antennas; and they can pass seamlessly through nonmetal barriers like walls and ceilings.

When you enter a command, such as a Web address in your browser, that information is sent out of your computer via an installed antenna (usually in the form of a PC Card). The command flies through the air and is picked up by the nearest "access point," which sends it to the main machine via a wired connection. The primary system then processes it and passes the information back to the access point nearest you, where it is then transmitted back to your computer.

In most cases, an installation will require multiple access points, which are situated in an overlapping manner so that as a user roams, he or she will maintain connectivity. Usually, you will find access points mounted as close to a ceiling as possible to help signals surmount cubicles and other interference. This is why the convent's bell tower was an ideal location.

Regardless of the number of steps or access points involved in the wireless transmission, the speed with which the data is passed back and forth now approaches the performance of a wired network and, as the next generation of technology is installed, will soon match it.

This standardization and accelerated data speeds are the result of a series of standards. The development of the standard is a long story. All that is helpful for you to know is that wireless networks got really interesting when the (rather geeky-sounding) 802.11b standard was introduced, along with its data rates of 11 to 22 Mbps (megabits per second). To understand what this rate means, let's compare it to the speed of a 56K modem, standard on most personal computers. With this analogy, 11 Mbps is equivalent to a 977K modem. Just so you have a complete picture, wireless loses about half its robustness owing to noise and other interfering variables. So even though a wireless network may be rated at 11 or 22 Mpbs, its throughput (actual speed) is closer to half that. So in this case, 11 Mbps is closer to 5 Mbps, which means that the "modem equivalent" would be around 488K. That's fine for basic data such as Web surfing, e-mail, and file sharing, but nothing you'd want to stream video on. By the way, it's handy to know that 802.11b is often also called WiFi, which stands for "wireless fidelity."

To return to our story, once 802.11b arrived with its much faster speeds and higher dependability, wireless local-area networks were embraced. They will become even more popular as the "next up" technology, 802.11a (yes, "a" after "b"), becomes available with its blazing speed of 54 Mbps (now picture your hair blowing back in the wind of your wireless connection). Additionally, 802.11a operates in the 5 GHz band, which is a frequency that is not currently crowded by other wireless technology.

Even though wireless networks run slower than their wired counterparts, most people feel that the convenience of wireless more than makes up for speed. The fact remains that they are still plenty fast for Internet access, which is why hotels, airports, and convention centers are investing in 802.11b networks.

The idea behind public area installations is that convention attendees and airline and hotel customers are able to access the Web, download files, or check their e-mail effortlessly as long as they have a WiFi PC Card. These cards are now relatively inexpensive but may not even be necessary for laptops purchased in 2001 and beyond, since the 802.11b technology is being preinstalled in many brands of laptops, such as IBM ThinkPads.

Interestingly, it should be noted that Apple Computer was one of the first to market with an 802.11b-standard wireless network solution that allows people to log on as long as they are within a certain range.

Launched in 1999, the product is called AirPort. It was originally marketed (and thus perceived) as a solution for homes, schools, and small businesses that wanted to share Internet access. In 2000, Apple gloriously proved the scalability of their product at their World Wide Developers Conference. Using 18 base stations, Apple easily accommodated 450 simultaneous wireless connections to the Net. At the conference's Internet Café, a 40,000-square-foot room, 4 AirPort base stations served up 150 users at one time. By the way, because Apple is using a non-proprietary standard (in this case 802.11b), any computer with any operating system, including PCs, would have the same access as a Macintosh. (And the walls come tumbling down.)

Some companies are also outfitting their satellite offices with wireless LANs. Doing so means that the headquarters can avoid the high cost of installing an expensive high-speed network. Anyone associated with the company, including visiting executives, can have access to the Internet, e-mail, even the office printers, without having to use a colleague's machine or find a spare Ethernet tap. The concept is termed "hot-desking." Wireless LANs are also popular with start-ups, which may move offices often as they grow (or can be quickly disassembled after they file for bankruptcy).

Many cities are also benefiting from wireless network connections. Greensboro, North Carolina, is one. Instead of reporting back to the home office to file inspection reports or review their day's itineraries, inspectors now drive to the nearest of eight "islands" to connect wirelessly. By avoiding multiple trips to headquarters daily, each inspector saves two hours per day. With a total of 32 inspectors, the enforcement manager for Greensboro calculated that "it's like getting eight new people without paying for them."

BUT ARE THEY SECURE?

Any time the subject of wireless networks is discussed, there is a mandatory dialogue regarding security. It's an important point, but one that keeps changing. The 802.11b security issues have received their share of bad press. Keeping in mind that stories with bold headlines sell more magazines and newspapers, I still believe the issues were real, but not nearly as serious as claimed.

Since security issues for wireless local-area networks are a moving target, any IT professional you work with can quickly educate you on what you need to be most aware of. Overall, I happen to agree with one of IBM's Mobile Market Development executives who feels that

"security is procedural issue . . . and if you have strong security procedures in place with your wired network, then augmenting that with a
wireless one should not pose any additional problems if you use the
security features that come with the technology." He adds that companies with higher-than-average security concerns should also consider
WEP, which stands for wired equivalent privacy, an encryption scheme
for WLANs. His feel is that an enterprise that couples these security features with existing ones has no reason to feel that their wireless LAN
cannot be as secure as their wired one. That said, he does have one
caveat: "Nothing is foolproof, wired or wireless."

WHAT DOES THIS HAVE TO DO WITH A TENTH-CENTURY DANISH KING?

There is one type of wireless network for which there are virtually no
security risks, one that corporate bookies are betting heavily on. This is
the personal-area network, which is focused on connecting devices
within 30 feet without cables, such as a computer to a printer, synchro-
nizing your Palm without having to use a cradle, or wirelessly connecting a headset to your cellular phone.

The consensus on personal networks is that we are on the right track
but using the wrong technology. It began with infrared/IrDA, but
infrared requires line of sight at a particular angle to work effectively,
which isn't always possible and is often cumbersome. The white knight
riding in to save the personal network is a technology developed in
1998 called Bluetooth. Bluetooth? Yes. It's named after the tenth-century
Danish king Harald Bluetooth, who was able to unite two opposing
countries to live in harmony, similar to the goal of the technology.

Eleven centuries later, Bluetooth is uniting technology using radio
waves, thus eliminating the line-of-sight issues of infrared. Bluetooth's
objective is to render cables obsolete. The performance runs at about 1
Mbps, which means that in sending a job to a printer, you wouldn't
notice much difference between using Bluetooth and using a cable connection. The heavyweights behind the development, standard, and
implementation include Ericsson, IBM, Intel, Nokia, and Toshiba. Given
this unprecedented level of support, the Cahners In-Stat Group estimates a $5 billion market for Bluetooth-enabled devices by 2005.

In the workplace, this will mean that as long as your equipment is
"Bluetooth enabled," you'll never need a physical cable to make connections. Need to print a document? Just make sure you're within 30

feet of the printer and click "print." Need to get a business-related photograph to a colleague right now? A Bluetooth-enabled cell phone can act as a modem and tap right into your digital camera. (As a quick aside, when Bluetooth enters the home, you'll never need cables to connect any of your Bluetooth-enabled components, which will include your VCR, stereo, TV, videocamera, and speakers.) Another Bluetooth benefit is peer-to-peer networking, which allows people to share files instantly as long as they are within 30 feet of one another. Think of it as a corporate version of Napster.

Essentially, Bluetooth is a quick and easy way to self-network. The advantage of this technology, along with local-area networks, is freedom. Freedom for your data. Freedom for colleagues to roam the workplace and interact more easily and efficiently. In this environment, when a co-worker asks for a copy of your PowerPoint presentation, you no longer have to jot a note to send it via e-mail when you return to your desk. Instead, with the aid of a personal- or local-area network, the files can be transferred on the spot. Better yet, consider how much more productive meetings can be when everyone's technology is interconnected automatically.

REALLY, REALLY BIG INSTALLATIONS

At the other end of the network spectrum are wide-area networks (WANs), a term whose definition depends entirely on who you ask, but is generally thought of as a network that spans a large geographical area. Cellular carriers such as Sprint and Cingular would be considered WANs; however, some consultants refer to a large corporate installation as a WAN, so go figure. There is one indisputable fact: The largest wide-area network in existence is the Internet.

Within the WAN landscape are WMANs, wireless metropolitan-area networks, which connect key buildings in a municipality. What makes these connections a growing trend is that they are significantly less expensive than the T1s (superspeedy connections to the Internet) most have now and can be even faster.

This is exactly what the city of Ventura, California, learned when it was in the process of upgrading its network of 11 of the city's remote geographical sites.

Before a wireless solution was considered, the Public Safety Department was initially campaigning for an upgrade of their existing 56K frame relay connectivity, which provided a barely acceptable level of speed, in exchange for T1s. They estimated that the upgrade would cost about $90,000 for the new hardware, with recurring annual costs of $24,000 for the high-speed connectivity.

When the proposal was reviewed by the city's information technology manager, he countered the request with the suggestion of using a wireless network connected via fixed wireless broadband. In simple terms, this means that instead of installing separate T1s into each building, all the buildings would share one T1 (which was plenty for their usage) by using omni-directional antennas mounted on top of each building.

Since they were just installing antennas, which was relatively easy and comparatively inexpensive, the IT manager also proposed expanding the project to include other key sites. The city agreed, and the project originally slated for 10 locations was now upped to 19.

Because of the sophistication of the project, the city of Ventura contracted with the Wireless Guys, who despite the look of their homespun Web site are respected experts for highly complex wireless networking installations anywhere in the world.

In 45 days, installation for the 19 sites was complete and included city hall, 6 fire stations, 2 parks, a water treatment facility, a senior center, and the city's police headquarters. Now, 680 of the city's employees are united and able to share data as well as Internet access at speeds higher than that of a T1. The expedited transfer rate is due to routers added at city hall that, by filtering network chatter and increasing the speed of data, can accelerate the throughput of the network to the look and feel of a 10 Mbps system, which is like having six T1s.

Better still, the system is never down. Maintenance can be handled remotely via the Internet, but it's virtually never needed since the antennas are not affected by bad weather. While the antennas do rely on line of sight, the city is able to circumvent interference because the network was designed to allow for powerful signals that are resistant to rain, fog, and wind.

If city employees were impressed by the elegance of their new, fixed wireless system, you can only imagine the glee of the city's treasurer, who crunched the numbers before the system was installed and discovered the impressive return on investment.

Total cost of ownership for the 19 sites in the city of Ventura was approximately $145,000 over five years, with recurring costs of $3,000 per year for maintenance and parts. Since the city had already approved the T1 upgrade plan that was budgeted for $90,000 plus $24,000 annually in recurring costs, the fixed wireless implementation would pay for itself in two years as a result of the amount saved from not having to upgrade and maintain the T1 system monthly. Once the city factored in the savings of the recurring T1 costs from the additional nine sites added to the original plan, the payback time improved to 14 months.

YOU CAN TAKE IT WITH YOU

Whether the wireless installation is a metropolitan-area network like the one just described in Ventura County; a corporate wireless-area network that spans buildings, campuses, or satellite offices; a public wireless-area network for Internet connectivity in facilities such as hotels, airports, and convention halls; or a personal-area network to connect printers, computers, Palms, and people, the benefits of wireless networking are extraordinary. In every scenario, wireless is a productivity-enhancing, cost-effective method of connecting people and the technology that fosters communication.

The bottom line for these networking options is that instead of constantly having to go to your office, your office is always with you. This advantage, though, goes beyond mere convenience. Consider the empowerment that stems from information available anytime, anywhere, and you understand how wireless in the corporate workplace is genuinely revolutionary.

For these reasons, *Communications News* reported that "almost all major research groups predict wireless networking growth to be 100% per year for the foreseeable future."

12

Pocketing the Company Intranet

NO BUSINESS HAS a good reason for not incorporating wireless access to their intranet. Complementing an existing system is cheap, literally only a fraction of what was spent to launch the system; therefore, not adding this option has to be a conspiracy to stifle the company's growth.

Okay, so I'm a little emphatic on this point. But my passion stems from stats. Productivity flourishes when data flows.

Ford Motor Company, in an effort to create a more connected workforce, agrees. The multinational corporation wanted to extend the company's intranet and groupware applications, like Microsoft Exchange and Lotus Notes, to mobile devices to give their employees a wider net of information, as well as create an easy way for executives around the world to wirelessly access key business metrics wherever they were on the planet.

Following the lead of 18 other Fortune 100 companies, Ford used AvantGo Enterprise, which is renowned for integrating existing HTML-based data (information formatted for Web sites and intranets) without investing additional developmental resources or writing any additional code. The complete installation took only a few weeks.

Ford's wireless integration is just one example of the ease with which a wireless groupware solution can be adapted by its users. This was unequivocally demonstrated at the 2001 World Economic Forum, where each of the 2,200 political, business, and academic leaders were given a Compaq iPAQ Pocket PC (courtesy of Compaq and Microsoft), an appropriate gesture given the event, "The Second Phase of the Digital Revolution."

Seamlessly connected via a wireless local-area network equipped with AvantGo Enterprise software, the world leaders were able to access their fellow delegates' biographical details (and photographs), as well as send one another e-mails directly from the devices to set up meetings. The delegates also received real-time session updates and news that they could coordinate with their personalized agenda and contact directories.

A similar success was realized by Alcatel, the telecommunications giant, at their Carrier Internetworking Division Conference. The conference had a two-part goal: first, be exclusively electronic and wireless (no paper was ever distributed); and second, use the conference to train and equip their sales and marketing delegates with their new handheld buddies.

About the same time the delegates at the World Economic Forum were having a handheld experience, Republican senators were having one, too. These members of the 107th Congress were determined to find an alternative to lugging around binders full of reports, daily agendas, press deployments, and published policy papers on more than 33 topics ranging from international affairs to the environment. The senators also required intranet access, allowing them to manage their contacts, scheduling, and other vital information accessible via their intranet and Web site.

Prior to their wireless launch, a survey indicated that 7 out of 10 employees in each of the Republican Senate offices were using a handheld (Palm OS and Pocket PC) to synchronize their calendars. With 70 percent of the users already equipped, the decision was predestined.

Since deployment cost was a significant consideration, the technology department of the Republican conference chose AvantGo's Enterprise software because it allowed the political organization to integrate their existing technology investment, easily justifying the expense.

One of the initiative's biggest advocates was Senator Rick Santorum (R-Pa.), who refers to the PDA deployment as an attempt "to bring Republican senators into the digital world." But the consideration goes well beyond digital literacy. Remember, these are Republican senators for whom fiscal advantages always prevail. Case in point: Santorum explained that when information packets were distributed when the Senate broke for recess, the cost to prepare them ran about $1,800. Instead, the identical material is posted and easily accessed with their PDAs . . . which they can reliably connect to from just about anywhere in D.C. except the Capitol Building's basement, according to Santorum. Even better, since handheld devices are not classified as computers by the Senate, they are not prohibited on the Senate floor, where laptops have been banished because they are considered a mechanical device that could "distract, interrupt, or inconvenience the business or Members of the Senate."

Handheld devices might get the same treatment if the Republicans aren't careful about how they show off their new technology. Apparently, during a pitch from New Mexico's Democratic senator Peter Domenici regarding the budget, Domenici remarked that the market was down by 400 points. This startling piece of information provoked Republican Santorum to access the Dow Jones chart via his Palm VII. At this point, the market was rebounding, and as Domenici finished his sentence about the plunge, Santorum announced, "No, Peter, the market is now down only a hundred."

By the way, even if a Democrat were to swipe a Republican's Palm VII, there would be no reconnaissance advantage. "There's nothing on the intranet of a sensitive nature that would prove dangerous for Republicans should someone heist one of our Palms," says Santorum.

UP AND RUNNING IN THREE WEEKS OR LESS

One point about wireless that deserves countless mentions is the ease with which the technology can be developed and deployed. It's common for a companywide conversion to take just a few weeks, sometimes even a few days, especially in the groupware arena.

Part of the reason for this has to do with the back-end technology to convert content into data that is accessible by handhelds. Parsing the data is generally fairly easy for wireless because software integrators such as AvantGo are able to write interfaces that repurpose the world's most popular software and groupware, such as Microsoft Exchange and Lotus Notes, which together own 85 percent of the market.

With regard to security, AvantGo Enterprise makes use of industry-standard communications protocols to enable secure, efficient access. Best of all, owing to the intuitive interface, deployment requires virtually no training. Another notable advantage of AvantGo's product is the multilingual option, with versions in French, German, and several other languages. At press time, AvantGo Enterprise software cost is about $40,000.

AvantGo is just one of the dozens of companies that provide wireless integration for corporate intranets and groupware applications. Wireless Knowledge (founded by Microsoft and Qualcomm in 1998) and ThinAirApps are two other big players, with GoldMine's Everywhere

Server handling the needs of smaller businesses that want to add mobile connectivity to their FrontOffice 2000 product for synching and live access. Also keep in mind that the companies that specialize in groupware and intranets, such as Lotus and Microsoft, are keenly aware of the markets and have added mobile support to their groupware products as well, which will allow e-mail retrieval from wireless devices. In fact, the next development will be a "virtual personal assistant," which will allow employees to call-in via their cell to have their corporate e-mail read aloud or to access company data using only their voice for timely information such as sales statistics.

THE "NO INTRANET" SOLUTION

Smaller businesses that don't have an intranet but do need to share files and documents with a mobile workforce should consider My Docs Online Enterprise edition.

My Docs Online gained notoriety as a consumer Web storage provider. Their service, which was voted number one by *PC Magazine,* allows users to store up to 20 MB of files for free, with additional megs available for a nominal fee. Users clamored for the product because of its reliability and ease of use. The files reside in a "folder" on your PC and look and act as if they are actually on your drive, even though they are homesteading in cyberspace on My Docs Online's server.

Capitalizing on this concept and their brand, My Docs Online introduced an Enterprise edition that puts the virtual-drive concept on steroids. The goal is simply to give you and your workgroup easy access to files and documents that can be shared with customers or co-workers. The beauty of their system is that it is compatible with any wireless device that has Web access, it does not require any special software downloads, and it is economical at $24.95 per person per year for 1 to 10 users $13.95 annually per user per year for groups of 100 or more.

All of the advantages of this system may not be obvious at first, but they are valued quickly. For example, because one file is being shared by many, you have complete control over out-of-date or redundant information; the documents, in addition to being available for download, can also be viewed on the Web.

THE LESS OBVIOUS ADVANTAGES

Since wireless intranet and groupware accessibility is an anytime, any-where, proposition, the mobile aspect is helping combat efficiency challenges that have arisen since the widespread use of e-mail. According to a survey performed by Gartner, respondents noted that only 27 percent of the e-mail they receive demanded attention and that a large percentage of people find themselves spending an hour a day or more managing the influx of electronic missives. With the aid of a mobile device, much of this less-than-necessary e-mail can be handled during downtime, such as during flight delays, before appointments, or when waiting in lines.

While it's undeniable that we need time to breathe during business hours (and these mini-respites are often necessary to maintain sanity), I believe there is also a benefit (in terms of stress reduction) in being able to handle three timely e-mails a few minutes before your son's Little League game.

Downtime can also be a revenue enhancer for professional service firms with workforces that need to keep track of the billable time they spend with clients. The makers of Timsolv, a mobile time and expense software program, estimate that up to 15 percent of a company's billable hours are lost when the mobile workforce loses receipts or simply fails to log billable hours or expenses. However, a mobile solution solves much of the problem because of its availability.

Lyne Berg, a fictitious litigation attorney, can illustrate this point. While heading to court for an appearance, she makes three cell phone calls on three separate client matters and is easily able to account for all of them because of the timer function built into the Timsolv's Mobile-TimeBilling software running on her Palm. She arrives at the courthouse and with a few taps on her handheld records the mileage for the trip. Next, Lyne triggers the time and billing clock to track her court-time hours by selecting the client *Widget Makers* v. *State of California* and then the task code representing "court appearance." At the end of the day, Lyne stops on the courthouse steps and quickly enters a description of the appearance events, then taps the "submit" button, whereby the information accumulated during the day is automatically sent and instantly integrated in the firm's accounts receivable system. All for less than $10 per month per user.

Attorneys are a natural choice to demonstrate the power of mobile time and billing because they are frequently away from their offices and have to account for dozens of clients and an equal number of incremental tasks. From what I understand from my friends who are legal secretaries, their bosses are notorious for failing to log billable time, and the end of the month is a time for high-stakes frustration as they try to piece together what they did for whom and when. Ditto for consultants, accountants, and the entire galaxy of service professionals.

Links to all the companies and products discussed can be found at *www.easton.com.*

13

Cordless Phones Save the Office

WHILE WIRELESS CAN'T cure every corporate ailment, it can certainly treat the primary ill of business—the tyranny of voice mail and phone tag. The solution is obvious and simple: cordless office phones. Why, then, has this staple of the average American home not yet migrated into the workplace? Answer: cost, security, and quality. Until now.

Just about every office phone system uses a technology called PBX, which stands for private branch exchange. Essentially, it is a private telephone network whereby a staff shares a certain number of outside lines. The reason virtually every company uses PBXs is that they are significantly cheaper than connecting everyone's phone to an external phone line, the same kind of connection you have in your home.

While PBX systems are comparatively less expensive than giving everyone their own phone line, the additional technology in wireless PBX systems is more expensive than their wired counterparts, by a factor of 25 percent, according to Bill Landis, president of TuWay Wireless in Pennsylvania. The manufacturers of these systems would argue that while there is a greater initial outlay of cash, the productivity increases and reduced long-distance call-back costs quickly make up the difference. With a wireless PBX handset, employees can roam anywhere in the company's building or corporate campus and have the full functionality of a PBX desktop phone.

I realize that trying to convince anyone of the advantages of a wireless phone in the workplace is like preaching to the choir. Most professionals want to be available. In fact, at least half of the executives I communicate with regularly offer their cell numbers on their outbound voice mail greetings to facilitate human contact.

While the cellular option is appreciated in an emergency, I rarely place calls to a mobile phone. Too many times when I have had only a quasi-timely, semi-important matter to discuss, I've found myself feeling as though I'm intruding by calling the person while he or she is rushing to a urgent meeting or confirming an order at a drive-through ("Super-size it, please").

IT'S MORE THAN A CONVENIENCE

For businesses that are highly service oriented, availability is the equiv-alent of responsiveness, and responsiveness is the test of service. For those companies or executives for whom customer contact is nil, the pitch for wireless office phones begins and ends on the productivity note.

Here's a typical statistic. When Hatfield Quality Meats in Hatfield, Pennsylvania, installed a wireless PBX, completion of first-attempt calls increased by nearly 200 percent.

On a more palatial note, when Biggs Hypermarket in Mason, Ohio, installed a SpectraLink wireless PBX system to service their 165,000-square-foot store, which houses 34 different departments, music replaced the screeching overhead paging, and customer hold-times dropped drastically. Now all 275 personnel are equipped with wireless handsets, which means that they can service customer calls without having to stop what they are doing to make the pilgrimage to the near-est wall phone.

THE CHALLENGES ARE OVERCOME

Despite the obvious advantages, there is still that nagging issue of cost. While most technology prices tumbled quickly, wireless PBX has remained consistent over the past five years because installations have remained flat. Needless to say, as the technology becomes more popular, a corresponding price decrease should follow. For the time being, the small user base leaves vendors without a way to offset research and development costs. Luckily, wireless PBX integration is gaining momentum. Executives for one major wireless PBX man-ufacturer are enthusiastic about the jump. Where a few years ago cus-tomers would supplement a wired PBX with 10 to 15 wireless connec-tions, the same type of customer now is adding 75 to 100 connections. The brightest note is the projections. According to Frost & Sullivan, revenues for wireless PBX systems are expected to reach $1.3 billion by 2005.

The lack of wireless PBX adoptions, however, isn't due just to the cost.

Companies that were willing to invest in these more expensive handsets may have initially rejected the idea because the first-generation wireless PBX handsets were highly limited and couldn't allow for many features of the PBX desktop phones, such as caller ID and conference calling. The other major issue for these lower-tech handsets was security related. Since these early units ran on analog signals, they could easily be tapped. However, now that the phones are digital, the encryption schemes allay this consideration.

Another issue related to the analog PBX wireless handsets was voice quality. The residential standard of 900 MHz is fine for chatting while unloading the dishwasher, but interference in the workplace is unacceptable.

The challenge for manufacturers when wireless PBX was first introduced was that the Federal Communications Commission (FCC) had not yet released spectrum that would support higher-quality connections. Meanwhile, the 900 MHz handsets were duking it out with bar code readers (think retail), pagers, and radio-based equipment like that found in hospital monitoring gear. Then in 1996 the clouds parted, the angels sang, and the FCC allocated the 1,900 MHz range (also known as 1.9 GHz) exclusively to telecommunications equipment. It was at this point that Nortel and Lucent began building wireless PBX products. Once you've had an experience with wireless PBX, you'll find that the voice quality and reliability approach that of wired connections.

The telecommunications manufacturers also understood that once security and quality issues were addressed, the demand for wireless PBX would eventually translate into big business, especially for corporations whose offices span acres.

HOW BIG IS BIG?

I've seen specs for wireless PBX systems from SpectraLink (the first and most respected of the wireless PBX companies) that cover as much as 100 million square feet and up to 3,200 handsets. While this installation is far more than you'd ever need (unless, of course, your office space needs exceed 2,300 acres), you can see that wireless PBX is ideal for corporate campuses and companies spread out over many floors. Furthermore, this is a perfect fit for employees who roam, meaning that their "office" extends over the entire complex or retail store.

Studies have shown that calls to employees in these palatial workplaces have a dismal first-time connect rate of 30 to 35 percent (the balance handled through voice mail). After the installation of a wireless PBX, the average skyrockets to 90 percent. As long as users are in range, they can have full access to all the features of their desktop phone. The employee's extension number and desktop features such as voice mail, call forwarding, caller ID, message waiting indication, call transfer, speed dialing, do not disturb, multiple lines, and three- or four-digit extension dialing are completely accessible. The battery charges vary, but a talk time of 4 hours and standby time of 50 hours is fairly standard.

Also standard are where these wireless PBX systems are cropping up. For example, you can find SpectraLink installations at Arthur Andersen, Smith Barney, the UCLA Medical Center, General Motors, Hormel, Whirlpool, Borders books, Marriott and Hilton Hotels, and Kmart, as well as Hewlett-Packard, IBM, and Microsoft. While this is just a partial list, it gives you an idea of the growing popularity of wireless PBX systems.

THE RADIO COMBO

There's another problem that wireless PBX solves, involving workplaces that need part of their staff on radio while the administrative team is on cordless phones (a scenario typical of industrial environments, which can span hundreds of thousands of feet). Years ago, this would have been an unsolvable problem. Now, however, it can easily be resolved with Motorola's Telario line of 1.9 GHz wireless PBX phones. What makes these handsets different from most is that they also integrate a radio system. This combination allows a person to be accessible to outside callers while staying in touch in two-way radio mode with internal operations. It works like this.

En route to a meeting down the hall, a manufacturing account executive takes a customer call inquiring about the status of an order. The executive puts the caller on hold, switches to radio mode on the same handset, and contacts a co-worker on the factory floor who is equipped with a Telario radio-only device. Since the executive is able to contact a floor manager quickly, within seconds he has an answer for the customer and relays the information instantly, thus saving a call-back and the aggravation of having to voice mail tag two people, the floor manager and the customer.

What is less obvious in this example is the alternate advantage of a wireless PBX/radio combination. Radio is broadcast technology, meaning that the executive can speak as one to many. In the described scenario, the executive happened to be paging one person in particular, but it's important to note that he had the option of expressing his request to an entire department or team, on the chance that the first person he wanted to speak with wasn't available and someone else could get him the information he needed.

These combination wireless PBX/radio phones should be considered for manufacturing, distribution/warehousing, car dealerships, and large retail operations. In fact, a manager for a Costco in Schaumburg, Illinois, found an added benefit of their Telario system. When a blackout occurred while he was on the receiving dock, he was able to stay in contact with his managers at the front of the store with instructions on how to reassure customers navigating their way in the darkness.

Added to a growing list of reasons to consider any wireless PBX installation is the fact that the system can be integrated piece by piece, overlaid on an existing PBX. Let's say only 25 percent of your office needs a mobile handset. You can purchase just what you need for now, with the balance being added over time. Furthermore, the installation involves only hanging antennas and their adjunct technology, which means that a system can take as little as a few days to install.

While wireless PBX is a panacea for employees in the office, let's look at an additional wireless technology that gets rids of the other chink in the productivity armor: handling calls while out of the office.

THEN THERE'S CELLULAR NIRVANA

If you're someone who frequently travels—in other words, you're not roaming the corporate campus but, instead, the city, state, or nation—you'll want to know about a special cellular phone integration available for PBXs that will let your mobile phone function in Manhattan as though it were on your desk in Milwaukee.

Welcome to PBX paradise, brought to you by WirelessConnect from Ascendent Telecommunications, Inc. I speak without hyperbole when I say that this invention may be the most liberating to corporate America since the introduction of the cell phone itself, because it gives your cell phone the core functionality of your corporate PBX connection. In other words, no matter where you are (as long as you have a cell connection), you can use your mobile phone just as you would your office phone.

What does this mean in day-to-day usage?

1) When someone calls your office phone, your cell phone rings simultaneously.

2) If you are unable to answer the call on your cell and it drops to voice mail, it transfers to your corporate system, thus simplifying retrieval to one voice mail box instead of two.

3) On your cell phone, you use the company's employee extension number to dial anyone in your company.

4) No matter where you are in the world (as long as your carrier offers coverage), your cell phone maintains the most-used features of your PBX system, including call transfer, call screening, call waiting, and caller ID.

5) When you need to make long-distance calls on your mobile phone, the calls are routed through the enterprise PBX trunk for the ultimate lowest rates. Think of the savings when an executive makes an international call. Instead of the cell carrier's rate of a few dollars per minute, the price could be as low as seven cents a minute.

The ease with which one taps into the corporate PBX is phenomenal. Literally, all you do is push one button, and the next dial tone you hear is coming from your office system. It should be noted that to prevent unauthorized use, before a dial tone is established, the phone is authenticated using caller ID, a PIN code, or both. Also, the system works with any brand of cell phone, any carrier, and just about any PBX system.

Ascendent Telecommunications invented WirelessConnect and is virtually the only company in the world that can offer this type of cell phone/PBX integration. Their system works with any brand of phone, even multiple brands and any cell company, even multiple mobile carriers.

The up-front base system ranges from $55,000 to $250,000, with an average cost per user of from $90 to $250. There are no monthly fees or recurring costs. For companies that prefer to lease, Ascendent offers a plan of $15 per user per month (based on 150 users). Smaller leases are also available.

Not surprisingly, corporations are clamoring for the technology. In fact, the cellular carrier Nextel was one of the first customers of the WirelessConnect system and were so thrilled with how well it worked and the quick return on their investment that they licensed the technology and are now offering it as Nextel Mobile Extension.

Another less obvious benefit of the WirelessConnect product is that it can give a corporate PBX extension number to mobile workers who don't even have a PBX desktop phone because they never work out of an office. This means that their only office connectivity is through their cell phone, but it has all the PBX benefits: an extension number, extension dialing, and so on.

An office furniture maker took advantage of this feature for key workers on their shop floor who don't have a desk and phone but need to be reachable. Now they carry a cell phone, have an extension number like their management counterparts, and are available to anyone in the company via four digits.

DECIDING BETWEEN THE TWO

Given the extraordinary benefits of the WirelessConnect system, one might wonder why anyone would consider a wireless PBX when this cell phone/PBX integration is far more cost-effective and flexible. The decision between the two is based on the answers to two questions.

First is the need for high-quality connections. Keep in mind that calls with WirelessConnect are simultaneously routed to cell phones, where voice quality and interference are considerable variables.

The second consideration is the need for specialized handsets, which SpectraLink customizes for vertical markets. For example, they offer a handset specific to health care, with support functions that integrate into a hospital's nurse call system (to beckon them to a certain room), as well as overhead central paging for physicians. Needless to say, these are not features one would need in a manufacturing plant. On the other hand, manufacturing companies can get SpectraLink handsets that are data enabled so that they can broadcast critical information.

Last, keep in mind that these wireless PBX handsets can easily be passed between workers from shift to shift.

While the productivity benefits of wireless phones are enough to champion the integration into enterprise life, it is the underlying wireless trends that make them inevitable: because it is possible, people are now demanding that communications follow them everywhere.

14

Printing Anything You Need...
Out of Thin Air

HERE'S A PROBABLE real-life scenario. Your flight has landed but is stuck on the tarmac because the gate isn't ready. The pilot forewarns that it could be as long as 30 minutes. The good news is that since you are on the ground, you can at least use your wireless device.

Nonetheless, your seatmate, in exasperation, strikes up a conversation with you and, as it turns out, has a need for your services. Given the dynamics of the situation, you would probably take her card and forward your sales materials when you returned to the office. But what if she could have the materials on her desk via e-mail or fax before the both of you deplane?

This is possible with wireless document management.

One of the forerunners in this area is Qxprint which will e-mail, snail mail, or FedEx any attachment you have in their system. It's all done via a virtual desktop feature that handles your documents as well as your contact information. So if you need to forward a PowerPoint presentation to a colleague, you can do so by clicking on the contact information, then selecting the presentation. Qxprint does the rest, sending you an e-mail confirming a successful document deployment. The company also offers a mail merge feature, which can be used to send a document or a quick e-mail (in this case, alerting everyone at the office to your "tarmac hostage" situation).

Field sales reps find wireless document management particularly useful to send follow-up letters without having to return to the office or to instantly e-mail, fax, or FedEx marketing materials.

(By the way, if you are outside your wireless coverage, you can always phone customer service using a landline.)

Another remote printing option is My Docs Online Enterprise/Premium, which offers a similar service (minus the FedEx and U.S. Postal

The Input Sequence You Use to Access Qxprint's Opportunity to Print Just about Everything from Just about Everywhere

```
      Delivery Method

Welcome. Select method
   to send document.

   Email          .25 ea
   Reg Mail      2.25 ea
   FedEx        16.00 ea
   Fax            .50 ea


       Main Menu
```

Select the type of service.

```
      Select a Contact

Doe, John
Drew, Nancy
Thomas, Dave
Smith, Ben
Lewis, Jerry


Quick Send
Search for a Contact
Main Menu
```

Choose the recipient.

```
      My Documents

--Invite
--Mletter
--Presentational
--MergClose
--Contract


Next
```

Indicate which document.

```
      Confirmation

Documents: 1
Contacts: 1
Delivery: Fax
Cost: $0.50


Send Now!
Send Documents Menu
Main Menu
```

Confirming your order.

Service options) for as little as $25 annually, or $13.95 if you have 100 or more users. In addition to the features noted above, their premium service will let you view Microsoft Word, WordPerfect, .rtf, and .pdf files and Excel and PowerPoint documents.

The advantage here is that anyone can send a document as an e-mail attachment to your My Docs Online Premium virtual drive (try saying that 10 times fast), and you can instantly view the file from any wireless device that supports Web access. If after you review the document you want a hard copy, with a few button presses you can fax for a printout (or pass it along to anyone you wish as an e-mail attachment).

My Docs Online's ability to let you view a document on your wireless device aids the time-sensitivity benefit of wireless. One such real-world example could play out like this. You're traveling in the field when an important prospective client e-mails you final revisions to your pending contract, with one caveat: He needs your approval today. Today? You can give him the approval he wants in minutes, even though you are 45th in line at Starbucks.

Speaking of faxes, wireless printing can also take place in proximity of a genuine printing device, not just when you're stuck in a car or airplane. Bachmann Software has introduced numerous printing applications that, while a little less glamorous than printing from the tarmac, lets handheld devices equipped with infrared (most are) print to any printer that also has an infrared interface, a feature becoming increasingly more common on mid- to high-level laser and inkjet printers.

15

Know More about Everything
(Including Your Competition)

TEN MINUTES AGO, Larry King mentioned your company on his nightly CNN show. How do I know this? I just received an alert from TVEyes on my Internet-enabled cell phone.

TVEyes is a service that monitors all the programming on the major broadcast and cable networks and then sends you alerts when a keyword or phrase you have preselected is mentioned. Their monitoring covers CNN, CNNfn, MSNBC, Bloomberg, ABC, NBC, CBS, Fox News, CSPAN, ESPN, the major stations in Chicago, Los Angeles, and New York, all the major Canadian channels, and several other international as well as some public television channels.

Because wireless is so well suited for time-sensitive information, TVEyes is the perfect 24-hour business intelligence tool. It can be used for any interest or topic—financial, political, entertainment, sports, lifestyle, shopping—or for other user-specified, keyword-based information.

The alerts are quite robust. The e-mail message shows your keyword in the context of a couple sentences. For example, one of my keywords (not surprisingly) is Palm. Here are the contents of a typical alert:

> Your keyword(s), PALM, was spoken on the Fox News Channel during FOX News Monday, Apr 23 at 1059 AM.
>
> For most people, it's scary that the government can use not only the mobile phone but your personal digital assistant, palm pilot, pda, and handspring devices and . . .
>
> For details, visit http//www.TVEyes.com/database/expand.asp?ln= 3215698&Key=palm.

Now, if you click on the "details link," you can get an expanded transcript (usually one to three paragraphs) of the mention. Using the above alert, here is the complete, expanded transcript:

> . . . accuracy could mean the difference between life and death, but in everyday life, improved tracking raises serious questions about privacy. >> For most people, it's scary that the government can use not only the mobile phone, but your personal digital assistant, palm pilot, pda, handspring devices and mobile devices, computers that now have wireless modems to track you. >> They plan commercial uses like directions, finding restaurants or family members. But what's to stop them from stealing information on the daily travels to merchants, insurance company, or abusive spouse? >> We, as a company, believe there will be privacy solutions, technology solutions that essentially allow consumers to opt-in and opt-out of these various services, but there's no doubt that privacy is an e911 mouse component going forward. >> The next generation of phones may very well make life convenient and save lives, but privacy advocates warn in the world of wireless, you can be mobile and can't hide. . . .

You can see from the above example that you get plenty of information to understand the context of a mention. Perhaps the best part of this alert is that I received it just two minutes after the term was uttered.

Now that you understand the service, I'll reveal the secret behind TVEyes. They monitor the closed-captioning portion of broadcasts. That's how they are able to spot the keywords so quickly (and why the transcripts are often all lowercase) and why you get the information in less than 30 minutes, as my example proves.

Obviously, the advantage to TVEyes is not just to learn about your company or product/service area, but to stay on top of your competition as well. But it's in watching your company's own interests that TVEyes really shines, because there are those rare occasions when the media is ahead of an event that involves your corporation.

Here's an example, a true story and the reason why a media-monitoring firm has come to depend on TVEyes for their clients. Like all mentions, the company was instantly alerted when a beverage, a product of one of its clients (which just happens to be one of the world's biggest manufacturers of consumer goods), was mentioned in an adverse context on a local television news show. In fact, it was this local program that broke the news allegations of significant health issues linked to the product.

The beverage manufacturer was caught completely off guard. Regardless of whether or not the allegations were true, the multinational manufacturer had a potential public relations nightmare at hand. However, because their monitoring firm learned of the news within minutes, the beverage's product manager was in turn alerted and able to undertake immediate action to counter the claims made on the newscast and prevent the spread of the adverse and, as it turns out, erroneous publicity.

A PR ANNEX … EVEN IN THE DELIVERY ROOM

To show you how wireless completes this scenario, it is interesting to see how wireless allows publicists to work anywhere, a necessity for this group of itinerant professionals. The product comes from Vocus, which is the first company to provide comprehensive public relations applications that are completely Web based. Using Vocus's wireless adjunct, media relations executives have access to a national media database of 250,000 unique editorial contacts updated daily; the ability to manage media inquiries through targeted distribution lists; and access to a personalized database of documents, photos, and other pertinent files that can be e-mailed anywhere via the Web site. You might note that these services are similar to the one My Docs Online offers, as discussed previously in "Wireless Document Management" (page 131).

Vocus's wireless solution was released just in time for one public relations executive for a major software publisher, whose son just happened to be born the same week the company launched two new products. His virtual press office consisted of a mobile phone and his Web-enabled PDA. While fielding reporters' calls during this busy, busy week, he remained calm. "I didn't have to worry about calling and being unprepared," he noted. With the ability to log in wirelessly to his Vocus database of documents, he knew he could forward to reporters any information they needed, such as a company history, statements, and media kits. Furthermore, he also had the ability to post a press release to their company's online news center wirelessly from the delivery room.

The most important aspect of a media relations professional is to be available, responsive, and proactive. Combine the ability to receive vital new alerts ("Your client's product is tainted!") with a defensive array of wireless technology (online PR databases, Web-based newsrooms), and you have an accurate picture of the power of this technology working to inform and disseminate.

Another less considered aspect of TVEyes is the opportunity to track your clients. In addition to keeping you current on your customer's business, being able to pass along a mention you have tracked is a relationship builder and an opportunity to make contact in a nonsales context.

The TVEyes basic edition is also available through SpyOnIt, which is another reconnaissance tool available for wireless devices that I highly recommend for fun and useful business intelligence. The free service offers recon notifications when your competition has updated their Web pages; alerts you when your Airborne, FedEx, or UPS packages have been delivered; or sends notification when a dot.com domain name you want becomes available. There are dozens of other options.

As we know, business intelligence is as much about companywide issues as it is about media mentions. It for this reason that we must remain cognizant of the timeliness with which information is received. All data has a limited shelf life, in some cases only a few hours. Having to wait to access the data the next time you're at your desktop makes no sense in a world that can pass along the information instantly no matter where you are.

Of course, media mentions are just a small part of the business intelligence package, so let's look at a completely different scenario.

GUARANTEEING GENUINE INTELLIGENCE FROM ALL YOUR SALES OUTLETS

If you can imagine having sales units scattered all over the country and having no idea of the details of your sales, you have a sympathetic ear in Rick Harris, manager of channel research at Dr Pepper. He says that thanks to wireless technology, for the first time he is getting "real data rather than ballpark figures on exactly what is going through our vending machines."

The data mess is understandable. Dr Pepper owns 17 brands and franchises bottling territories for each. For this reason, tracking sales of a single brand at different locations and for different demographic profiles was impossible, at least for accurate data. Information was being gathered, but it was inconsistent from bottler to bottler.

To relieve their frustration, Dr Pepper hired wireless vending experts Isochron Data Corp., which installed VendCast Software and a Motorola Reflex protocol two-way pager in each vending machine. The installation takes 12 minutes, costs $340 for the hardware, and has a monthly fee of only $6.50. The return on the investment is measured in percentages. For the vending machine channel, profit margins of 14 to 15 percent are common; Dr Pepper brings in 20 percent more, at 19 percent.

The vending machines are polled daily. The information collected includes inventory, sales, and machine health. This data, is then uploaded to a Web site provided by Isochron and, secured by 56-bit encryption, personalized to the client. Executives can query their data, view preconfigured reports, generate new reports, or download the information to import into additional business applications like Excel spreadsheets.

In addition to highly valuable marketing and sales data, the vending machine application helps with the placement of new machines and the refilling of current ones. The latter point is a great boon to the distributors. In a perfect world, vending machine operators like to fill 80 percent empty machines, not ones depleted only 30 percent, which is more typical.

INTELLIGENCE IN WAR AND LAW

While Dr Pepper is extracting front-line data, wireless business intelligence applications also apply to those literally on the front lines. There is no place like the battlefield to illustrate the need for up-to-the-minute information and the benefits of wireless business intelligence.

While handhelds are the perfect solution for military personnel in the trenches, they offer an additional advantage to help protect troops: the opportunity for a two-way data exchange. In addition to receiving maps of the terrain, locations of hostile and friendly forces, and supply line and other critical logistic info, soldiers in harm's way can be updating the information based on what they are actually seeing on the battlefield. Geodyn Research Group, which developed this military application, notes that this bidirectional synchronization of data from field to command center and back to field is the only accurate way to provide soldiers with real-time situational awareness.

By the way, it's not just the soldiers who have handhelds; the medics have them as well, with access to key medical information on each member of the battalion, including blood type and medication allergies. These corpsmen can also message the medical facility with a complete description so that triage can begin before the injured soldier even arrives.

Last, there is the more obvious aspect of business intelligence research. Wireless connectivity means getting the data you need exactly when you need it. The law figures into this scenario well. Westlaw, the preeminent online business and research tool, now offers a wireless service that allows access to their 13,000 databases from any mobile device with online connectivity. If in-court opposing counsel cites a case, you can enter the law citation and obtain a synopsis of the case, with a full text available if necessary. Getting the goods on the backgrounds of lawyers on the opposing side is also a snap using Westlaw's Legal Directory.

As you can see from these examples, we are at the point where virtually any business intelligence application available on the desktop is also available on the wireless laptop or handheld device. Considering the timeliness of such information, the value of this data increases exponentially when we have it available to us exactly when we need it.

WHAT TO DO IF YOUR EMPLOYEES REBEL

Since the name of the game in business intelligence is data that is highly perishable, having every entity in the loop is paramount. Wireless can solve this problem, too, even if the employees don't want to have anything to do with technology.

This story focuses on Landstar, a $1.4 billion freight-hauling company that deployed mobile Internet devices to their fleet of 7,300 drivers. However, this initiative originally began when the company wanted to outfit their fleet of independent owner/operators with laptops. It didn't work because the barriers were too high. The laptops required the drivers to have access to a landline to send and retrieve data, they didn't offer any location sensitivity, and frankly, they were daunting to the drivers, most of whom considered themselves "nontechnical." (Think of Susan Hawk from *Survivor*.)

After working with Phone Online, a software developer that specializes in wireless, Landstar discovered that the Web-enabled cell phone was the solution. At a cost to the truckers of a few hundred dollars instead of a few thousand, it is a device they have been using for years and are totally comfortable with. Furthermore, the embedded technology allows for location-based information, which enables the drivers and Landstar's agents to be significantly more efficient because the non-mobile agents know exactly on what route and where the drivers are traveling.

This information comes into play when a Landstar agent logs on to the company's intranet to find the nearest truck to assign a shipment. Since Landstar's drivers are independent owners, the quicker the company can match a shipment with an available trucker, the more cargo the company can move, and the more money the driver earns. Once again, we see evidence of how wireless connects the company, even when the company's 7,000 employees are scattered over thousands of miles.

AND NOW A WORD FROM THE CEO

Corporate broadcasting is next on the wireless business intelligence horizon. This will occur as soon as video-enabled smart devices move from the beta stage to widespread use. What exists now are not only primitive, they are also expensive and require much more bandwidth than the wireless networks currently offer.

That said, right now owners of Pocket PCs can use a technology called PacketVideo, which streams video to your handheld. It works by downloading a free PV Player to your CE-based device (Compaq, Casio, or HP); afterward, you can access extended clips of video-based information such as financial news, sports, and weather, just as if you were streaming them from your wired desktop PC. While this information may be helpful to your business, it's still not about your business specifically, which is where corporate narrowcasting (streaming video to just a few) and corporate broadcasting (streaming to the whole company) come into play.

Uses for wireless video via portable devices range from videoconferencing among colleagues and clients, to product and corporate training, to the dissemination of company intelligence, all delivered almost as though they were traditional TV broadcasts. Messages from the president no longer have to be lifeless e-mails, but instead can be multimedia messages full of enthusiastic intonation and eye-popping visuals.

We all know that when information is communicated in a media-rich environment, comprehension and retention improve dramatically. For this reason, wireless business intelligence applications may prove to be the biggest innovative factor of the mobile technology convergence. The more information a company's workforce is introduced to and the quicker they can integrate it into their work and build upon it, the faster the company grows.

16

Data Collection with Mobile Devices Is So Cheap, It's Fun

THERE IS NO bigger headache for drug companies than clinical trials. For a patient waiting for the approval of a medication in a clinical trial, there is no wait longer. What many people don't realize is that the bulk of the time consumed in the multiyear studies is actually absorbed in inputting, compiling, and analyzing the data. And it's not just time. The labor costs associated with these data collection procedures are daunting.

I'm specifically using pharmaceutical trials as an example because they are some of the most costly and exacting in terms of data management and collection. If there is a solution that benefits this industry, it can be adopted to nearly any other vertical market with identical benefits.

The leader is in this area is Numoda, which is setting the standard for wireless data capture and can miraculously get a typical project into a wireless environment in as little as three weeks (case histories of a few days exist).

While Numoda offers services for the financial community, government, insurance, and especially industries focused on sales or other types of businesses that rely on field reps, their work in pharmaceuticals is particularly notable, especially for their extraordinary returns on investment, which are guaranteed (for any industry segment) at a minimum of 200 percent and have been documented as high as 1,000 percent.

Anyone in the pharmaceutical industry can attest that clinical trials are the ultimate data management nightmare. I have never read of a procedure more prone to errors. To better understand the variables, one must grasp the depth and length of a clinical trial to fully appreciate the beyond belief improvement that wireless technology contributes to the process. Moreover, Food and Drug Administration (FDA) regulations regarding data integrity, which include special verification procedures, bump the herculean data management task of a regulator-compliant trial into the near impossible.

With the introduction of mobile handheld devices, clinical trials have leaped not by years, but by decades. Numoda's solution enables data to be entered while a study coordinator sits with a clinical trial subject. Double data entry/transfer/faxing is eliminated. If there is a data discrepancy, it is resolved within hours or days, not months or years. The coordinators who are interviewing the subjects are forced to categorize responses from the screen of their handhelds using drop-down lists and checkboxes so the basic data is always clean and legible. Also eliminated are incomplete forms, since a caseworker can't officially finish with a patient until all the input fields have been assigned a value or have the reason marked for the incomplete entry.

While clinical trials for different drugs vary greatly in their duration, a trial for a drug in its final stages of testing prior to FDA approval (known as a Stage 3 or 4) generally lasts one to three years.

Prior to the mobile solution, the information was compiled via patient case report forms (CRFs). These CRFs were voluminous. For instance, at the end of a trial, a paper patient case report form could build to 100 to 300 pages for just that one patient. This data was then inputted for tracking, analysis, and review. Consider the margin for error when inputting hundreds of pages for each of the hundreds of CRFs.

Exacerbating the data collection process are amendments to the type of data being collected. Because the protocol for the study is put together by committee, a lack of consensus at the beginning often begets changes during the actual trial.

Pre-wireless, new forms had to be printed and distributed to account for the addition or deletion of patient information. With a wireless solution in place, amendments are no longer encumbering in the least, since all that is required is an interface update, which can be handled when the data from the device is uploaded. Gone is the expense of designing new forms, printing updated ones, or storing new and old versions.

Furthermore, these fully electronic studies greatly enhance the security of CRFs because no one has physical access to the paperwork. Since the data is completely digital, the CRFs do not have to be physically stored, nor do they ever have to be accounted for or eventually destroyed at the end of the trial. The processes described, which include protocol preparation and case report form preparation, database programming and data entry cleanup, and costs related to incom-

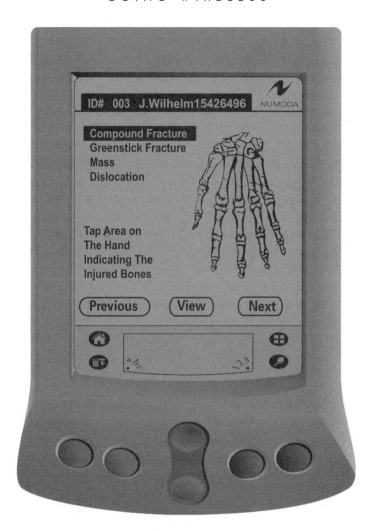

A typical Numoda input screen used by a caseworker during a clinical drug trial.

plete paperwork, typically total about $680,000 for a manually con-
ducted trial. However, this figure is reduced to a mere $29,500, about 95
percent less, with the introduction of Numoda's mobile technology.

However, the biggest expense is incurred in relation to managing the
up to 30 sites typical of a larger trial. A budget of about $3 million is
average for site monitoring and management as well as general project
management.

The reason these expenses are so high is that clinical trials have complex requirements. Patients have to be seen at different times, in differ-

ent stages of the trial. For example, at a particular site there are 4 investigators, each screening 40 patients; each investigator conducting the trial on the 38 of those who make it through screening, all coming in at different dates, days, weeks, months, and even years apart. Each patient has to come in for four or more visits, all within a precise and documented time frame. Now keep in mind that this could be happening in as many as 30 sites in 30 different states.

Before the integration of a wireless solution, it was impossible for a site monitor, the person who oversees the trial, to be certain all the CRFs were being completed by the appropriate person at the appropriate time in accordance with protocols, their amendments, and the rigorous standards for controls, blinding, randomization, and size. It is the responsibility of the site monitors to ensure and eventually prove the integrity of the data; therefore, they tend to be a fastidious group, traveling constantly from site to site to ensure accuracy during the manual data collection process.

The frequent flier accounts of site monitors are not what they used to be for those who use Numoda's solution. Now much of the monitoring is done remotely, by viewing the results electronically. Because the inefficiencies have been eliminated (most notably the accuracy of the inputted data), the monitor has complete confidence in the interim results viewed without having to physically check the patient case report forms. Being able to catch potential errors in near real time avoids fines for FDA violations due to nonadherence to FDA guidelines, something often discovered months or years into a trial, when it's close to impossible to fix.

The biggest benefit outside of the monetary advantage is that Numoda's real-time reporting assures that the clinical trial is maintaining its goals and quality of data today, not four months later when the paper trail catches up and it is determined that an amendment is necessary. Using the nonwireless, nonelectronic method, in just four months several dozens of patients could be enrolled, several hundreds of pages of data collected, and several millions of dollars wasted.

Now, instead of millions being frittered away, millions are saved. The bottom line is that even with Numoda's service fee of $366,000 (based on the parameters above), the net cost reduction totals more than $2.6 million. This means that a budget of $4.75 million for a manual trial is reduced to about $2.15 million, a 63 percent savings, and a return on investment of 712 percent.

Does Numoda's solution always work? It doesn't matter. The company offers a guarantee of at least a 200 percent return on investment.

This policy was a result of a sensitivity to managers who have become risk-averse after years of paying for technology that failed to deliver on its promise.

There's also the human element. Numoda's technology can dramatically hasten the time a drug gets approved and into the hands of those who need it most.

REDUCING CHOW LINE TIME

While Numoda's work in pharmaceuticals is about reducing costs, shortening time to market, and ensuring data accuracy, better data collection for some companies is about having information to make better decisions. That's exactly what army food service managers had in mind when they implemented a handheld data collection initiative at their 12 dining halls at Fort Hood. The bottleneck in the food line occurred at the checkout, when cashiers had to sift through paperwork filled out by the soldiers to determine the amount, if any, of subsistence allowance they were to receive and then collect the difference.

The prehandheld method was to have the soldiers write their Social Security number, rank, service, and entitlement on a clipboard upon entering the dining facility. They were required to do this for each meal.

At the end of the day, a data entry clerk spent approximately two hours entering the soldier-provided information into a database. This occurred daily at each of the 12 facilities at Fort Hood, each of which served about 1,200 meals a day. At the end of the month, the dining facility manager would then manually sift through the inputted data to produce a monthly report indicating how many meals were served and verifying soldiers' stated entitlement.

While the army was aware of point-of-sales systems that could help solve their clipboard issues, the solution was too expensive to implement. Instead, Fort Hood equipped each of their cashiers with a Palm device complete with bar code reader; the soldiers just swipe their ID cards to provide all the necessary information for a successful and speedy transaction. Over time, the system included a feature that allows for the soldiers to have their meal contribution payment deducted from their paychecks; eliminating the cash transaction moves the lines along even faster.

Now the Fort Hood food service managers can determine in real time how many meals have been served and whether to prepare more food, thus making it possible for the first time to actually improve meal planning and reduce food waste. They also know if there are any discrepancies in the amount of cash collected and if any of the soldiers used the wrong entitlement code.

LETTING THE DATA SUPPLIER DO THE INPUTTING

In both these examples, data collection is being handled by company representatives. However, the simplicity of handheld devices is such that some of the labor may be absorbed by the person from whom the data is being collected.

For instance, in the near future, during a doctor's visit you may be handed a Palm-type device that offers a survey of symptoms. You would respond by clicking checkboxes and drop-down lists to zero in on the health issues and problems you want to discuss with your doctor. This is far less tedious for the patient who doesn't have to wait while a nurse notes responses on a form. Next, the nurse would beam the inputted data to a nearby printer and then hand this report to your physician. This data would then be uploaded to your digital chart.

Data collection is a mundane task, and mobile technology's ability to eliminate routine chores frees the worker to do that which is more beneficial to the company and its clients. Instead of spending 15 minutes interviewing a patient, a nurse can devote that time to patient follow-up, a service painfully lacking in our current health care system. Another example occurs each time I pay a restaurant check, when I see a missed opportunity on the part of the eatery. Along with the bill there should be a Palm device, asking a handful of questions about the experience, service, food quality, and other dining-defining characteristics. A paper survey is costly to maintain, while the handheld requires only a multisecond synch at the end of the day and provides astounding data in which the restaurant managers can, in real time, rate their establishments in areas other than gross sales.

17

Perfect Inspections Every Time

INSPECTION PROCEDURES IS not a glamorous topic. But quality control and efficiency are, so here we go.

As most of us know, Volvo's cars are considered some of the safest in the world, and for this reason they were striving to improve the inspection of new vehicles by eliminating the three weeks that would pass from inspection to the final data compilation that determines if the vehicle has potential problems.

Similar to the data collection issues just covered, Volvo was desperate to get rid of their multipage paper forms, which were then manually inputted into a database. While this is standard for most automakers, Volvo always distances itself from the ordinary.

In an attempt to find a solution, Volvo first considered laptops, but then was attracted to the durability of a handheld (given the lack of moving parts and keyboards that are prone to damage). It was these advantages that convinced the carmaker to integrate mobile devices into their inspection routine.

In addition to being able to analyze data more quickly, Volvo was able for the first time to effortlessly and inexpensively tailor their inspections to particular models without technical assistance or additional development costs, since the forms are easy enough for nontechnical managers to program themselves.

Not only has the handheld solution eliminated new forms, the need to update them, and the manual entry involved in the paperwork, the data turnaround time of three weeks was reduced to one day. This means that if an inspector notices an anomaly, Volvo can resolve it immediately, continuing to make their cars the safest in the world.

WHEN THERE'S NO TIME

While Volvo's inspections are performed without any notable time constraints, BFGoodrich not only needs to input their inspection data accurately, they have to do it in a few minutes, and even this 180 seconds
was a time they were desperate to trim.

The scenario occurs at racetracks, where members of the BFGoodrich
design team wait in the pits along with the team mechanics. Their man-
date is to measure temperatures and pressures of all four tires when the
cars come in for a pit stop. By combining this data with lap times, track
temperature, and weather, designers are able to evaluate a tire's durability. These findings are then applied to their next generation of tires.

What was frustrating for the BFGoodrich team, as well as the race
car's mechanics, was that this info-gathering process took much longer
than they wanted. Each tire has to be checked three times in one pit
stop, during which the technicians would scrawl the data on a clipboard
as they moved from tire to tire. Because the data was noted on the fly,
it was often illegible and prone to errors, with the results worthless and
scrapped.

Like Volvo, BFGoodrich considered laptops but knew they were too
large, too expensive, and far too fragile for the racing pit.

The first stage in their handheld evolution utilized drop-down menus
to enter data, which saved a precious five to six seconds per tire per pit
stop. Next, BFGoodrich discovered and implemented a Versid Temperature Acquisition Module from Tangent Systems, which allows engineers to attach test probes directly to the Palm devices for automatic
temperature and pressure readings, thus eliminating data entry entirely
and reducing what was a minutes-long procedure to one that now takes
seconds and is markedly more accurate.

The financial payback is less easy to determine in this BFGoodrich
example because the data is used for research and development, but
one certainty is that the tire company can now leverage performance
information fully, which ultimately leads to the manufacturing of better,
safer tires.

PLUS GET STANDARIZED DATA,
WHICH MEANS A BETTER ANALYSIS

While Volvo was most interested in eliminating inspection forms and
their inherent time delays and associated costs, BFGoodrich was
focused on gathering the most accurate data in as few seconds as pos-

sible. However, there is another inspection scenario to be considered as well for mobile devices, and that is the standardization of data, vital for analyzing inspection information.

Now we turn to ServiceMaster, which owns such brand-dominating companies as Terminix, Merry Maids, Rescue Rooter, and the parent company, which provides janitorial and other commercial cleaning services. Operating in more than 40 countries with over 10.5 million customers, this corporation clearly has the resources to implement the best IT strategy necessary to solve an internal problem.

The challenge in this case was improving the quality of cleaning inspections for their client, the Greyhound bus company, for whom ServiceMaster provides cleaning crews at 19 stations throughout the country. As with most companies, the inspection was performed by a manager using paper-based forms, all of which were inputted weekly in a Microsoft Access database by an administrative assistant. The account manager could then generate whatever reports he or she wished. And that was the problem. Greyhound wanted to automate this auditing procedure and generate standardized reports for higher-integrity data.

ServiceMaster, like most companies launching a wireless/handheld initiative, considered units running Microsoft's CE operating system, which you can find on higher-end devices made by companies such as Compaq and Casio. Because many of their staff members were already using CE-based handhelds, this was the first solution ServiceMaster considered. However, the extra features offered were deemed unnecessary in light of the extra cost; therefore, a Palm device was judged the appropriate and economical choice. In fact, they chose one of Palm's lowest-end models because they were especially small and light.

In just eight weeks, ServiceMaster had their application up and running. Each bus inspection manager navigates 22 screens, which they maneuver with an ease especially notable for a workforce that is (in general) less than computer literate and for whom English is not the first language.

With the handheld solution in place, Greyhound can now access the service reports daily instead of weekly, which allows them to not only monitor the inspection scores, but also spot trends by site, shift, and supervisor.

The handheld solution cured a nagging issue of data disparity for Greyhound, which needed and wanted to better evaluate their outsourced cleaning crews. The result for Greyhound was higher quality control of this extended workforce. As one executive noted, "If you can't measure it, you can't manage it."

18

Supply Chain Paradise
(and Procurement, Too)

YOU NEVER WOULD have guessed that a British surgical supply company found their wireless solution in an American supermarket.

The company is Ethicon, and when they studied the companies with forward-thinking mobile plans, the one with which they felt they had the best fit was Safeway. As it turns out, the two had similar goals: to automate their stock and inventory management systems. While Safeway wants to make sure they have enough Cheerios and Pop-Tarts, Ethicon is focused on keeping hospitals stocked with bandages, gauze pads, and cotton balls.

Ethicon, a subsidiary of global pharmaceutical giant Johnson & Johnson, was quick to realize that the retail sector, and supermarkets in particular, would be an excellent source for lessons in best practices. They were right. Both are dealing with timely stocking issues and "clients" who demand just-in-time inventory.

As one of the world's largest manufacturers and suppliers of sutures and related wound closure products, Ethicon services customers that range from small health care organizations to large hospitals. Because of the disparity in size, it was essential that the system Ethicon developed and implemented be an end-to-end wireless network that would work on the client side, whether or not they possessed an existing network, Internet technology, or other expansive IT system.

Ethicon's aim was to enhance its relations with health care organizations by providing them with a new, automated stock and inventory management system that would always keep the facility's critical health supplies fully stocked. At the same time, this system would need to keep stock inventory costs to a minimum. To reflect the simplicity of this solution, it was eventually named E-sy Scan.

The handheld devices are situated within stock areas. As each product is used, it is swiped with a bar code reader. When the majority of the stock has been exhausted, Ethicon replenishes the supply automatically. That's it.

Using IBM Mobile Connect technology, the entire order process from the hospital's supply cupboard to Ethicon's supply dispatch is seamlessly activated, thus ensuring that the critical surgical supplies arrive in the right place at the right time.

Because Ethicon already had an established relationship with IBM, they turned to them for their solution. But contrary to the popular perception about IBM that new projects are implemented later rather than sooner because the company is so large, it should be noted that the Blue Behemoth had E-sy Scan designed and implemented in just six weeks. This speed is indicative not only of what a large vendor such as IBM is capable of, but also of the simplicity of wireless solutions in general.

For Ethicon, E-sy Scan has reinforced its brand presence, and its customer interface is now far more efficient and effective. Meanwhile, their customers have found real cost and time savings. When compared to the manual ordering process, the time required was reduced by an average of 30 minutes.

Perhaps most impressive is that Ethicon has automated their customers' procurement process by taking the day-to-day orders away from both the health care organizations and their own Ethicon call centers and converted them into a series of paperless transactions.

PAPERLESS PROCUREMENT A REALITY

Paperless procurement is precisely the goal of Core Harbor, an applications service provider whose focus is exclusively on B2B markets. One of their most impressive products is ProcureEdge, because it was the first to offer a wireless component to the wildly popular Ariba Buyer ASP. While Ariba Buyer is designed to save money by streamlining the purchasing of operating resources, it also allows wireless access to Ariba's Commerce Service Network, a gateway to over 30,000 suppliers.

Looking at the ProcureEdge/Ariba combo in broad strokes, the wireless e-procurement opportunity gives an organization three types of functions. The first is On-Demand, where users can check the status of their requisitions. The second is Notification, which alerts managers to the need for their approval along with a detail of the requisition. This is just an alert that is activated automatically when a requisition has been made. Last, there is Approval, in which management logs in, then views and approves the requisitions. While management loves exchanging mounds of procurement paperwork for the ease of wireless's anytime, anywhere, reviews and approvals, employees are equally thrilled to have access to the condition of their request no matter where they are as well. For example, a worker on the shop floor with a wireless device can check the status of a requisition without having to walk to the business office to access Ariba Buyer.

ProcureEdge, like most wireless deployments, is a snap. It is not carrier dependent, which means a company can use any cell service company (Nextel, Sprint, A&T) in conjunction with any device (any brand of cell phone or PDA).

Solutions like ProcureEdge that offer wireless access to employees and suppliers can significantly reduce a company's supply chain/procurement friction, thus making their organizations far more nimble.

This was the case for Digital Insight, which provides e-finance solutions for banks and credit unions (which rebrand the service). Despite the technological moxie of the company, they were slaves to a 100 percent paper-driven environment, with a procurement staff walking the halls seeking purchase approval signatures. Once they implemented wirelessly enabled ProcureEdge, they reported significantly reduced purchase cycle times, as well as notably improved service and prices from their suppliers.

Despite the growing popularity of wireless procurement within an organization, the greater benefit may be to suppliers that introduce a wireless initiative for their business customers. To prove this point, our story begins with PurchasePro, a company that provides public and private electronic marketplaces for suppliers involved in business-to-business transactions. The benefit is that a business, no matter the size, can buy and sell products and services to companies throughout the country and, conversely, can respond quickly to bids and easily create purchase orders. Monetarily speaking, the procurement paradigm reduces costs through streamlined transaction processes between suppliers and manufacturers.

PurchasePro runs over 291 e-marketplaces, serving 140,000 businesses, the roster of which includes Hilton, Office Depot, Honeywell, and Computer Associates. Naturally PurchasePro quickly launched its wireless application PurchasePro Anywhere, which allows the entire client base (one of the largest in the industry) to access the marketplaces and exchanges with full functionality from any Web-enabled cell phone, personal digital assistant (Palm, Handspring), or Pocket PC (Compaq, Casio). While this certainly sounds good, let's look at what it means in real-world terms.

For just a moment, pretend you are a manager for a large resort in

Hawaii and that you own the latest and greatest cell phone with an integrated Palm-type device that allows you to access the Web.

It's 10:00 A.M., and you are five minutes early for your dental appointment, more than enough time to handle an important matter. On the drive over, you remembered that the hotel is running dangerously low on tiki torches. You retrieve your smart phone and log in to your PurchasePro account and create a PO for 500 tiki torches by browsing the online catalog. After inputting the payment information, payment terms, and shipping information, you add a memo to your order indicating the need for rush delivery. You click "submit" just as the receptionist calls your name.

Meanwhile, across the ocean in Wichita, Kansas, Matthew Flambe, owner of Just Tiki Torches, is starting a round of 18 holes with a client. While waiting on the tee box, he decides to check in, not with his administrative assistant, but with his PurchasePro account to view and approve POs that may have transacted while he was on the green.

He immediately notes your order, approves it, and calls his warehouse manager to both alert him and request a tracking number.

Moments later, as you walk out of the dental office, your smart phone signals an alert notifying you that there is a message waiting. You look at the display to see that your tiki torch order has been approved, along with the shipment tracking number so that you can monitor the progress of your order.

Five minutes of downtime in a dental office waiting room was transformed into five productive minutes.

WHEN YOU HAVE ZERO DESK TIME

While in your role as hotel manager you get at least a few hours of desk time each day, consider the benefits of wireless e-procurement and supply chain management for mobile professionals who have intense buying requirements, such as construction contractors.

Wickes, a $1 billion-a-year leading distributor of building materials and related components, recognized this need. Realizing the huge void wireless was filling for out-of-office management, such as contractors, the company partnered with Buildscape to offer a sophisticated procurement system that could be accessed by any wireless device that allowed for Web browsing. By doing so, construction professionals could order materials from their 120,000-item catalog anytime, anywhere, then have it charged to their account and delivered directly to an office or job site.

As it turns out, construction is a hotbed for handhelds. Webcor Builders (which named their company in 1971) are gaining renown for finishing their jobs early. And these are no small projects—consider the 236-room Serrano Hotel in San Francisco that they completed 60 days ahead of schedule. Their secret is making sure all the key people involved in the project are communicating, including the customers, who are given Palm devices at the beginning of the project, courtesy of Webcor. Webcor's president notes that in addition to goodwill and smooth-running construction sites, the financial benefits have been glorious. The same number of managers that used to be required for a $20 million job can now easily handle a $60 million one. Given the company's enthusiasm for handhelds, it should be no surprise that they won the bid for a coveted job: building the Santa Clara campus for Palm, Inc.

The $726 billion construction industry is just a slice of the $5.7 trillion B2B commerce pie estimated (by AMR research) by the year 2004. Now consider that if a mere 1 percent of those transactions are conducted wirelessly, we're looking at a $57 billion market . . . and perhaps all the incentive you may need to be sure that both your company and your suppliers can process orders wirelessly.

SOLVING THE PROBLEMS FOR ALL

These supply chain and procurement examples have purposely cast a wide net to make a point. There are few norms in the minutiae of procurement and supply chain execution; nonetheless, the general problems are similar for all.

If you were to ask a supply chain executive for a wish list of problems to be solved, he or she would respond, "Timely information, anytime access to that timely information, and being able to act immediately on the timely information accessed."

Of course, this scenario is of most value to mission-critical goods. It's one thing to know an order hasn't arrived, it's another to be able to find out in real time that it hasn't arrived, discover where it was last seen, and obtain or issue a revised schedule. In other words, "If it didn't happen, when didn't it happen?" so that corrective actions can happen immediately.

These perspectives come from Narry Singh, a business technology authority who suggests that wireless transactions play a key role but that it's the information associated with the pre- and post-transaction stages (such as tracking) that may be where the most wealth is reaped.

"Everyone's supply chain needs are different," he explains. "But everyone has a need for connectivity to information, usable information once connected, and the ability to take action."

And what happens once wireless is applied in this way? "Simple," he notes. "Wireless will make the supply 'unchained.' "

For direct links to all the companies
discussed in this book, visit
www.easton.com.

19

The Efficiency Miracle
of the Wireless Warehouse

IT'S BAD ENOUGH that you've got so much inventory coming in that you can hardly keep track of it, but imagine that your warehouse had to be hastily built during a devastating flood, fire, or hurricane. Oh, and there's no electricity.

These are the typical working conditions the Red Cross faces daily as part of their disaster service operation. No matter how bad the physical landscape, they must instantly set up a mechanism for receiving and storing thousands of pallets of food, supplies, and equipment, then efficiently distribute these items to the disaster's victims.

It's precisely these extreme situations that led the Red Cross to find a solution for keeping track of what they have without having to pull in telephone and network cable. That solution was obvious: wireless.

From high school basements to million-square-foot warehouses, the bigger the disaster, the bigger the need for an automated system that would not only serve the temporary warehouse, but be able to shuttle the data back to the central database regardless of the challenging conditions.

Furthermore, because many of the goods are donated, the Red Cross must always keep scrupulous records of the materials used, since the IRS requires extraordinarily detailed information.

The Red Cross found their solution with Proxim's RangeLAN2 products, selected for their ability to handle the widest range, which was the major consideration for the Red Cross because of the size of the facilities they often use.

They got what they wished for in a system that was also mobile, reliable, and easy enough for a staff of volunteer workers with limited computer experience. Using a combination of equipment that includes rugged laptops, bar code scanners, long-life batteries, and a wireless local-area network, the Red Cross can now keep track of inventory and distribution of relief supplies regardless of the conditions inside the facility or horrific weather conditions outside. Perhaps the system's two best features are its scalability (being able to add additional equipment effortlessly) and the ease with which it can be disassembled and moved to the next disaster.

SOLVING THE COMMON PROBLEMS

While no company has to endure the overwhelming logistical challenges that the Red Cross faces daily, having an endless stream of inbound and outbound stock that must be properly tracked can sometimes seem equally challenging. Such were the warehouse management and inventory control issues faced by Ocean Spray, Kraft, and Ingram Micro, and all were solved by a wireless technology.

Let's begin with Ingram Micro, a Fortune 50 company that is one of the largest global wholesale providers of technology solutions, products, and services. With sales of over $30 billion in fiscal year 2000, the company sought to implement a system that provided near perfect inventory and order accuracy.

With an arsenal of bar code scanners, handheld computers with integrated scanners, and a wireless network to upload the data, wireless is the first line of defense against errors of inbound inventory, which is doubled-checked using bar code scanners and then verified against the main database. It's a two-part process, the first of which involves scanning the inbound order's paperwork in all its detail. If this first stage matches, the actual order itself is scanned to make sure that the vendor part number, UPC, or Ingram SKU also matches.

A similar procedure is used on outbound inventory, which is also double-verified using wireless. First, an operator verifies an order after it has been picked by scanning the order ticket. The order is then double-checked by a shipping clerk, who scans both the order ticket and the product box and compares them. If what is scanned doesn't match, the system rejects the order. If it does match, the order is shipped at the same time the system tracking the match generates a packing slip, bills the customer, and assigns a carrier.

With these wireless checks in place, Ingram has rated their Canada facilities with 99 percent accuracy on the 4,000 to 5,000 orders they fill each day. "The only errors we're finding are when a customer ordered the wrong time or a product is defective," remarks an Ingram Micro executive.

Similar kudos have been noted with respect to inventory accuracy, which they once considered "atrocious" but is now near 99 percent.

Ultimately, the real measurement of a wireless system is the degree to which it benefits customers, and that's where the wireless system shines brightest. Pre-wireless, it was a three-day cycle from the time the order was placed to shipment. Now, if Ingram Micro receives an order by 2:00 P.M., they can ship it the same day.

WHAT OCEAN SPRAY DID ABOUT THEIR PERISHABLE INVENTORY

While Ingram Micro was dealing with the challenges of carrying thousands of different products, Ocean Spray's warehouse management issues stemmed from the storage of perishable goods—in this case, fresh cranberries and related products such as juice drinks, sauces, and dried fruit. Exacerbating the problem was a customer base that was increasingly demanding just-in-time deliveries on smaller orders with even smaller lead times. But this is no small business, with annual sales in excess of $1.4 billion.

Previous to their wireless implementation, the agriculture cooperative (Ocean Spray is owned by nearly 900 cranberry and citrus fruit growers) used paper-based procedures to fill 1,200 orders daily. When inventory arrived, forklift operators would literally roam the warehouse looking for an empty row to deposit the goods, making first-in, first-out initiatives nearly impossible.

The wireless warehouse makeover has been extraordinarily successful. Now the epitome of efficiency, the company uses procedures similar to Ingram Micro's to verify all inbound and outbound inventory, including order verification and invoicing and a guarantee that the oldest product is picked first.

Ocean Spray's wireless warehouse has translated into lovable numbers for the cooperative. Total output rose 15 percent; the warehouse was able to ship 1.8 million more cases with 2,200 fewer man-hours; productivity per warehouse worker rose from 451 cases per hour to 551; inventory accuracy is better than 98 percent; and inventory levels declined by 121,000 cases.

Along with their happy warehouses are equally happy customers who have noticed even better service, fresher product, and fewer order errors.

THE "VAST INVENTORY–SHORT SHELF LIFE SOLUTION"

Last, there is Kraft Canada, which had problems similar to those of both Ingram Micro (lots of different products) and Ocean Spray (products with a short shelf life). Kraft Canada also realized massive improvements once they started using wireless terminals for data collection, inventory, and space management.

Theirs is also a wireless system from start to finish. Kraft Canada's installation is highlighted by the 65 forklift-mounted data terminals that dynamically direct the forklift operators to complete specific tasks, such as put-away instructions indicating the precise location. Order fulfillment works similarly and can direct the forklift operators to exactly where they need to load. Furthermore, the system is so smart that it knows when to direct the forklift operator to a full-pallet pick location versus a case-packing one, the latter used for multiple product picks. Wireless checkpoints from the dispatcher to the shipping docks continue the verification process.

Internally, the forklift data terminals also use the wireless system to optimize space. Periodically, trip tasks are downloaded to the terminals, directing the forklift operators to move pallets according to lot number and rotation date.

Kraft's Montview distribution center's inventory accuracy has risen to 98 percent. Moreover, now that every warehouse function is recorded, inventory status can be consulted with confidence.

The end benefit of the wireless warehouse management system was best described by a relieved Kraft executive who said, "Now we know we're shipping the right product in the right quantity to the right customer at the right time."

20

Always Knowing Exactly Where
Your Mobile Assets Are

THERE'S NO MYSTERY to this story. The motive was obvious, proven by the fact that this laptop was stolen while three others, also left unattended, were ignored. The owner of the abducted ThinkPad was Irwin Jacobs, CEO of Qualcomm, the communications company giant. According to the Associated Press, after speaking to 90 members of the Society of American Business Editors, Mr. Jacobs stepped down from the podium to talk to a small group, at which point the laptop was heisted.

Since the data was completely backed-up, the real loss was the corporate secrets stored on the system's hard drive, proprietary information that Jacobs admitted would be valuable to foreign governments.

What might be more infuriating for Qualcomm shareholders is that the theft of the data could easily have been prevented even though the machine itself had been stolen.

Using wireless tracking technology and other sophisticaed microprocessors, Mr. Jacobs could have initiated two messages to his ThinkPad the moment he realized the laptop had been seized. The first would have been an instruction to the drive to overwrite all the data, and the second would have queried the location-sensitive component to determine exactly where the machine was to an accuracy of within 10 feet. As long as the unit was between the Pacific Coast and the East Coast, Nova Scotia and Chiapas, Mexico, it could have been located within seconds.

MOBILE AND EXPENSIVE

Given the nature of Mr. Jacobs's work and the fact that Qualcomm is highly involved in tracking devices, he would have been aware of this technology, which was commonly available in September 2000, when the laptop was stolen. But asset tracking, even if you run a communications empire, is not part of your day-to-day thinking in this kind of scenario. Wireless asset tracking is usually associated with high-value or highly dangerous goods.

For example, a railcar carrying hazardous, high-volume chemicals traverses the tracks between Wyoming and Nevada. Despite the fact that these states form a corridor for highly dangerous chemical travel, the risks never diminish. Given the cargo, the train is highly monitored. Even the slightest mishap in a populated area would be catastrophic.

With the aid of a wireless identification system, this shipment is being tracked in real time, with crews on call should there be any aberration in the precisely planned routing. Management, however, does not need to stand by and stare at beeping lights on a wall-size electronic map. Instead they are free to roam, secure that they will instantly and automatically be notified via their cell, pager, or other wireless communicator if even a blip is out of the ordinary. Even better, management can receive periodic notifications assuring them that all is functioning as planned.

It's official. The twenty-first century is here, and wireless asset tracking, which means always knowing where you can find what's valuable to you, is proof. While it's currently being relegated to the expensive stuff, as chip prices continue to fall and the transmission technology continues to standardize, the practice will eventually be ubiquitous.

In other words, asset tracking via wireless technology isn't just about the location of a railcar of titanium tetrachloride, a construction company's untethered trailers, or other high-value mobile assets. The next uses will include location-sensitive chips to track your company's internal assets such as tools, printers, desk chairs, and file folders, as well as the laptop of your CEO. Granted, the cost of a ThinkPad can't be compared to a $100,000-plus forklift, but the information contained in the unit could easily be worth 10 times that.

Justifying the minimal cost of asset tracking is easy when complemented by its return on investment. According to the National Equipment Register, nationwide theft of heavy equipment is estimated at $1 billion annually, and the FBI claims that at least $9 billion worth of freight is stolen from transportation companies in a typical year.

FINDING YOUR FLEET

It's also helpful to note that asset tracking can include people in the vehicles owned by your organization. Install in any vehicle a product called AssetVision made by Wireless Link, and an automatic alert system can notify whoever is in charge of monitoring usage if the vehicle is driven more than a particular distance away from a particular point (your offices) or if it travels outside a specified geographic region (across state lines, for example). If you don't want your vehicles driven at all during certain times, National Systems and Research Company will be happy to install a "virtual security fence" for you. If the area it covers is penetrated, you get an instant alert in addition to the tracking of the vehicle.

How this asset tracking works is astounding in its simplicity and indicative of how big and fast asset tracking will eventually be. The leader is Aeris.net, which has put together the information network that the data travels on. As such, Aeris.net provides service to the companies or products you will use to track assets. Aeris.net is well ahead of the curve owing to its extensive coverage (most of the United States and huge chunks of Canada and Mexico) and the extreme reliability necessary for the technology to make any sense. For this reason, they are usually the first-choice provider.

As you can see, one of the most popular areas of asset tracking is fleet management, which can include robust information to prevent theft and misuse as well as flag risky driving habits. Using the Mobile Trak device by NeoTech Products, Inc., a fleet owner can incorporate trip logging (start time, end time, max speed, distance traveled) as well as driver abuse (speed violations and even unnecessarily abrupt acceleration and deceleration). These reports translate into savings for the company using the technology. Here are two examples:

A delivery service had a fleet of 15 trucks. Using Mobile Trak, the system revealed two hours per month of misuses at a cost to the company of $22 per hour. By reining in the offenders based on the report, the total savings in a year is approximately $8,000. This is a substantial savings over time when you consider that the cost for 15 devices totals $4,485 (15 at $299 per unit), netting $3,515 the first year and $8,000 in subsequent years.

Another case study of employee mileage reimbursement for 10 people found that, on average, they each misreported their mileage by 100 miles a month at a cost savings of 30 cents per mile. In the latter scenario, the savings is less, at $61 for the first year and $360 for each year per employee that follows; however, it's the cumulative that keeps this in perspective.

While these investment returns and payback times are drawn from small business, consider the financial benefits when a Mobil Trak–type device is deployed over the fleet of an enterprise. Say it with me: "Cha-ching."

SMALL ASSETS COUNT, TOO

On a smaller scale, the U.S. Postal Service (USPS) is now using a wireless tracking solution for their international mail. Unlike Federal Express, the U.S. Postal Service is not an integrated carrier with its own fleet of planes. Instead they rely on a variety of resources to transport mail to and from their international destinations, thus increasing the chances for shipment mishandling. (That explains it!)

When a "mail handling irregularity" (their term, not mine) occurred, a ramp clerk filled out paper forms to document the delayed flight carrying the mail. The forms were later given to employees to input.

That was then. Now, using Symbol handheld devices and Aether's ScoutSync technology, ramp clerks scan bar-coded mail containers before they are loaded onto aircrafts, thus making the information instantly available to the entire network.

In addition to tracking mail handling irregularities such as an airline's failure to load a bag of mail on a flight, weather damage, or mechanical problems, USPS managers also have a handle on the degree and number of mishaps that occurred, allowing them to ascertain the root of the negligence.

KNOWING WHERE TO FIND 300,000 EMPTY BEER BARRELS

While bar codes are at the heart of the postal service solution, yet another technology is big in the asset tracking world. It's called RFID (radio frequency identification), and it's expected eventually to replace bar codes. While bar codes are by far the cheapest wireless tracking method available, they have two major drawbacks. First, they have to be read by line of sight; and second, bar codes become unreadable if they are altered or damaged, the latter common when products are being handled by machines.

RFID is thought of by some as the technology that can do no wrong. The tags are cheap (usually under a dollar), and because of their size and construction, they are virtually impossible to damage. They are small, the size of two matches side-by-side, and they also do not need line of sight to be read because they use radio frequency and need to be only within a certain number of feet of a reader to be processed. Furthermore, the tags can be programmed with information about the product to which they are attached.

Let me give you an example. The United Kingdom brewing industry was having a heck of a time keeping track of 300,000 empty beer barrels worth over $21 million (U.S.). While many are simply misplaced, others are stolen, melted down, and sold as scrap metal. Scottish Courage, one of Britain's largest brewers, started attaching the tags to their barrels to keep track of the barrels themselves in addition to following the whereabouts of every single keg. Apparently, some industrious pub owners were breaking their trade agreements by reselling the beer, and kegs delivered to one pub were showing up at another.

Using RFID technology, which holds plenty of pertinent information about the keg as well as the customer to whom the barrel was delivered, Scottish Courage can now identify customers that appear to be big buyers and are getting big discounts but in fact are using only a small amount themselves because the kegs are being retrieved from pubs that are not customers.

For their internal processes, Scottish Courage also has an ongoing record of the life of the barrel, including the weight of the empty barrel to prevent over- or underfilling, the cleaning and maintenance records, and the entire itinerary of the barrel from the day it was initially tagged. This translates to phenomenal efficiency in their tracking progress, including where they can be found (on premises or off) at any moment.

DECIDING BETWEEN CELLULAR-EQUIPPED CHIPS AND TAGS

Essentially, you have two choices for wireless asset tracking: chips and tags.

Cellular-enabled chipsets are far more robust and equally more expensive. Their technology works in such a way that at any point you can send a message to the chip asking where it is, and in a second it will respond. Furthermore, when the chipsets are attached to other chips, additional information is available.

For example, if a tracking chipset is linked to the processor of a computer, questions about the status of the machine (for instance, which components are working, which ones are not) can be answered even if it is turned off. Commands can also be originated, such as "overwrite the drive" for a stolen machine. You now also have a glimpse of wireless tech support in the years to come. Another example would come from a boat owner with a wireless chip installed on her yacht. She may be on land while a friend has taken the vessel out to sea but can query the status of any of the computer-enabled instruments, including engine temperature, speed, and the boat's precise location.

In other words, tracking with cellular-equipped chips is highly sophisticated because they operate autonomously. Once attached to an item, the item can roam, but you still have instant access to critical information.

With tags, you don't necessarily know exactly where the item is, but you know where it was last seen. How we view overnight delivery tracking logs is a good example of how tags operate. When you view the log, you might learn that your package has been loaded onto the delivery truck, but you have no idea where the truck is. That's "don't know where it is now, but know where it was last."

Tags run less than a dollar, and these cellular chipsets cost upward of $30 to $60. That's why you find chips on high-value assets and tags on products where general "where is it" information and durability are key.

Interestingly, both of these tracking technologies create the same result. RFID and cellular-enabled chips are not a new technology, they are a new paradigm. Never before have companies had access to data and of such high quality and precision. Since asset tracking is specific and reliable, corporations can now analyze that which they have never had the opportunity to before, including cracking down on black market beer and bad employee driving habits. Either way, companies can now save money in facets of their business where they never could before.

21

Wirelessly Being Where You
Can't Possibly Be

THERE'S A SNICKERS bar caught in rung G2 of your office vending machine, and Doug, who fills the machine, was just paged . . . not by your assistant, who is staring at her 4:00 P.M. sugar rush as it dangles by the wrapper, but by a chip in the machine that literally sensed the problem and wirelessly alerted Doug with an exact description of the problem.

Meet telemetrics, a term that describes what happens when, without any human intervention, information is exchanged remotely, a device is remotely controlled, or a condition is remotely measured.

The telemetric aspect of the vending machine scenario occurred when the machine sensed the distressed Snickers and alerted Doug. The core of this communication transaction was strictly machine-to-human, versus assistant-to-dispatcher-to-Doug, which, naturally, would be human-to-human-to-human. Even more *Star Trek*–like, Doug can query the chip to determine if any of the snacks in the machine holding the Snickers hostage are running low, so while releasing the captive candy bar, he can have with him items that need to be restocked.

As with wireless asset tracking, telemetrics is about cost savings via reduced labor and location awareness and the priceless value of peace of mind, knowing that those who need to be in the know will be alerted proactively when necessary. In addition, it often removes at least one layer of labor, as with the dispatcher in our vending machine example.

The vending machine scenario describes only a fraction of the potential of telemetrics. While the vending machine uses are certainly a boon, telemetrics's biggest fanfare is trumpeted in security/alarm monitoring, utility metering, and the general surveying of machines in business environments such as copiers. As you can see by these examples, remote monitoring is one of the many hallmarks of telemetrics.

In the metering realm, telemetrics can wirelessly alert a utility company if there is an outage; if the meter has not been authorized for connection and one has been made; or, worse, if the meter has been disconnected or tampered with. And thanks to telemetrics, by using remote diagnostics, technicians can be apprised of any of the above without human intervention.

Interestingly, statistics for the telemetrics industry often revolve around meters. When analysts project a market for 289 million telemetric units, you should note that while this number is considered accurate, it includes 242 million meters, many of which will not replaced until they wear out at the end of their average life of 25 years.

THE EASY CHOICE

The wow factor of telemetrics is its simplicity and effectiveness. In other words, if you ever have to make a choice, and telemetrics is one of your options, grab it.

Security alarms are a perfect example. If your office is protected by one, chances are it was installed over traditional phone lines. If a break-in occurs, the system would respond by sending an alert message over these telephone lines to a central processing station, where a human operator responds by dispatching the police.

While this solution has worked well, there are paramount considerations. For example, landlines can be tampered with, thus rendering even the most secure system useless. Meanwhile, in a wireless scenario, the link can never be severed because there is nothing to "sever." Furthermore, wireless alarm systems can send what network provider Aeris.net refers to as "heartbeat" messages, which indicate that the unit is healthy. By the way, "I'm here and so far have not been vandalized" messages are sent all day long by the Statue of Liberty, which has telemetric sensors located from the tip of her torch down to the museum hall on which she sits.

In fact, all historic facilities are optimum candidates for telemetric fire, security, and early warning alarms because they invisibly eliminate the aesthetic challenges posed by exposed wired conduit and represent a significant savings in refurbishment costs and interruption of operations during installation.

Telemetric early warning systems have also been a boon for hotels, such as Walt Disney World's Royal Plaza Hotel, as well as many Best Westerns, Holiday Inns, and Radisson Resorts, many of which now have a completely wireless fire and security system.

WINE TIME

Wireless via telemetrics is also gaining users outside industry and is moving into the agricultural field owing to its ability to measure climatic changes. The return on investment is eye-opening for pricey crops. Wente Vineyards in Livermore, California, is in an ongoing war against the cleistothecium fungus, more commonly known as powdery mildew, which ravages the grapes while they are still growing on the vine. Undetected, cleistothecium fungus can cost a single winery thousands of dollars and, in severe cases, even millions.

This problem has been nearly solved by a combination of the Aeris Network and a solar-powered Strison wirefree weather station, which measures all the atmospheric conditions, including rain, degree of wetness on the plant, temperature, wind speed, and so forth.

Because powdery mildew can thrive only in certain climatic spectrums, having this information in real time allows the vineyard to monitor at-risk vines. Since the 3,000-acre Wente vineyard is comprised of subclimates, it is nearly impossible to manage this with standard weather reports (which don't accurately reflect miniclimates scattered throughout the fields).

Now, however, the vineyard's project manager can get hourly reports via the Web and instant alerts via his cell phone or other wireless device anytime a predetermined set of conditions manifests, such as a drop in temperature in a particular part of the field.

This is yet another example of wireless freeing workers from the mundane. Now the vineyard manager's time can be much better spent at his desk strategizing than in the field collecting routine data.

Understanding the overall cost savings of wireless in these telemetric

Time	Temperature	Leaf Wetness	Humidity	Solar Radiation	Wind Speed	Rain
2/23 10:14	43	11	91	0.0	3	0.81
2/23 11:15	47	0	73	0.3	2	0.00
2/23 12:16	44	11	85	0.0	4	0.04
2/23 13:17	45	7	78	0.5	2	0.02
2/23 14:18	47	7	76	0.3	2	0.05
2/23 15:19	46	0	75	0.2	3	0.00
2/23 16:20	48	0	74	0.2	1	0.00
2/23 17:21	47	0	69	0.0	4	0.00
2/23 18:22	44	0	78	0.0	3	0.00
2/23 19:08	42	0	82	0.0	2	0.00

A typical Wente Vineyards data log from one of their wireless weather stations.

scenarios is best illustrated by the fact that these wireless devices are stand-alone; therefore, a problem with one device does not impact the integrity of any other part of the system. This is also the reason they are so reliable. For example, if one of the vineyard weather sensors goes down, the balance continue working; the same is true for fire alarms or any other telemetric measuring device. The failure is always isolated to the one inoperable unit.

PLENTY OF WARNING

This is just one of the reasons wireless flexibility is so inspiring. Nothing encumbers the technology. Thus, calamity warning systems are instantly and effortlessly installed in facilities as large as 700 acres, with as many as 60 buildings.

World Electronics Inc., based in Coral Springs, Florida, installs such systems routinely for clients like Reynolds Aluminum, Monsanto, and Sears. Forerunners in this arena, they own over 20 telemetric patents, and their technology is accepted by all regional code authorities in the United States.

However, it's their pioneering work in employee accident detection and safety that is particularly notable. One of their clients, a plant concerned with chemical spills, used World Electronics telemetric equipment in all of their emergency shower stalls. The moment a shower is activated, medical assistance is immediately notified and dispatched, thus reducing the risk of perilous injury to the employee.

WHERE THE MONEY IS MADE AND SAVED

While saving lives is always a good marketing angle, let me show more straightforward, revenue-based approaches using the technology.

In the vending machine scenario cited earlier, the data collected can also report on product preferences based on location, thus possibly yielding not one but two Snickers sections in a vending machine if the unit reports an overwhelming demand for the candy bar but less-than-stellar sales of Fritos.

In fact, it was reported that Coca-Cola was considering adjusting their vending machine prices to weather conditions, upping the cost of their sodas when the temperature reached a certain level. This can be controlled internally in the machines or, theoretically, via telemetrics based on the location of the machine and the event involved.

Let's say the machine is located in a popular sports park, but seat sales for a particular event were minimal. Telemetrically, the prices could be lowered to promote sales to the small crowd. Conversely, on a sell-out on a hot day when soda demand is high, the machines could adjust the price to reflect demand.

Perhaps the most dazzling feature of telemetrics is its reliability. Since most systems run on radio signals, the technology can use redundant paths for both reporting and remote control functions without any additional costs.

In a nonwireless environment, the same coverage would require two separate wire runs and, hence, would not be financially feasible. Furthermore, with wires there are risks of corrosion, electrical fires, ground faults, and power outages. Telemetrics runs none of these risks.

Bottom line, telemetrics saves money, saves lives, works proactively, provides peace of mind, and allows the highest level of service available in the area in which it serves. And according to World Electronics, the estimated cost is three times less than any wired system.

Assessing the average price of a telemetric unit is tough because there are so many variables. Asking how much a system costs is as difficult as responding to the question "What is the average price of a house in the United States?" That said, the Yankee Group, in their most recent wireless report, estimates the average unit costs approximately $675; but, as they note, prices are quickly dropping.

An investment in telemetrics always pays off, especially in cases where humans are required to gather information. By way of example, let's look at the labor involved in reading copier meters and how the process is improved by installing telemetric devices.

A telemetric-equipped copier can now have its meter read remotely; the primary advantage is that it gives the leasing company instant access to the billing data without having to dispatch a technician. With wireless technology, on a specific day each month the usage statistics for each machine are uploaded automatically to the leasing company and integrated automatically into their billing system. This seamless flow in turn produces an improved cash flow from the expedited billing cycles because the leasing company no longer has to wait for a human to read a meter.

In addition to the reduction in labor costs from the meter readings and the improved cash flow, the leasing company found a less expected advantage: the elimination of "by the way" service calls, which would occur when technicians appeared on-site to read the meters.

Telemetric devices are gaining popularity, and according to the Yankee Group, it is expected that there will be a day when a person makes use of tens of hundreds of telemetric devices without ever knowing it.

A FAVORITE SUCCESS STORY

Before I move on from this aspect of telemetrics, I want to share with you a remarkable case study that illustrates the extraordinary financial gains the technology can realize.

The company is Packaged Ice/Reddy Ice, Inc. (PI), and you can find their machines in 74,000 locations that in addition to consumer outlets, such as grocery and convenience stores, include restaurants and agriculture. Their sheer ubiquity in part accounts for their $244 million in revenue for 2000.

The units found in retail stores are part of what they call their Ice Factory Program. These machines were designed with the goal of increasing volume while reducing distribution by combining three functions: making the ice, bagging the ice, and storing the ice where it is sold.

Before the telemetric installation, retailers would contact PI when an Ice Factory was not working properly. During the 1990s, Packaged Ice/Reddy Ice, Inc., had two options for servicing their machines.

The first, personal visits were prioritized by the highest-volume machines. In a typical day, a technician would service 20 machines. Not only was this scenario inadvertently discriminating against the lower-volume units, it also lacked efficiency and was costly.

The second solution was remote monitoring using land-based phone lines and modems. These installations were expensive because they required a dedicated phone line, long-distance charges to dial-up for information, and the cost of the modem. Accurate status reports required that the machines be called-in to, which could take all day for a few hundred. PI had 2,800 in service at this point. While this option was sophisticated, technologically it was not especially useful or dependable.

Packaged Ice/Reddy Ice, Inc., was desperate for a comprehensive yet inexpensive technology. Their savior was Isochron Data Corporation, which was able to deliver their dream solution, one that satisfied all their requirements as well as items on their wish list. Appropriately, Isochron named it PolarCast. PolarCast service integrates a wireless two-way pager with Isochron's VendCast software, which can provide virtually as much data as PI could ever need or want. In addition to the expected statistics, PolarCast provides alerts and real-time information on hundreds of machine functions from air temperature to door status to bagging seal rate to hourly ice production. It can even report if the lightbulb has burned out. As one Packaged Ice executive noted, "[We] can remotely monitor millions of dollars' worth of assets daily."

Each morning, PI consults the "snapshots" information culled and ready to view in report form on Isochron's secure Web site. When a system alert has been identified, Packaged Ice/Reddy Ice, Inc., dispatches a service technician. During the day, alerts can also be sent directly to PI headquarters. Now, instead of the retailer contacting PI with a problem, PI finds itself on the phone to the retailer, relaying timely information such as the Ice Factory's door being open.

Customer satisfaction is not a concept upon which we can impose a monetary metric, but numbers do tell us much, and the ones associated with PolarCast are exhilarating.

Owing to the efficiencies of the PolarCast system, PI saves $194 in annual service costs per machine, or an estimated $582,000 gross savings total for the 3,000 units that are in the installation plan. Once the annual services costs of the PolarCast systems are factored in, the annual savings net to $222,000.

Morever, PI estimates an additional 10 percent in productivity for each Ice Factory. This is because with Isochron's technology, the units have little or no downtime, hence higher ice production as well as a more efficient use of technicians to manage the machines.

This 10 percent higher yield adds $924 per year per machine in annual revenue, for a total of $2.7 million per year for all 3,000 installations. At a 25 percent net profit, the increased production nets $700,000 in additional gross profit. Therefore, the bottom line is that the net service cost savings, combined with the additional gross revenue, approaches $1 million per year.

In other words, PolarCast produces cold cash.

To see additional photos about
wireless tracking, visit
www.easton.com.

22

Wirelessly Automating Business Transactions

JUST WHEN YOU thought there couldn't possibly be another blank-to-blank acronym such as B2B and B2C, along comes A2B, which expands to "automated-to-business."

The company responsible for the term is also the one that trade-marked it. Their name is Questra, and their raison d'être is integrating telemetrics with a company's existing enterprise systems. The result is a hub that profoundly affects the workforce and its customers. What makes Questra's technology so notable is that it perfectly integrates technology, people, and the needs of the enterprise.

The basic premise is actually a glimpse of what I call "next-generation telemetrics." Unlike telemetric sensors that communicate back and forth like a Ping-Pong ball, such as vending machines and photocopier meters, A2B responds to the collected information by actually triggering business processes, some of which are so complex that they involve several integrated steps.

A simple example would be a toner cartridge in a laser printer. Equipped with a telemetric sensor, the cartridge, at the point it senses its toner is running low, could send a signal to the company's enterprise system. The system would then query the company's approved suppliers for the lowest price replacement, place the order, and then alert the employees who use that particular printer that toner in the cartridge is running low, but fret not, a replacement is on the way. The entire process requires no human intervention.

Questra refers to this procurement miracle as Transparent Commerce (another of their trademarks) and sees the technology being implemented in any device that uses consumables, which in addition to office equipment includes (but is not limited to) industrial gas tanks, home appliances, and medical devices.

Questra, which was founded in 1990 and whose customer list includes all the major technology players you would expect to see, developed A2B to extend telemetrics from a source of no-frills data into a system where an appliance or device actually extends itself into the commerce system. It's this integration that spawned the term *A2B* as well as the phrase *Transparent Commerce,* because the process takes place without any human intervention.

THE REVENUE OPPS ON CONSUMABLES AND MORE

In my opinion, Transparent Commerce could theoretically also be called Transparent e-Business because the commerce angle is about not just purchasing, but revenue generation as well.

Using a blood transfusion machine as an example, not only would the replacement consumables for the device be reordered automatically, as demonstrated in the toner cartridge example, but the usage metrics would be uploaded for billing and data mining (to capitalize on future sales opportunities). Questra considers the scenario a win-win. Customers benefit from the personalization as well as the overall maintenance convenience and minimal inventory. The company integrating the A2B solution into their product gains a high degree of customer loyalty with little or no sales costs.

A2B is not just about consumables. It can also play a part in preventive maintenance. If, by way of example, a manufacturer integrates A2B capabilities into highly technical equipment, such as the MRIs found in most hospitals, the technology would allow the machines to virtually service themselves by self-diagnosing problems, submitting autonomous service requests, updating their firmware automatically, and collecting and analyzing historical data that could be used to forecast the need for preventive maintenance and actually predict when a system is most likely to fail.

The company selling the MRI will be kept in the loop indefinitely by the A2B technology, remaining in constant contact with the machines via imbedded telemetric technology. In fact, they are "in touch," theoretically, for the life of the machine. Instead of a onetime sale, the manufacturer or distributor has a recurring revenue stream from ongoing service.

LETTING HUMANS DO WHAT HUMANS DO BEST

While the examples cited are noteworthy, it's the more complex A2B installations that are the most inspirational.

Our story begins with a genuine case history that uses a pseudonym of Semiconductor International (SI) as a stand-in for the company's actual name.

Semiconductor International, as the name implies, supplies, manufacturers, and markets sophisticated equipment used in the primary stages of semiconductor manufacturing. To service the equipment, the company employs over 2,000 field technicians, whom they refer to as CEs, or customer engineers.

In the course of their day, CEs interface with four different applications in their enterprise system that cover every aspect of their jobs, including parts availability, parts ordering, equipment histories, expense reports, and time sheets. The problem was, the CEs rarely used the system. None of the components were integrated; therefore, each function required a separate log-in. One technician noted that it was far easier and faster to call-in to the inventory department than to tap into two or three separate programs.

Aggravating an already frustrated CE was the fact that these systems could be accessed only at the office, not a small deterrent when CEs spend their days in the field.

After identifying the entire spectrum of SI's inefficiencies, the company proposed a complete overhaul, which incorporated A2B technology that would trigger a sophisticated process.

This process begins when a diagnostic application being used by the CE determines the need for a part. This information is uploaded wirelessly to the enterprise system that carries parts information for an automatic query regarding availability.

Once the part is identified, the enterprise system responds by ordering the part, either automatically or with the approval of a CE.

When the part arrives, this information is communicated wirelessly to the customer engineer via pager, cell, or other device at the same time the enterprise system books an appointment for installation on the CE's calendar.

Not only is this a multifaceted process that could theoretically span days or weeks, it is a process with a built-in revenue generation model.

Questra was quick to point out to this semiconductor client that in addition to overcoming their core inefficiencies with their legacy system, they could make money by offering their customers premium services, such as remote monitoring and diagnostic equipment that specifically benefits those clients. These options would include regularly scheduled maintenance and preventive maintenance services (automatically order and schedule installation of parts that have reached 90 percent or more of their estimated useful life), as well as remote monitoring services that will automatically alert SI of imminent failures.

Questra and SI estimated a magnitude of savings in operations of over $5 million based on the improved utilization numbers, a payback from implementation costs of close to six months after full deployment; this doesn't even include the potential gains in revenue, which the companies estimate at $125 million annually.

The premise of Questra's technology is simple and sincere: Instead of you working the Web, the "Web works for you." In other words, "the Web is a 'utility' used by people, enterprises, and all types of intelligent devices to deliver information, conduct transactions, provide services, and improve productivity." This lofty goal, while being realized in the twenty-first century, would not have been possible much before. The key ingredient is wireless, which provides anytime, anywhere, access and universal conductivity necessary to let the machines operate autonomously.

23

Government Services:
Shockingly Ahead of the Mobile Curve

IT SEEMS APPROPRIATE to end this section with the country's largest enterprise, government services.

First off, I must admit how surprised I was to discover the extent to which government services have been leading the wireless technology revolution. Because of the double-digit percentages in efficiency and astronomical cost savings, law enforcement, fire, emergency medical services, and others are the crucial group of early adapters, proving the degree of wealth accessible to every enterprise when devices and data are allowed to roam.

ON THE BEAT

The first focus is on law enforcement, which has the epitome of the mobile office and the corollary need for access to information anytime, anywhere.

One of my favorite examples comes from the Colorado State Patrol, whose squad cars are equipped with Panasonic Toughbooks linked via a cellular network covering the entire state's 104,000 square miles. Because of wireless technology, the troopers are experiencing at least a 35 percent increase in productivity on accident reports (up to 50 percent with the younger troopers), which according to the manager for Mobile Data Systems for the Colorado State Patrol is saving at least $800,000 on just the one application.

But the savings are not just financial. The time savings figures are astonishing. Pre-wireless, when a trooper wrote an accident report, it took about six months for the process to filter through the Colorado Department of Revenue, as well as the Colorado Department of Transportation (CDOT) if it involved property damage. Now, from beginning to end, the process has been whittled down from 6 months (or 4,320 hours) to 72 hours. And it gets better. Because CDOT has a jump on the claims process, they estimate saving an additional $1 million per year in collections. Now, consider the ways in which mobile technology might streamline receivables for your company.

Colorado is just one of many cities dispatching wirelessly enabled squad cars. In Raleigh, North Carolina, officers can tap into the FBI's National Crime Information Center databases and in only 12 seconds or less know if they are about to confront a suspect with a criminal record. Soon, officers will be able to get mug shots in the field as well.

In Miami, the U.S. Justice Department's $9.5 million grant was used to install a mobile data network, which will eventually include a facial recognition system, crime analysis mapping, and a data-sharing project called, not surprisingly, the High Intensity Drug Trafficking Area.

As a result of having access to this data, something as simple as a traffic stop now produces staggering results in the arrests of fugitives and criminals. Quality intelligence always breeds productivity.

Similarly, GPS technology is also helping them do their jobs better.

A favorite example cited by Aether Systems, makers of PacketCluster Patrol, whose product is used by more than 2,700 public safety agencies, is an incident cited by an officer called to a domestic dispute at one of the mobile home parks in Poughkeepsie, New York. This particular community housed over 300 trailers spread across four square miles.

Since the trailer numbers are in no particular order, it's nearly impossible for the officers to arrive at a scene there with any timeliness. Using PacketCluster Patrol, officers can download full-color maps within 10 seconds, which they estimate in a typical scenario can save up to 5 minutes in arrival time. There's also the advantage for dispatchers who can know instantly which officer is closest to the location of an incident.

The bottom line is that wireless technology in law enforcement means more criminals get caught. For example, in Flint, Michigan, the police department has doubled its warranted arrests because they are able to get critical information more quickly. Part of this may be due to the fact that officers are now more comfortable backing each other up, according to the Flint police captain. "They can maintain a better sense of one another's situations with wireless communications and mobile data . . . it's a real boost in morale."

After reading case history after case history of law enforcement's use of wireless, I was struck by a particular statistic that occurred in nearly

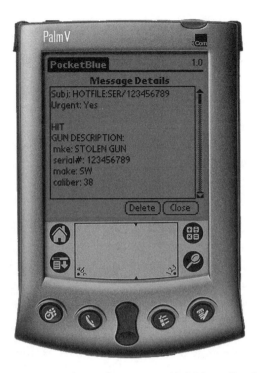

Wireless empowers law enforcement with high-quality data
that drastically reduces risk of harm to police officers.

every installation: The officers were up on the systems in just days.
Even those who "hated computers" were embracing the technology for
all the benefits, especially the added safety it brings. Information is an
officer's secret weapon and best protection. What's interesting is how
the experience law enforcement is having parallels that of virtually all
mobile professionals. Companies rarely have to convince any of their
mobile employees to use wireless devices, and in fact, in many cases
the workforce itself is initiating a wireless installation. When word of
wireless benefits spreads, employees line up.

One such example occurred after fellow officers learned of an incident in Carmel, Indiana. Again, by using the PacketCluster Patrol technology, patrol officers can access multiple government information
systems, including the National Crime Information Center. One day, an
officer ran a routine license plate check on a 1987 Buick driving U.S.
Route 31. When the license plate did not match the vehicle registration,
the officer signaled the driver to pull over, requested the driver's
license, and returned to his wirelessly enabled squad car. The response

to the routine check showed that the driver was wanted for an outstanding warrant in a Los Angeles murder case. Before returning to the suspect, the officer alerted all on-duty officers by flashing the information on their patrol car–based laptops, which are wirelessly connected. Within minutes, more than half a dozen back-up patrol cars arrived on the scene, allowing the initial officer to arrest the suspect without incident.

Routine traffic stops are the epicenter of law enforcement's use of wireless, especially with respect to racial profiling. In an effort to comply with pending legislation, as well as vindicate their own precincts, most police who use the PacketCluster Patrol technology do so to give information about every traffic stop, including the race of the person in question. Furthermore, wireless helps officers to identify suspects with digital mug shots or specific (rather than vague) vehicle descriptions, increasing the likelihood that the person detained is, in fact, the suspect in question.

A reduction of racial profiling translates to less litigation, the cost savings of which has not yet been measured but can confidently be assumed.

While officers certainly feel safer with wireless technology working to their benefit, the natural question is the one of data security. It's law enforcement's job to outsmart the bad guy, and that can be done only when the criminal does not have access to the same data as the officers. According to Aether, PacketCluster Patrol is virtually 100 percent secure and light-years ahead of analog communications, which are susceptible to voice-based radio scanning technology, an unpleasant element police deal with daily.

Furthermore, Aether is proud to note that in the period since the mid-1990s, when, over time, 50,000 users started utilizing PacketCluster daily, there has never been a security breach. They attribute this security success to three factors: the quality of their data encryption technology, their use of advanced data compression techniques, and the requirement of full user log-ins (user names, passwords, and so on). These same security precautions apply to enterprise as well.

Perhaps PacketCluster's most valuable endorsement of the breadth and depth of their security comes from the federal government, which has entrusted the technology with the right to provide access to law enforcement databases in 47 states.

FIRE FIGHTING INTELLIGENCE

To the same degree that law enforcement has benefited from wireless, so have fire departments, but how they apply the technology differs.

If we think of the police as the epitome of itinerant professionals who rely completely on a mobile office, then firefighting services are best associated with sales force automation. Their goal is "bigger picture" and more reconnaissance based. Like sales professionals, they need to know as much about the customer as possible before they meet—only in this case, the "customer" is a burning building.

With wireless technology in tow, firefighters have access to critical data before they arrive, which includes prefire plans, occupancy demographics (helpful to know if a chemical company is operating out of a warehouse in flames), building inspection information, and hydrant locations.

In the future, fire personnel will have additional data. Using telemetric sensors embedded in the sprinkler or smoke alarm system, smoke levels, a room's temperature reading, and a digital image of the room would be available before fire personnel even enter the building. Once there, GPS-type sensors on utility belts of the firefighters will give central command the exact whereabouts of each person, which can substantially help avoid fatalities for both these men and the people they may be rescuing. Knowing where your resources are is as important to emergency services as it is to any company.

Because of the outstanding difference wireless is making for certain government and public safety agencies, when redistributing channels for high-density television the FCC set aside a new spectrum for these organizations, more than doubling what was previously available. The greatest benefit is that these agencies can build larger systems and share networks (such as police, fire, and emergency medical), thus netting additional savings, efficiencies, and community protection.

OTHER WIRELESS GOVERNMENT TRENDS

But government use of wireless is not just about public safety. The technology is infiltrating cities in less obvious places with outstanding fiscal success. For example, Burlingame, California, is one of the first cities in the country to install wirelessly regulated parking meters. The units were installed with two goals: to stop meter theft and to be able to monitor coin deposits. After a test period, not one of the meters was vandalized or stolen, a notable statistic for a municipality that had recently lost $60,000 over six months from these offenses. Because of the wireless technology embedded in the meters, if one had been stolen a transmitter would have revealed its precise location. Not happy news for fraternities.

In terms of coin collection, Burlingame found that they were better able to monitor the deposits, which allowed them to better manage the collection and revenue accounting. In fact, a related benefit was also realized. When parking meters became inoperable, the units sent out a signal requesting a replacement. In a fraction of the time it took previously, the city had a unit in place, ready to continue generating revenue.

In the earlier discussion about wireless in the firefighting arena, I spoke of inspection reports. Even that process is moving to a mobile procedure.

The Los Angeles City Fire Department conducts annual brush clearance inspections via 40 field inspectors who prowl the area's most high risk properties to make sure they are clear of fire hazards.

Prior to adapting a handheld strategy, the less-than-high-tech clipboard and manually filled multipart forms were routine for inspection data. While a thorough process, it was woefully inefficient because data entry clerks were required to input the data into the fire department computer systems, causing significant delays between the time of the inspection and the issuance of a noncompliance notice to the homeowner who had too much brush. Moreover, there was no way to know how many properties inspectors had visited, since they were generating paperwork only for properties in violation of code.

Now, using the Palm computing platform and Satellite Forms Software from Puma Technology, the inspectors simply click and check such hazards as "grass too high" or "brush too close to the road." The pull-down menus also include verbs like "cut down" and "remove" and adjective-noun combos such as "dead tree" and "near fence." This data is then merged into a central server, which automatically generates notices of noncompliance and sends them within 24 hours of the inspection. To date, the city's collection rates for violations has improved substantially, which, coupled with the $123,000 yearly minimum savings for data entry and inspections, has allowed the devices to quickly pay for themselves.

According to the city, the new system delivered an 11-month payback and a 109 percent return on investment that they estimate will soar to at least 302 percent after three years.

These examples are just a small, small percentage of equally impressive government service case histories. Because the government is such an easy target to demonstrate inefficiencies, it is wonderfully refreshing that their adoption of wireless technology is one view government as a mentor.

For additional screen shots of
wireless in government, visit
www.easton.com.

Section 3

■

NEW BUSINESSES,

NEW MARKETS,

NEW CHALLENGES

24

New Businesses:
Entertainment—Wireless's Most
Fun Killer App

I CONFESS. WHEN I bought my Handspring Visor, the first couple weeks I spent more time playing Bubblet than I did sleeping. It's the blessing and curse of mobile technology. But for those supplying entertainment, it's a cash cow.

An ARC Group survey of industry professionals proved what those in the wireless know have always known, that by 2004 entertainment services will be the most important source of reveunue from the wireless consumer mass markets.

Using gaming and entertainment on mobile phones as an example, consider that people already own the devices, always have them with them, and (because of the convenience) always have a few moments to spare. The infrastructure for collecting revenue is already in place as well, since the fees can be added to a subscriber's existing service bill.

It's actually rather simple, and when you consider the desire for entertainment and gaming, the fact that it transcends age and demographics, and its addictive appeal (I beg of you, no Bubblet on cell phones), the prognostications made by the ARC Group study are on track.

What's most interesting is how wireless gaming and other forms of mobile entertainment will evolve along with new business opportunities. Furthermore, it's not just about revenue generation, it's also about marketing. For example, any handheld owner through AvantGo can play "the Nissan Sentra Rock and Roll JEOPARDY! Wireless Road Challenge." Since the game can be played offline via a PDA, there's no profit potential for carriers, but it is a great marketing vehicle for Nissan.

In fact, free gaming plays a big part in the mobile sandbox. It is believed that carriers will offer most games for free for a specified time period (excluding connect charges) as a way to get people hooked. Then, at the addiction point, the meter will kick in.

LOCATION-SENSITIVE GAMING

The unique selling proposition formula for mobile gaming is a combination of anytime, anywhere, of huge interest to gamers, along with the concept of being able to participate in games based on the player's precise location (which adds another level of reality).

It's Alive, a Swedish gaming company, was the first to develop a mobile, location-sensitive amusement, which they named Botfighters. It is described by the developers as "an action game with a robot theme for hardcore gamers."

To play Botfighters, the players locate and shoot at each other with their mobile phones out on the streets via short message service (which works like Instant Messaging), while mobile positioning determines if users are close enough to each other to be able to hit. The game was so successful when first tested that participants admitted to driving out of their way for the chance of a showdown with another bot.

What It's Alive wants to show is that the most successful aspect of mobile gaming is not transporting checkers, chess, and Parcheesi to handsets, but using the actual environment the players are in at the moment they are playing.

There is one exception, however, to the concept of porting board games to handsets, and that is when handsets and carriers have adapted the technology so that voice and data can be mixed. In other words, when you are playing mobile Monopoly, you can talk to your opponents simultaneously. By combining real-time voice chat with wireless's anywhere opportunity, you have a huge lead over gaming on stationary PCs.

FREE FILMS FOR A SYNCH

Owners of more sophisticated handhelds, such as Windows CE devices with robust processors and vivid LCD displays, can enjoy movies on the go for free right now. The idea is that the content is downloaded to a PC, then synched into the CE portable, hence making it mobile. Some sources include Atom Films, who make their independently produced animations and short films available for downloading (at four minutes or less each). Selections include *Louie the Fly Guy* and *Two Guys on an Elephant.*

Free full-length features are available from Filmspeed. Their eventual goal is to charge for each download, but in the meantime, they want to eliminate the risk so that people will get used to the method and the medium. Such classics as Bruce Lee's *The Chinese Connection, A Christmas Carol,* and *Nosferatu* are among the selections.

The big studios are also getting involved early. Warner Bros. is teaming with PacketVideo (more about them in a moment) to offer 30- to 60-second Looney Tunes clips. Executives at the company feels that wireless will serve a different entertainment niche from that of TV (30 minutes) or the Internet (2 to 4 minutes), so they are scaling down even more to accommodate the capacity of wireless and what they believe will be beget even shorter attention spans.

Meanwhile, Sony is using the medium at first as a promotional tool, starting with movie promos, something they did in mid-2000 with the trailer for *Hollow Man.*

Expected to be the forerunners of streaming media to Internet-connected and mobile devices, PacketVideo has figured out how feasibly to broadcast wirelessly much like the streaming video you see on the Net. First you download a player to your mobile device, and then you either access the content live, via a wireless Internet connection, or you can download it to your PC and move the content to your mobile on your next synch.

Even in mid-2001, at the predawn of wireless streaming video, PacketVideo had more than 45 content developers, including every entertainment company of significance (such as AOL Time Warner, Viacom, and Fox). PacketVideo was founded in 1998 by two former Motorola executives, with investments from Qualcomm, Intel, and Texas Instruments.

From a business perspective, this accounts for the inevitable. The world will be consuming more entertainment than ever before. And what is the yang to entertainment's yin? Advertising, which will probably look similar to the type of sponsorship we see on TV today. Interestingly, stand-alone advertising, similar to infomercials, could become equally popular. For example, if you are car shopping, you might use your wireless device to tap into an extended video that describes each and every detail of the make and model that interests you.

ORBITING ENTERTAINMENT

While cellular technology is a great play for mobile gaming and quickie video, look to the sky for the bigger picture of long-play multimedia entertainment.

Death certificates for video rental stores have been prematurely issued several times, the last being the advent of on-demand first-run films, now available from many cable companies. This was in addition to the economic pricing of new video and DVD releases at $20 or less. But if you look closely at these models, you notice the lack of back catalog. Rentals are not just about new releases, they have just as much to do with old favorites.

A preview of what this could be like is possible by looking at a landline trial from 2001, when Blockbuster began offering video rentals on demand over high-speed data lines (such as DSL) to people in the Pacific Northwest whose homes were also equipped with a special Motorola set-top box.

The experience was eerily similar to that of using an actual videocassette or DVD, because it allows for full control of the playback, including pause, rewind, and fast forward. This was accomplished by using an extremely high quality form of data streaming, which you could think of as a sophisticated version of online Real Player or Windows Media player. The cost for rentals (above the weekly freebies the households were given for participating) was $6 per rental for a film that could be watched as many times as desired in 24 hours.

If you take a snapshot of this Blockbuster trial and substitute a satellite feed for a landline as the conduit for the movie, you have a picture of the possibilities.

The receiving units will vary and will definitely include television, as we've already seen with the combination of DirecTV and Tivo. But since the hallmark of wireless is mobility, look to streaming to any mobile device using high-speed cellular connectivity (such as the promised 3G networks with data rates of 384K, which is similar to DSL or cable modem rates) via the Internet as the standard.

Because feature film loses much of its appeal on the three-inch screens of a PDA or cell phone, you might look to the forthcoming tablet PCs, with screen sizes similar to the size of a sheet of paper, to function as the mobile monitor that can be enjoyed anytime, anyplace.

MOBILE MATCHING

Another less obvious form of entertainment is dating, and in 1998 the Japanese were introduced to a wireless device that allowed this to happen with alacrity and panache.

Appropriately called the Lovegety, the oval-shaped, cigarette pack–size device lets owners select from one of three dating preferences: talk, date, or romance. A sensor beeps discreetly with one tone when two Lovegeties are in the same room and another when the preferences match. It's a simple concept that has been a raging success in Japan.

The Lovegety is actually a prognosticator of similar mobile technologies that will match people. Since people will not carry a dozen devices, a stand-alone concept such as the Lovegety probably won't work. Instead we will buy adds to our cell phone or PDA that will allow us to download applications to a device that uses radio frequencies to detect and alert us to the geographic desirability of another person. For example, friends or relatives also equipped with the same technology will elicit one type of tone, potential suitors another, and someone with similar interests whom we have never met yet another. For example, avid golfers might belong to a service to identify each other (as if it's a challenge to find two of them in the same room), passionate yoga practitioners another, and fans of *Fawlty Towers* yet another. When the compatible party is identified, your alert tone will include the approximate distance of the other half so that you can more easily find each other.

When you consider it, mobile matching is not only a form of entertainment, it is also essentially an offshoot of location-based commerce.

MAKING IT HAPPEN FASTER

Entertainment has a history of pushing the perceived limits of technology. For example, the gamers' zeal and need for better playing experience created more powerful processors, video components such as 3D graphics, and advanced audio, all of which were in turn largely responsible for the strides made in desktop computing. Expect the same in the development of mobile devices. Better screens, better ergonomics, and durability will be enhanced to meet the demands of heavy-duty players.

Because of the revenue potential attached to gaming, wireless network providers also have all the impetus they need to improve connectivity speed. While some in the business world believe that m-commerce applications will hasten the development of faster wireless connections, the truth is that entertainment, even adult fare, will be far more responsible.

A mobile entertainment executive offers a reminder of how wireless entertainment fits into a bigger picture. "New media has always been driven by two things," he says. "Sex and games."

To check out Bubblet and other
fun mobile entertainment downloads, visit
www.easton.com.

25

New Businesses: Automobiles and the Wireless Value Adds

"FOUR-WHEELED VEHICLE portal."

"Mobile consumer connectivity unit."

"Bulky steel cell phones with wheels."

This is a sample of the terms technology journalists use to describe cars crammed with wireless technology. The technical wording for these installations is *telematics,* and giving it a definitive definition is ill-advised. As *Commverge* magazine noted, "Telematics is whatever you want it to be if it somehow involves a computer, a wireless telephone, a GPS receiver and an automobile."

The reason we want to be careful not to pigeonhole telematics is that we need to keep open to the endless financial opportunities it offers. Essentially, telematics is the auto industry's play at capitalizing on exploding wireless markets. The carmakers perceive it as a stronger way to maintain customer relationships after a sale while increasing profits from this new revenue stream of subscribers.

To date, the telematics market has been dominated by one brand: OnStar. In fact, when asked to describe the term, I usually just mention OnStar, which renders an instant and complete understanding, though a dozen car brands offer this or another similar service.

Launched by General Motors in fall 1996, OnStar offers a combination of global positioning system technology and a hands-free, voice-activated cellular phone link that connects both the driver and the innards of the car to OnStar's center 24/7/365.

THE FEATURES ARE ENDLESS

To best understand the opportunity of a wireless value add like tele-matics, it is helpful to describe the various features the service offers so you realize how the value add now could eventually become a third-party bonanza.

OnStar is a dealer-installed three-button system. The factory-installed hardware runs $695 and requires one of two service packages.

The basic option is referred to as Safety and Security and costs $199 year. There are three especially notable features in this service.

The first is Automatic Notification of Air Bag Deployment, which immediately connects an adviser via the vehicle's hands-free cell phone system with the occupants. The response is near instantaneous. Case in point: One gentleman was driving in a remote area in Oregon when his car hit a deer. The animal crashed through the windshield, setting off the air bag, the deployment of which automatically contacted the OnStar service center. Before the vehicle had even stopped, an adviser announced herself through the hands-free technology to ask the driver if he needed help. Had there been no response, or had the car's occu-pants reported an emergency, the adviser, who is able to determine the exact location of the vehicle using GPS, would have contacted the near-est emergency services provider.

Next is Emergency Services, which is activated the moment the driver touches a dedicated button. This immediately establishes a connection to an OnStar adviser, who can locate the vehicle's position on a digital map and alert the nearest emergency services provider.

Third is Stolen Vehicle Tracking, which allows an adviser to track a vehicle while simultaneously contacting the nearest police department. This feature was especially appreciated by a Tennessee woman driving an OnStar-equipped Cadillac that was carjacked. After holding her at gunpoint, the thieves let her go and drove off in the Cadillac, at which point she called in to the OnStar center and reported the theft. The OnStar center adviser began tracking the car, called the local police, and gave them the location of the Cadillac. In about 20 minutes, the police found the abandoned car, minus its wheels and tires but otherwise undamaged.

Other popular features include Remote Door Unlock, which allows an OnStar adviser to remotely open the doors for a keyless owner; MED-NET, which provides a hospital emergency room with detailed medical info in the event of a serious accident (10 percent of all acci-dents); and AccidentAssist, which provides step-by-step guidance after a minor traffic incident (including insurance company notification and a police report checklist).

Last, the Safety and Security package includes remote diagnostics, which lets an OnStar adviser remotely query a vehicle when one of the dashboard indicators light. While the advisers are unable to determine the cause, they can recommend the best action, ranging from turning off the car and waiting for roadside assistance to having the problem checked during the next scheduled maintenance visit.

The Safety and Security package annual fee of $199 can be partially offset by insurance companies, which are aware of the benefits of the OnStar vehicle tracking capability and its ability to reduce losses. As an incentive, insurers such as Progressive, Liberty Mutual, and USAA, among others, offer discounts of 15 to 30 percent on the comprehensive portion of the OnStar-equipped cars.

Subscribers who want "productive services" and are willing to spend $399 per year—$200 more than the Safety and Security package—can order OnStar's Premium Service, which includes all the safety features already described plus further interactive assistance.

The first of the two highlights of this option is Routing and Location Assistance, which pinpoints your car's location and provides voice routing and navigation assistance and can even help find an alternate route if you are caught in traffic.

The second is Information/Convenience Service, which ranges from suggesting a restaurant to booking travel reservations to ordering tickets to hard-to-get events. Using a database of 11 million listings, these concierge advisers have access to hotels, restaurants, entertainment companies, and other service providers around the world. The only downside to the service is that it closes at midnight EST. So if, at the end of an enchanting evening, you decide to send your date flowers and it's 9:01 P.M. PST, pick up your cell phone and dial 1-800-FLOWERS instead.

With the exception of the concierge services just described, most of OnStar features can't be replicated by a cell phone, because their magic is based on technology that is integrated into the car. While there are plenty of arguments and hope for open standards and third-party (non-factory-installed) telematic options, for the time being these features are available only to those cars that are equipped with OnStar-integrated systems. Of course, this thrills the car manufacturers, who believe that integrating telematics into their vehicles will promote brand loyalty. They may be right, but only for early adopters.

Before I made my last car purchase, I considered all the OnStar-equipped car lines, which at that time were Cadillac, Buick, Pontiac-

GMC, Oldsmobile, and Chevrolet. Problem was, I couldn't find one car among these brands that I liked well enough to buy, despite my zeal for the OnStar system. This is much less of an issue now that other automakers such as Lexus, Saab, Acura, Honda, and Toyota now offer the service.

Realizing the potential of the telematics market and the perceived brand loyalty that can ensue, Ford Motors in 2001 partnered with cellular behemoth Qualcomm to introduce a OnStar-like service called Wingcast, which dramatically opens the options for factory-installed telematic services. By 2005, the division expects to have outfitted 9 million cars.

WINGCAST AND OTHER CHALLENGES

Despite these big plays, analysts rightfully anticipate challenges for OnStar, Wingcast, and other proprietary telematic services. The real action, these experts assert, is with telematics as an after-market product rather than an OEM'ed one, given that after-market companies move far more quickly and efficiently. This, too, was proved by the car phone industry as cell phones migrated from built-in units to portable devices. The consensus: The OEMs have a 5-year window, at best. Part of this is due to the long shelf life of automobiles of 10, 15, or 20 years (or more) as compared to electronics, which are upgraded every 18 months with new wizardry. The automakers claim they can circumvent this obsolescence problem by using modular components that can easily be swapped for more sophisticated, current-generation equipment.

These technological advances are far more important than many automakers are willing to own up to. Wireless technology is, by many standards, in its infancy, and robust connections can still be scarce. This is far less of a problem when you and a colleague are disconnected when one of you enters a tunnel, but consider the implications of a route navigation device's data stream being cut off just before you are faced with a "must turn" option.

Another still unanswered question focuses on the willingness of cell phone owners to pay for a telematic services. While OnStar and similar companies offer features that require the factory-installed system, such as air bag deployment alerts and remote diagnostics, there is speculation about whether or not this is enough of an incentive when mobile phone owners already have the most cherished emergency feature: a connection to 911.

According to *EyeForAuto* magazine, there is no compelling body of research to indicate that consumers would prefer their car to a cell phone or PDA. Furthermore, it is believed that for many the car is a cocoon—a place to escape to, not connect from—hence another antitelematic argument.

Nonetheless, the future revenue from telematics as a wireless value add for car manufacturers is promising, especially in the early stages. The situation is similar to that of the introduction of air-conditioning: automakers are in a position to reap hefty profits and charge what they like while the novelty factor is high. Historically, early adopters are more concerned with the features than the price, especially if the selling proposition is easy to justify.

Not surprisingly, the telematics chief marketing angle is safety, safety, safety. You may recall a similar sentiment for cell phone purchases, and it was this incentive that propelled the devices into mass acceptance and sales. At the time reasonably priced models were introduced, cell phones were not about yapping with Aunt Joyce when caught in traffic, but instead were bought to save or preserve life and limb. Both the cell phone and telematic marketers always remember that peace of mind is a commodity that people are willing to pay for. In fact, when focus groups were asked to associate a famous figure to personify the OnStar system, they cited Mother Teresa and Colin Powell.

The safety marketing angle is irresistible to those who can afford it and precisely the reasoning behind the debut of telematics in high-end vehicle brands such as Lincoln, Cadillac, and Mercedes-Benz. Research shows that the demographic most interested in telematics are couples earning $50,000 or more who spend at least half an hour daily commuting in minivans, SUVs, or upper-midrange- and luxury-model cars.

While no one can argue with safety angle, the reality is that telematics will eventually be cherished for its productivity advantage, and that's the greatest value in the value add. This will mirror the situation with cell phones, which evolved from safety devices to mobile offices. For example, OnStar subscribers who are also Fidelity Investments customers have full access to their accounts and can do everything from trade stocks to manage their 401(k) plans while cruising into the office.

If you have any doubt about the future of telematics, just consider the 500 million hours a week that Americans spend in their car. It's stats like these that have the auto industry pumped with anticipation.

WHY AUTOMAKERS SHOULDN'T GET TOO COMFORTABLE

However, this greed may be the carmakers' undoing as well. So far, they have been giddy over their new revenue stream. But as *EyeForAuto* magazine's editor in chief, Tim Moron, points out, "If telematics systems become ubiquitous . . . there's no premium effect. The market will drive toward an open-standard, and these nimble third party service providers can run rings around the automaker community. Bang goes the new revenue stream balloon." Technology forerunner Motorola (whose first product was a car radio in the 1920s) and Clarion (who partnered with Microsoft) are standing by with the pin in the form of after-market telematic products.

Whether the telematics service company is an OEM or a third party, all are in agreement with OnStar's CEO, Chet Huber, who has declared, "The car deserves a dial tone! It deserves to be a node on the network! It wasn't to be a part of the infrastructure!"

What telematics also proves is that wireless technology can enhance our experience of the ordinary and give it new meaning. And there is one of the biggest secrets to success in wireless. Find the untapped but obvious solution by looking at the world's most used technologies and give it an additional function and a new convenience. No technology is easier to deploy or integrate than wireless because it is autonomous, meaning that it rarely needs input from anything else to work, even though it offers a whole new feature set.

Watch as airlines use wireless as a value add as they begin to deploy wireless high-speed Internet access on board their planes for passenger use. It's a simple installation because it requires little wiring and is expected to use the same Internet wireless local-area network connectivity already discussed. The ones who offer it first have the competitive advantage, of course, and soon it will become a consumer expectation.

Now that you are aware of the trend, you are bound to notice it often. You can use these examples in addition to the telematics scenario just described as inspiration to find ways to add value to your products or services by including a wireless component.

Not only will it add an irresistible sheen, as telematics does for cars, it may also, like telematics, produce an additional revenue stream as well.

26

New Businesses: Tracking What
Matters to You Most

THINK OF WHAT is most valuable to you, then consider the peaceful-
ness from always knowing exactly where to find that which, to you, is
priceless: your kids, your pets . . . your luggage when traveling.

Along with entertainment and telematics, personal tracking represents
another colossal opportunity for the ingenious. In other words, the following examples are just a peek at how wireless technology has thus far
been applied in the personal tracking and monitoring arena. You could
take this much further. In fact, the biggest moneymakers don't even
have to have practical uses of the technology. For example, you could
challenge yourself to create a new game that incorporates personal
tracking or monitoring to beget an entirely new form of entertainment.

For this reason, consider the information that follows as a primer of
what is possible and that the next chapter in its history could easily be
something invented by your company.

CHILDREN FIRST

For the same safety justification behind early cell phone sales, expect
child-locating devices to hit with equal velocity. This may be due in part
to the fact that parents are being introduced to the devices via amusement parks, who rent them for the day. A typical success story occurred
at the 65-acre Hyland Hills Water World, America's largest water park,
located near Denver, Colorado. Because of its size, Water World offers
daily "ParkWatch" rentals for $3. Powered by WhereNet's real-time loca-
tion tracking technology, these watchlike devices can be worn by parent or child or both, allowing them easily to find each other.

The success story focuses on a young girl who was part of a group of summer day camp kids who were being chaperoned by a group of parents. The entourage included the mother of the little girl, who, while playing with some of the kids, fell, hurt herself, and panicked when she couldn't find her mom nearby.

Noticing that the upset child was wearing a ParkWatch, a counselor immediately led the frightened youngster to a ParkWatch video monitor kiosk. Her watch was scanned, immediately triggering a real-time graphical view of the water park, which included a precise location of the injured girl's mother. The two were reunited minutes later.

Realizing the value of this technology for the other 360-plus days a year a child is not at an amusement park, Whereify Wireless has developed devices specifically to track kids in their day-to-day lives. When you consider the statistics, that a child is reported missing every 18 seconds and that each year over 359,000 of them are kidnapped, you recognize that the market for this kind of device is, sadly, built in.

While these solutions are perfect for older children, expect PacketVideo's NannyCam technology to be a winner with parents of toddlers or infants. Although video surveillance technology has been around for years, to actually view the video you have to log in via a landline connection to the Net, because the images require the processing power found on a computer (versus a handheld) as well as the faster speeds of a wired Internet connection.

PacketVideo, which specializes in streaming video to mobile devices, can provide your cell phone or PDA with the same video feed previously available only at your desk. Of course, this means that Mom and Dad can see that their kids are well and enjoy their night out without phoning in constantly for reports from the sitter.

BENEFITING THE HEALTH CHALLENGED, TOO

Tracking devices are really about freedom for the tracker and the trackee. But there is another level of data available that gives these calculable benefits a third dimension. The technology in play, biosensors, are capable of monitoring the most common health-related data, including blood glucose levels for diabetics, heart sensors for cardiology monitoring, and basic vitals such as blood pressure for those convalescing out of physician range but still in need of care.

The company on the forefront here is Digital Angel, producers of chips the size of a grain of rice that can do all described and more. Powered by body heat, the chips store data that can be retrieved on request by those authorized to do so (caregivers and doctors) or transmitted automatically on a periodic basis. For example, parents of a diabetic child who happens to be across town at school could get multiple blood sugar readings automatically via a pager or cell phone.

Integrated tracking technology is also a benefit to seniors. Not only can we make sure that Grandpa's vitals are in check, we can reassure ourselves that his dementia hasn't caused him to get confused and wander out of the house. If the recipient of the technology were to stray either geographically or outside given health parameters, those who are designated would be notified instantly.

NONHUMAN TRACKING

Though I discussed tracking extensively in the enterprise section, the important difference to note is that the devices and the networks that track the devices are large-scale operations. Companies are buying hundreds, if not thousands, of tracking units at a time and contracting with companies who own large networks to keep them activated (think of it as buying telephones and then needing monthly phone service).

The windfall from consumers will come when you and I can walk into a general merchandise store such as Wal-Mart and buy a location-enabled cellular chipset for personal use. Theoretically, you could tag whatever you wanted, from a favorite book (the tags are reusable) to a bicycle to your key chain to your laptop computer. The tracking sensitivity would be to within 10 feet and easily determined by logging on to the network's Web site and giving a code number of the device. The info is delivered in less than a minute.

According to Aeris.net, one of the country's biggest cellular tracking networks, by 2005 we should be able to make these one-off purchases for about $15 to $30 each, with the price eventually dropping to as little as $10 in the years that follow.

The big win for consumers, other than no longer having to spend an hour looking for lost keys (which you swear you left on the counter when you walked in), is the insurance benefit. To the same degree that LoJack tracking on cars has reduced auto insurance premiums, these chipsets could reduce the premiums on homeowners' policies covering such high-value items as collectibles, fur coats, and luggage when traveling. In fact, if you put a tracking chip in your luggage, when the airline calls to sadly inform you that they are not sure where your bag is, *you can tell them* within a 10-foot radius.

The consumer arena is just busting with opportunities for wireless tracking and monitoring. In the foreseeable future, you will be able to use your cell phone to monitor what your children are watching on the home TV sets, control home appliances, even unlock your front door.

In the meantime, until the more sophisticated gadgets are here, some people are finding fun wireless work-arounds to relieve everyday inconveniences. Here's one such example.

A couple years ago, when sophisticated tracking instrumentation for tracking pets was just a glimmer, a friend of mine had a problem with a dog who loved to roam. And roam he did, well beyond shouting distance of his owner, even beyond the sound of the electric can opener, the universal canine signal for mealtime.

Since the neighborhood was a safe one, bursting with kids and drivers equally cognizant of young ones and pets, the fact that the dog strayed was not as much of a concern as the fact that he was impossible to find at feeding time.

My friend found her solution no farther than the kids with whom the dog would play. So she did what the other parents did to let their kids know it was time to come home. She bought a beeper, one of those nifty teeny-tiny ones. And with the help of her vet, she found a safe way to keep the device attached to the dog's collar. Now, when it's time for dinner, she doesn't shout, she dials—activating the beeper, which vibrates, letting Shakti the dog know that it's time for dinner.

To see additional photos of tracking devices, visit
www.easton.com.

27

New Markets: Generation Y-erless

THE STUDENTS MUST have known that the day would come when there would be a ban against mobile phones inside the school building.

"Enough was enough," barked the Croatian elementary school principal. "Mobile phones were ringing all during lessons."

This noise from inbound calls was not the only barrier to better learning, the principal explains. "I caught two girls actually phoning their parents during a chemistry exam to ask for the right formulas, and when I confiscated the mobile the parents came straight to school and complained that I was stealing private property."

The Croatian principal's plight is simply a preview of how wireless communication will affect U.S. teens as well.

"When I went to school, class began with the Pledge of Alligiance," voices a frustrated U.S. high school teacher. "Now class begins with a reminder to kids to turn off their cell phones and pagers."

This should not be surprising when you consider that a bewildering 42 percent of kids born between 1971 and 1985 already own a mobile phone or pager. This age group is also referred to as Generation Y or, considering their swift adoption of mobile communications, "Generation Wireless." For 66 percent of them, communicating is a top priority, and they spend more than half their time online each week, e-mailing, chatting, and sending instant messages.

Now that this savvy group has been identified, there is a race to gain their consumer loyalty. Needless to say, they are a choice demographic. They have disposable income, spending an average of $89 per week, as well as their youth working for them, meaning that they are the darlings of advertisers who want to establish brand allegiance now for the ultimate revenue longevity. To entice them, communications companies are offering features that appeal to their spirit. For example, Nokia lets them create custom faceplates for the Nokia 5100 series of phones, while Samsung has released a cell phone that doubles as an MP3 player.

THE PERFECT FIT

While hardware is one conduit to Generation Y, giving them new, creative, and useful ways to use their technology is another, and that is precisely the niche of Upoc, the first company with any sensibility to understand how to facilitate one ubiquitous aspect of teenhood: the relentless need to constantly communicate.

Upoc (which stands for "universal point of contact") is a free membership service that allows teens (or any age group, for that matter) to build lists of people to broadcast to and hear from. Think of them as private communications communities. If one kid has a core group of eight friends, all eight would belong to a particular list. If one of the members has information the group should know, let's say "I got an A on my science report," that data appears instantly on the displays of the other seven members' cellular handsets or alpha-numeric pages.

The advantage of Upoc is that it gets around the lack of standards among cellular carriers. For example, if I want to send you a text message from my Sprint PCS phone and you are an AT&T subscriber, that's not possible. I can send you an e-mail, which is ridiculously cumbersome and time-consuming, but not an instant text message.

As mentioned before, with Upoc you can establish a private list of contacts and send messages to the group or to one person in the group. These can be text or voice messages.

The corollary is that members can join public groups with different interests and functions, such as movie ratings (where you can announce a movie you saw and what you thought of it), Bushisms (self-explanatory), or pickup lines you've just heard. Since this is a free service, in a moment you will learn how this is monetized.

Essentially, what has been described is a mobile community, and how it works in the real world is a communications nirvana. The following example is tendered by Upoc's VP of marketing, Greg Clayman. As you read it, maintain a teen's perspective.

> You leave your house on Friday night and get a text message on your phone telling you that a band you want to see is playing nearby. You get a message from a friend who also got the band alert, asking whether you plan to go. You do want to go and send a message to another group of friends asking whether any of them are interested.

On your way you receive a message that your mother has sent to the whole family asking if you would like to have dinner Sunday night. You quickly reply. Someone has sent a message to a group of pop culture enthusiasts asking what brand of retro '80s sunglasses the group might recommend she purchase. Someone else beats you to the reply and lets the group know that a new store just opened on Canal Street with a slew of vintage shades.

What Clayman astutely points out is that to influence the behavior of a group, particularly teens, you must become part of the group. "A phone that beeps with a coupon every time you pass a Starbucks is a nuisance," he says. "A wireless forum for planning coffee breaks with a friend that is brought to you by Starbucks is not."

That said, let's go back-up to the previous example of messaging in a community and see the branding opportunities there. According to Clayman, "The band alert could have come from Sony, Ticketmaster, or Pepsi; the group the mother started for the family could have been sponsored by the Family Channel or McDonald's; the pop culture group could be a service of MTV, Old Navy, or *Maxim* magazine."

What seem like branding opps actually go far beyond, since sponsoring a group is usually part of a bigger package of community-based communications. In addition to branding a group, companies buy channels, which allow them to broadcast information about something or someone. For example, Epic Records has a channel for just J. Lo (that's code for Jennifer Lopez). Epic describes it as a way to "keep up with your favorite girl 24/7 and be the first to know when J. Lo's got a new video, single, or movie out, where she's touring, what she's doing!"

Companies who buy channels have sign-up and other channel interactivity on their site in addition to the traffic that Upoc funnels into them.

It's with channels that "calls to action" occur, since the participants are 100 percent opt-in and therefore are giving permission to have the brand communicate with them (which includes incentives such as couponing). Development of a channel ranges from $25,000 to $50,000 and beyond, plus a monthly fee based on activity, with a set minimum of $1,000 and a set maximum so companies can determine and maintain a budget.

Even though Upoc offers dozens and dozens of paid channels, to date their most famous group is a grassroots forum called NYC Celeb Sightings, which boasts a membership in the thousands. When members spot a famous person, they send an instant message via Upoc to the other members.

Kris Konno, the list's founder, who happens to work at Upoc, has spotted and alerted the group to such high-profile celeb sightings as Robert De Niro, Denzel Washington, and Sarah Jessica Parker and explains that the messages are straight to the point: "Janeane Garofalo @ LaGuardia Airport held up at security."

One of her favorite NYC Celeb Sightings messages was about a Lenny Kravitz incident from a member shopping at a Kmart. Apparently, the store had announced Mr. Kravitz's presence over the loudspeaker, then at the last minute decided to add, "But please don't look at him."

THE TRICKLE-UP INFLUENCE

To understand how wireless will be introduced into the lives of some adult consumers, simply look to their offspring. For example, in many cases, parents bought pagers for their kids so that they could find them. After a while, they found enough utilitarian value in pagers to buy one for themselves. Ditto for cell phones; they were initially bought for safety considerations for teens at night, but a short while later Mom bought one for herself, too. Thus, much of what is invented or marketed to children and teens can and will be co-opted by the parents.

It's possible that after reading the detailed description of Upoc, you thought of various ways it could help with your business communication, such as being able to easily text message a group of colleagues on different short message service systems. Go ahead. Upoc encourages adults to set up their own private group on the service for free as well.

The point is that what was developed primarily for teenagers' high-drama need for instant communication with each other will trickle up and influence parents as well.

With that in mind, I want to introduce you to a spectacular experiment being conducted by the Illinois Consolidated High School District 230. It evolves each year, but for the past couple has included over 2,200 students and over 400 teachers and a few thousand PalmPilots. The idea is to put computing into the hands of each student, instead of expecting students to share a few coveted desktops. By doing this, the district feels they can make technology a beneficial part of students' lives in every respect. (The units can be bought for $225, leased for the year for $75, or used for free at the school only.)

Deployment of the units goes far beyond scheduling classes and accounting for homework assignments in the handheld's to-do list. The

Typical Short Messages from Teens to Teens
Using Upoc's Free Message Network

Actual Messages from Upoc's
NYC Celeb Sightings Group

to : celeb_sightings

sarah jessica parker from
sex in the city just took
my table at bottino!

to : celeb_sightings

johnny depp, SOHO,
looks gorgeous 2 me
and I am a straight
guy !!

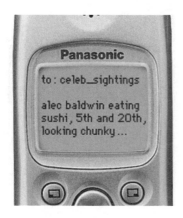

to : celeb_sightings

alec baldwin eating
sushi, 5th and 20th,
looking chunky ...

You have a voicemail
from Jennifer Lopez.
Dial 877-550-Upoc
to listen.

software that accompanies each unit was very well thought out and is clearly meant to be of assistance in every aspect of the students' lives.

The preloaded software included what you would expect, like Quick-Office for creating and editing Word and Excel files; Due Yesterday, which is a homework manager; and PrintBoy, which lets one print documents from the Palm directly to any infrared-enabled printer.

Along with the student necessities just noted were some more worldly choices. For example, students get exhausting detail about their eating and exercise regimes for a complete fitness program using Vivonic's planner; there's also Accounts and Loans for tracking finances; and AvantGo has a program for reading the daily news (this last software is attractive to adults as well). As these kids begin to integrate their Palm devices into every aspect of their lives, it's bound to catch the attention of parents, who may previously have thought of the devices as glorified organizers but will be dazzled by their additional functionality. There lies the trickle-up.

The real advantage here is for companies with products or services that appeal to both kids and adults. If you can create a "teen" version of a program at the right price, you may have a built-in cross-sell to parents as well.

THE EXPECTATION

Some analysts see teens' attachment to cell phones and pagers as more of a fascination with technology. Those who think that are wrong. These devices are simply conduits to community and communication. Without them, a teen is out of the social loop, which is a devastating proposition.

The level of fear of alienation can be relayed in this story about a 16-year-old girl from Brest, France. In March 2001, Deutsche Presse-Agentur reported that she filed a complaint against her father for stopping her cell phone service.

Apparently, he had given the teen a cell phone a month earlier, along with a subscription in her name and, as part of the present, promised to pay the cost of her calls—until he saw the first bill, which was much higher than he had anticipated. To avoid any more fiscal surprises, he canceled the contract by falsifying his daughter's signature. And that was the big mistake.

Enraged, the daughter, accompanied by her mother, went to the police and filed a complaint against her father. The charge? Forgery.

Remember, any company or organization is welcome to set up a free Upoc text messaging group. Visit www.upoc.com.

28

New Challenges: The Cell Phone Etiquette Business Challenge

"IT STRIKES ME as funny that so many people are under the impression that once they are engaged in a cell phone conversation, the rest of the world is unable to hear them," notes a poster in an Internet forum about cell phone use on trains. "It's as if some *Get Smart*–style 'Cone of Silence' drops down over them while they blithely prattle on about the most personal issues with grotesquely intimate details."

Unfortunately, this mirrors the sentiments of much of the public, and the result is a growing group protesting the unconscious use of cell phones.

The reason cell phone etiquette is of interest in a business context is that it has the potential to pinch the growth of wireless. It won't stunt growth at any alarming rate, but it will make a difference, so you should be aware of the implications. Eventually, businesses may have no choice but to jam cell signals, prohibiting inbound and outbound connections.

Though it is currently illegal to jam cell signals in the United States (a point we will come back to) and many other parts of the world, for those places where it is legal, it is becoming a necessity.

Such is the case in Hong Kong, considered one of the most densely wireless places in the world, where as of the beginning of 2002, almost 7 million people owned approximately 5.2 million cell phones and the public disruptions were growing intolerable. In fact, reports of people actually answering calls in the middle of a movie are common. What's worse, they would chat for several minutes, often making plans for later in the evening despite the crowd surrounding them.

India's parliament had a similar problem after the members repeatedly ignored pleas to turn off their phones. With no options left, they installed jammers in the halls, making it impossible to place or receive calls.

Award-winning actor Laurence Fishburne would love to be able to follow India's lead and have Broadway theaters establish jammers as a routine practice. This after it was widely reported that Fishburne literally stopped in the middle of a performance of *Lion in Winter* not only to ask an attendee to "turn off the [expletive] phone, please," but to actually have the man removed from the theater.

Unfortunately, legally installing jammers in the United States is impossible. Cell phones come under the jurisdiction of the Telecommunications Act, which makes it illegal to interfere with any licensed signal (like that of a radio station). Cellular carrier networks fall under this amendment and therefore it would require an act of congress to defeat. Given the increasing problems cell phones are creating, some analysts believe this just might happen.

Meanwhile, despite the fact that it is illegal to use a jammer, and illegal to sell one in the United States, many journalists have proved that jammers can easily be bought via the Net for well under $1,000 from countries like Israel, where they are legal. In fact, portable units the size of a paperback book are also available for a few hundred dollars (which may mean some militant anticell proponents could take signals into their own hands and jam them wherever they go).

While cell phones are still considered just an annoyance, what is most frightening is that considerably less than half the United States population owns one. What happens when the user base doubles and then triples? This means that however bad you think it can get, it's going to be much worse than your worst-case scenario. This will happen not only because more people start carrying the devices, but because the devices will get more sophisticated as well. For example, in this decade, expect to see two-way video capabilities in addition to streaming audio (favorite songs, audiobooks) and video streams (TV shows, movies). The seemingly relentless noise quotient will get exponentially worse.

We might look to Japan for a preview, since they have the most progressive wireless devices and a large percentage of their population is equipped with them. Their capacity-filled trains—once noted for an uncharacteristic silence, considering the number of people—have metamorphosed into a cell phone free-for-all. Apparently, the noise is so deafening at times that seats near the handicapped and the elderly were marked "no phone" zones. This was ignored, as were the pleas from loudspeakers asking people to switch off their phones to avoid irritating other passengers.

The company responsible for the bullet trains were left with no choice but to shame these surgically attached cell phone users into being more courteous. Now, if someone uses a mobile phone within 30 feet of a cellular sensing device, a red signal light flashes, which in turn causes fellow passengers to stare at the offender. (CBS.com reported a similar tactic used by a Chicago train commuter when disturbed by obnoxious cell phone users. The gentleman whips out a notebook, leans in closer, and exaggeratedly takes notes of the conversation.)

Despite the railway's attempts, they were overloaded with complaints from passengers who insist that they must stay in touch. This will certainly hasten the inevitable: dividing trains into cars for those who want to talk and those who prefer precellular silence.

Separate railcars is a growing trend in the United States as well, and those in the "talker cars" are using their phones to further commerce en route. This was noted by a passenger waiting for a late train in Ardmore, Oklahoma, at an unmanned Amtrak station. "We were unsure of when the train would arrive until a pizza man showed up at the platform," he explains. "Seems riders were ordering from the train using their cell phones."

The concept of a phone/no phone section is strikingly similar to the smoking/nonsmoking segregation scenario that began in the 1980s. Fittingly, offering a cell-free dining experience is now a marketing initiative, as noted by the owner of Vox 646 in Manhattan, who, while he doesn't allow cell phones at his tables, offers a glass-encased cell phone lounge for diners to take calls.

Like restaurants, movie theaters are another rough spot for the Hatfields and McCoys of the cellular age. The annoyance factor is likely far worse than many movie house owners realize. According to a Pacific Bell survey released in mid-2001, 60 percent of Californians surveyed would rather visit the dentist than sit next to someone talking on a wireless phone in a movie theater.

In fact, one of the most horrifying stories I have ever heard related to cell phone use was posted on an MSNBC bulletin board devoted to the topic. It too involves a movie theater and summarizes the growing problem of how cell phones interfere with every aspect of business.

Amber from Flagstaff, Arizona, wrote:

I work in a movie theater and I was in the concession stand where it was really busy and the lines were very long. I had one man approach my counter and say, "F*****g A! What's wrong with you people, can't you move any faster?!" I ignored the man's rude comment and said, "What can I get for you?" in my sweetest voice. He went ahead and started to give me his order. I already knew his drink and popcorn order, but needed to know if he wanted butter.

Just as I turned back to ask, his cell phone rang. I let him answer it and then got his attention to ask about the butter. I said, "Would you like but—" when he cut me off. "Dammit, can't you see that I'm on the phone? You can wait just a goddamn minute!" I replied in a very controlled voice, "Were you not the person who just complained about us going faster?" "That doesn't matter, I am on the phone!"

I walked off and told my manager the story and that they would have to deal with him. When my manager walked up, the guy was still on the phone. My manager said, "Excuse me, sir . . . excuse me?" The man shot him a dirty look and turned away.

My manager simply took the man's popcorn, threw it away, poured out the drink, and told me to help another customer. I called another customer forward. And my manager walked out of the concession stand into the lobby to stand next to the man. The man became enraged when I started to help the next person and he finally told the person on the phone he had to go. The man turned to me and started to complain, but my manager cut him off. "I'm sorry, sir, but you have been unforgivably rude, and will have to leave the theater immediately." One can imagine the argument that ensued.

My manager, Ben, is not a small man. He stands at 6 feet 4 inches, is thin but muscular, and 22. This man was probably in his mid-thirties, about 5 feet 6, and painfully thin. When the man demanded his money back for his ticket, Ben explained that since he was being kicked out he didn't get his money back.

The man took a swing at Ben, who avoided it and immediately turned to tell someone to call the cops. When he turned the man threw his cell phone and hit Ben in the side of the head. Ben turned back to dodge another swing. Ben started to take a swing at the man but thought better of it. By that time another male manager had come to back him up.

The guy grabbed his cell phone off the ground and dialed 911. Once the operator was on the line he would only scream obscenities at her, so she hung up on him. By then the police had gotten there. The man threw the phone at one of the cops and hit the guy in the face. In order to subdue and arrest the man, the police had to chase him across our lobby, tackle him, and hog-tie him. The whole time he kept screaming, "I was making a phone call! You never interrupt someone on the phone!"

He got nine months in jail for public misconduct and resisting arrest.

29

New Challenges: Security, Authentication, and Viruses, Oh My!

BEFORE I BEGIN this chapter, I want to ask you a question. What do you think is the biggest security risk related to wireless?

We'll come back to the answer in a moment.

Meanwhile, you should know that the quantity of data that will move across wireless networks will eclipse anything the wired world will ever see. Just consider the breadth of innovation you've been introduced to in the previous pages. Because of the anytime, anywhere, aspect of wireless, people will exponentially generate more network traffic, especially with more sensitive data related to banking, gaming, commerce, and health. This makes solving wireless security issues of paramount importance. Nonetheless, it doesn't warrant anywhere near the hysteria headlines provoke.

It reminds me of the late 1990s, when I was hired by a multinational financial organization for a nationwide radio and television tour of the United States. The goal was to educate people about the safety of using their credit cards online. Ironically, I was putting out this company's own fire, one they stoked only a few years earlier when e-commerce was dawning and they were caught totally by surprise. After declaring the Internet a haven for credit card fraud (in reality, at this time, Internet fraud was a fraction of that in the real world), the financial organization backtracked when they realized the revenue they could lose as online purchasing grew in popularity.

So I was dispatched to undo the damage. I explained to the masses that they were actually safer using their credit cards online than in a real store, thanks to the benefit of secure technology that allowed the card number to be transmitted from computer to store with no risk of interception. "Compare that," I would add with a flourish, "to handing your credit card to a waiter who not only has your physical card, but your signature on the back."

As people began to realize that they weren't responsible for any fraudulent charges (not even the first $50, as long as the fraud is reported in a reasonable time frame), and that the Net was as safe as, if not safer than, the other ways we used our card, the issue cooled, and consumers found new comfort using their credit cards for electronic commerce.

That was then and this is now, and headlines about security are periodically caught in the klieg lights. The catalyst is wireless, and the statistics today remind me of the numbers we saw years ago. In fact, I've seen surveys that show that up to 70 percent of wireless users are concerned about security.

While security in the wired world is pretty much centered on data theft and viruses, wireless by its very nature presents entirely new challenges, which is why it's important to understand the differences and the solutions.

My goal is to give you a broad strokes vista of the issues. Nonetheless, security, authentication, and viruses together is a technical topic I have whittled down for simplicity's sake. Even with this consideration, there are plenty of scary, mega-syllabic terms such as "nonrepudiation" and "digital certificates."

So if this is more terminology than you have the mental bandwidth for at the moment, I'll happily bottom-line it for you: In time, wireless will be just as secure as wired. This is true as long as those responsible for the back end of the technology take all the precautions available to them (using prophylactic software and keeping it updated) and users do their part by securing their mobile information devices.

THE BIGGEST SECURITY PROBLEM IS ...
PROBABLY NOT WHAT YOU THINK

Now let's get back to the opening question. What do you think is wireless technology's biggest security risk?

The most common response is sending personal or financial information using a mobile device. Actually, this quite low risk. It is nearly impossible to heist information out of thin air.

So here is the answer. If you use any type of device for mobile data (Palm, Windows CE, Handspring, and so on), the person you should fear most is yourself. You are the biggest security risk to yourself and your company.

According to Pointsec Mobile Technologies, Ltd., if you carry a hand-held with only 8 MB of storage (considered the minimum), you could easily be toting thousands of personal and company addresses, hundreds of e-mail messages, as well as hundreds of documents with notes. That's equivalent to your entire Rolodex and office files. Consider the implications of a loss, especially if the data fell into the hands of your primary competitor. Now you understand why PDAs represent one of the most ignored yet biggest security holes in the corporate world.

Despite the danger of losing this mobile data, few people take steps to correct the problem. It's an easy fix, with a buffet of encryption software now available for all handheld computers. The only flaw in the technology is that users don't like it. It's a hassle to enter a password each time you turn on your Palm. And wasn't this "instant on" characteristic one of the reasons you bought the device in the first place?

Now, I realize that some use the password protection that comes with the handheld. The problem here is that it's an easy hack to get beyond. While it is a deterrent, it lacks any real security.

This is why encryption software is so important. Let's use a house as an analogy. Think of the front door as general password protection. With the right tools and a little time, just about anyone can break in.

Now imagine that once you're in the house, everything—and I mean everything—is bolted down. Not only is each item locked, it requires a 12-digit alpha-numeric password that looks something like a nuclear launch code to release each bolt. That's encryption.

Encryption software works by descrambling what you need as you use it and then rescrambling it after you are done with the application or data. That's why if someone was successful in getting "through the front door," he or she would lack the necessary codes to get to anything else. To achieve this level of protection, all you need to do is enter a password once, when you turn on your unit. The protection far out-weighs the inconvenience.

If you are wondering why no handheld operating systems, including Palm, have encryption built in, it's because it takes expert third parties to find a way to incorporate the technology without slowing down the device. Encrypting and de-encrypting takes a lot of processing power, and it's not easy to find a work-around.

Now that you understand the importance of encrypting mobile data, here's a plan that will help move this discussion into an actionable concept.

Magnus Ahlberg of Pointsec Mobile Technologies has outlined an extremely thorough blueprint, of which the following are the most important points to consider:

1) Your staff must be educated about the volatility of the information they are carrying with them. Until they are made to realize the quantity and quality of the mobile data, the seriousness of a loss may not be realized.

2) All mobile devices should be equipped with encryption software that prevents the data from being accessed by anyone other than the user.

3) Since handhelds are inexpensive and people are buying them for work, companies need to inventory who is using one.

4) All employees should be banned from using mobile devices for business purposes unless security software has been installed.

5) Use one brand of security software so that it can be managed centrally.

By the way, Palms and other PDAs are not the only means through which a mobile data breach can occur. Mobile mouths yapping on cell phones in public can cause them, too.

On a recent commuter flight from San Francisco to Los Angeles, I was seated in front of an executive who was having an animated discussion on his cell phone about a pending press release. Because the plane was still at the gate, it was a lengthy conversation with enough detail that I was able quickly to identify the company based on the details he was broadcasting. While I could care less, and in fact turned around several times to give him a look of exasperation, I could only think of the competition surrounding him and hope that his lack of etiquette would have karmic consequences and that his competitors were taking notes. Think about it. A flight from San Francisco. A discussion about a technology. Statistically, chances were great that business foes, or even friends of business foes, could have been taking copious notes.

All of which reminds us that security's weakest link is the user.

A 60-SECOND PRIMER ON SECURE WIRELESS CONNECTIONS

Data security in a wired connection is as secure as many think possible. While wireless has its own idiosyncrasies, with time the challenges have given way to robust solutions.

For example, we want to be sure that the company we are talking to is who it says it is; we want our data, as it travels from our handheld computers to the host machines, not to be intercepted; and we want our data to arrive in the exact same state as when it left—completely unaltered.

The wired world has depended on a technology called secured socket layer, also known as SSL. Because of wireless's challenge of significantly slower connection rates than wired Internet data exchanges, SSL is too complex for wireless. For this reason, a wireless version was developed, what we could think of as a leaner version of SSL, that works just as well but is a much better fit for slow speeds. It is called wireless transport layer security (WTLS).

When WTLS was introduced, it had a few minor holes that were quickly identified and rectified. The reason for mentioning this is to remind of us of the big upside to wireless security—awareness of the problems while the technology itself is being perfected. Instead of the technology trying to catch up to the user (what we saw with the wired Internet in the mid-1990s), in wireless the security technology is just slightly ahead of usage, which means wireless has a bit more development breathing room.

I AM WHO I SAY I AM

Once the routes and gateways are secured, the next security issue is authentication. Authentication is proving you are who you say you are; that the company you are connecting to is really that company. In the wired world, we use something called digital certificates to validate a user's identity. Think of digital certificates as unalterable passports that authenticate you to anyone.

The security comes from the fact that you are the only person to whom a digital certificate can be issued, much like a passport. The companies that issue certificates are uninterested third parties, and one of the most famous is VeriSign.

Here again, the low processing capability of mobile devices was a challenge, so certificates for mobile devices that require less power and bandwidth were created.

Another solution to authentication are smart cards. These devices allow for 100 percent nonrepudiation (denial of involvement by either party). The card carries all the information to securely authenticate the user so that all the customer would have to do is enter an account number and PIN, which could be information available from another source, a serious consideration if the device is stolen.

For all these reasons, many authentication experts will say that a near

100 percent solution is the biometric device. In other words, depending on fingerprints, thumbs, and retina scanners to validate our existence with an infinitesimally low false-positive and false-negative rate. Theoretically, fingerprint readers could easily be incorporated into PDAs and cell phones, and voiceprints are a snap—you would simply say your name for authentication by having matched against a verified voiceprint, which can take as little as half a second. To the degree that this all sounds like a *Star Trek* scenario, consider the convenience.

By the way, another of type of wireless authentication are digital signatures. Not only can you receive the document, contract, or PO from anywhere, you can sign it, too. Thanks in part to Clinton's signing into law the legality of digital signatures, these authenticators will also be admissible in a court of law.

Here's an example of how it could work. When a remote transaction is performed by a wireless device, confirmation of the order could be sent back to the device on file by the credit card company. The user would then legitimize the transaction by sending his or her digital signature via a few taps on a wireless device, which binds the transaction— valuable data in a world of high-risk "card not present" transactions.

As we leave this security discussion, I'd like to do so with the most hopeful of thoughts. That is, as next-generation infrastructure ensues (also called 3G), the devices used to access these high-bandwidth networks will be equally powerful. As such, it is expected that implementing end-to-end solutions will (comparatively) be a snap because there are many more robust solutions in the presence of greater power.

INOCULATING MOBILE VIRUSES

Though there were only four reports of infiltration before an antidote was prepared, it was a sign that wireless had arrived. The culprit was a worm called Timofónica, and in June 2000 it affected mobile phones that used the Telefónica network in Spain. Similar to wired viruses, the infection tapped into the Microsoft Outlook address book and sent e-mail to each of the e-mail addresses. The twist was that at the same time, it sent thousands of text messages to randomly generated cell phone numbers that said (in Spanish), "Information for you. Telefónica is fooling you."

By definition it was not a true virus because it was not directly infecting the phones themselves, but it was, according to one observer, "the first virus in history that attacks mobile users by sending them annoying messages."

Unfortunately, those annoying messages can have financial implications for the users who pay for each message and the cellular providers whose network could be rendered inoperable from the bottleneck.

Despite the annoyance, cell phones are safe for now—they aren't yet sophisticated enough to be reprogrammable, therefore they cannot be attacked and made unserviceable. Of course, the next generation of more sophisticated wireless devices may be far more susceptible to infection because they may have faster processing and storage capabilities.

But Palms and related handhelds are well poised for attack, with 10 viruses (including their various strains) identified by the end of 2001. This has prompted a slew of antivirus software for mobile devices.

The infiltrations are not by definition viruses because they don't re-create themselves from machine to machine. The ILOVEYOU PC virus of 2000, which spread by infiltrating the Microsoft Outlook phone book and sending itself to all e-mail addresses, was an example of a replicating virus. The problem in handhelds are Trojan horses, programs that affect only the one device. In fact, they are more mischievous than damaging.

For example, the first malicious program for the Palm was discovered on August 28, 2000, disguised as a patch to a program called Liberty that lets you play Game Boy games on a Palm device. What the "patch" did was delete all the third-party applications and personal information. Because the damaging program entered the device disguised as something else and because it did not replicate like a virus, it was called a Trojan horse.

In the case of the Liberty "patch," the device itself was not damaged, and as long as the data in the device was backed-up, the Trojan horse it was more of a nuisance and inconvenience. Ditto for Vapor, which was discovered a month after Liberty. Vapor was less malicious; it simply hid your program icons without deleting the programs.

Trojan horses are certainly irritating, but viruses can be catastrophic—not only do they wreak havoc on individual machines, they also spread from one machine to another (hence their name). The first one discovered that was intended for handhelds (PalmPilots, specifically) was Phage.963, documented on September 21, 2000. While Phage is technically a virus, it actually stops itself from being spread. According to McAfee, the leaders in antivirus software, this is what happens:

> You must execute an already infected file that someone has sent to you (beamed, emailed, etc.). Once executed, the virus spreads to all other infected files. If you forwarded any "executable," the infection

will spread; but this is a moot point since the device is now functionally not usable and therefore you can't spread it any further.

Always ready to fill a need, both McAfee and Symantec (another popular software publisher) now offer antivirus software specifically for handhelds. Even though the risk at this point is extremely low, there are two ways to inherit a virus: 1) through an application beamed to you (similar to the Trojan horse concept—never accept beams from a stranger); or 2) by downloading an application to your handheld via a synch or from a direct Internet connection. Antivirus software protects the device by screening the downloaded content as well as data being synched.

Fortunately, if one doesn't have disinfecting software in place, eliminating a virus on a handheld is simple. You simply perform a hard reset of the device, which erases everything but the applications that came on the handheld when you bought it. You should know that doing this not only gets rid of the file containing the virus, it also wipes out all of your data and third-party programs, which can be reinstalled on your next synch. The tangible loss, then, is data that has been inputted but not synched and therefore not backed-up. It is gone forever.

Despite the inconvenience of Trojan horses and viruses, there is one aspect of them relative to handhelds that is not true with PCs: No matter how malicious the virus, it cannot physically damage the mobile device.

This is what is so comforting about viruses for many handhelds. They can't affect the operating system because, unlike the OS on a PC, the operating system on a handheld is burned onto something called ROM (read-only memory). Because the operating system controls the device, and because it cannot be altered, neither can the critical workings of the handheld. In other words, while a PC virus can actually render a computer inoperable (though they rarely do), the worst that can ever happen to a mobile device is that data or applications are lost and need to be resynched. The devices themselves can never be physically damaged.

On a final note, to keep the mobile virus threat in perspective, you should know that in the third quarter of 2001, according to McAfee, there were a total of 10 mobile viruses. Compare that to the 57,000 identified for all other types of computers and the fact that viruses proliferate at a rate of 100 per week.

For the time being, the risk of infection is virtually imperceptible.

30

New Challenges:

The Wireless Privacy Primer

IT'S PROBABLY NOT a very good sign when the president of a country swears off e-mail, citing privacy concerns.

In this case, the country was the United States and it was George W. Bush who, after less than 100 days in office, stated, "I used to be an avid e-mailer. I e-mailed my daughters or e-mailed my father. . . . I don't want those letters to be in the public domain."

President Bush's concern is that since there is no set policy for a president's electronic communications, whatever he writes could be subject to Freedom of Information laws and therefore be made available to the public.

It's interesting how Bush's concerns so perfectly match those of the consumers who fear being tracked when they least expect it.

It's precisely this ambush quality that is the biggest offense, according to electronic marketing master Seth Godin. "Consumers don't care about privacy," he asserts. "They care about being surprised. If you look at all the hassles that have arisen from the privacy debate, they've always been about consumers who get surprised by something a company did that they didn't think it was going to do." It's exactly this "surprise" factor that George W. Bush is protecting himself from.

The degree to which we have to protect ourselves as m-consumers and as wireless users in enterprise is a subject that will be metamorphosing along with the technology. And like politics, privacy is fraught with opinion and often a lack of understanding.

That said, my goal is simply to highlight the most far-reaching issues and their resolutions and in doing so to demonstrate that privacy and wireless are highly compatible.

THE LOCATION VIOLATION

Consider this report of a small auto alarm installation business located in Dallas, Texas. The story was relayed by *The New York Times* and told of how the owner, David Hancock, decided to install tracking devices on his trucks (similar to those discussed on page 171) to keep tabs on his equipment as well as his employees' whereabouts. The latter fact was imparted to his staff when Hancock declared, "Big Brother's keeping an eye on you, and I'm Big Brother."

Well, the Orwellian threat must not have persuaded one of his bunch, because the renegade employee was soon pinpointed at the Million Dollar Saloon strip club, thanks to the tracking device in the company's Dodge pickup truck. "After I fired that one fellow, you bet they all believed me."

Herein lies the debate. Wireless technology allows employers to monitor employees with a dazzling combination of precision equipment that is economically feasible for any company. Employees may not like this, but if they are fully informed, especially before they accept a job, then there isn't a whole lot they can do about it. Corporations would also add that if an employee has nothing to hide, then there's nothing to worry about.

Ever since the Internet entered the workplace, privacy concerns for both employee and employer have mounted, provoked by many companies' desire to monitor electronic mail. Experts for both sides argue the fairness factor effectively, but members of Congress intend to take the issue straight into legislation. This may put the necessary structure in place for the reasonable use of location-sensitivity equipment such as the tracking devices used by the Texas businessman.

The legislation is called the Notice of Electronic Monitoring Act (H.R. 4098). It is a bipartisan bill (most privacy initiatives are) that would require companies to disclose all electronic monitoring practices to their employees. The act does not prohibit any particular type of monitoring, so the use of vehicle tracking devices and location-enabled cell phones in the work environment would still be legal. However, if passed, the employee must be notified of the monitoring frequency, the kind of information collected, and how the information will be stored and used.

Declan McCullagh, *Wired* magazine's Washington bureau head, who specializes in technology and politics, believes that monitoring employees is unobjectionable—as long as employees are informed about it. "It becomes a contractual issue, much like salary, vacation days, and so on," he notes. "All of which are probably more important to an employee than monitoring!" He also adds that while employers have the right, they should be careful, and he questions whether monitoring benefits employers in the long run. "If it becomes too intrusive, employees will rebel and take measures to cloak their activities or communications or, in extremis, simply decide not to work there."

While location tracking and other wireless technologies in the workplace are bothersome, most people agree that they do not constitute an invasion of privacy because the usage is completely disclosed.

While many experts have cooled their opinions on wireless monitoring, they still maintain that if it's not handled properly, it's the consumers who might actually mutiny. I don't think so. The "horrifying scenarios" often paraded in the press are marketing related (like receiving a location-based coupon, such as a pizza deal when you are within geographic range of the restaurant). The descriptions lead you to believe that consumers will have no choice in the matter. They are wrong.

Admittedly, no one is certain how location sensitivity will play out in the consumer arena over the long run, but the consensus is that location-sensitivity marketing will be a completely opt-in arrangement—like a radio, you'll have to tune in and choose your stations. In other words, the handset's location-sensitivity setting will be factory set in the "off" position and the consumer will opt-in and -out by turning the setting off and on. The only exception will be when the numbers *911* are dialed, in which case the location sensitivity will activate automatically.

What's the exception? Look to cell carriers to offer deals to those people who opt for lower cell rates in exchange for the opportunity to be marketed, especially Generation Y and beyond. The location-sensitivity setting on these handsets will always be turned on, with no way to turn off the time-sensitive ads. According to Seth Godin, consumers will get so attached to the advertising that if the ad servers should go down, people will actually call and complain. "That's what advertisers want: consumers complaining when the ads go away."

PRIVACY ON THE WIRELESS WEB

When you consider the anytime, anywhere, functionality of the wireless Web, you get an idea of the frequency with which it will be accessed. It's exactly this exponential increase in usage that alarms pundits who predict an exponential opportunity for privacy violations.

Again, unlikely. I actually predict that privacy will become a marketing advantage as retailers and content sites brag about their lack of tracking features and other noninvasive procedures to demonstrate their superiority over the competition.

What will make this easy to implement is the Platform for Privacy Preferences Project (or P3P), the brainchild of one of the most influential governing bodies of the Internet, the World Wide Web Consortium. P3P is an elegant solution that attempts to let users maintain control over the personal information Web sites glean from their visits. And if you as a visitor don't like the site's policies, you can opt-out before you even enter.

In simple terms, P3P is a privacy matching service, only the matching is speedy and transparent. You, as a user, would sign on to the P3P site, and answer a set of multiple-choice questions regarding your attitudes toward traditional privacy policies. For example, you may be asked if you'd be willing to shop at a site that collects your personally identifiable information forever, or if it's okay with you that a Web site aggregates information about your buying habits so that they can tailor special offers to you based on your interests (but does not sell or share the data with third parties).

Just as you, the user, establish your preferences, Web site owners also respond to a lengthy query that focuses on how they handle the data. This is done so that (according to the P3P mission statement) the user can establish a "clear snapshot of how a site handles personal information about its users," instead of the site's interminably long legalese.

The results of the visitor's answers and the Web site's policies are what they term "snapshots," which are read automatically by a P3P-enabled browser. If there is an incompatibility (such as the fact that the site sells their e-mails' addresses to third parties), you are made aware of the discrepancy as soon as you hit the home page.

The concept solves myriad problems, and it shows promise for a seamless implementation since the technology and is standardization are backed by techno-heavyweights such as Microsoft, America Online, and hard-to-impress organizations like the Center for Democracy and Technology.

Needless to say, P3P also has its critics, and their points are well taken. They say that P3P is just another effort to self-regulate in an effort to circumvent far more strict federal laws.

Another weakness is that no one is auditing or authenticating the sites' compliance. P3P, then, in fact is an honor policy system, not much different from the privacy infrastructure in effect now. It is for this reason that P3P promises, such as "a user having control over their personal information," gives P3P adversaries the heebie-jeebies. While P3P was originally developed for the wired world, its timing is perfect for the wireless revolution.

Most Web-enabled devices lack the screen real estate required to download a privacy policy in just a few clicks. In fact, most policies, when actually printed on standard letter-size paper, exceed six pages. Clearly, this won't work on a cell phone's four-line display. Therefore, if consumers want a base-level assurance of privacy compatibility between them and your site, P3P is a viable solution.

THOSE UNEXPECTED PRIVACY VIOLATIONS

While I focused on the possibility of a strict privacy policy as a marketing point and how a program such as P3P would support that, I don't want to imply that this wraps up the issue of wireless technology and privacy.

Quite the contrary. I would wager that there will be many privacy glitches as the technology get adopted. A perfect example occurred in 2000 (when the wireless Web was still new), eliciting a major techno-guffaw from two of the country's biggest cell phone companies.

It was discovered in 2000 that Sprint PCS and AT&T users, when visiting a Web site using their Internet-enabled phones, were automatically giving dot.coms their cell phone numbers. The root of the problem was attached to the microbrowser that was being used by most cellular carriers. Programmed at the time by Phone.com (now Openwave), the microbrowser required a unique identifier when Web pages were downloaded to the cellular device. While some carriers such as Bell Atlantic and AirTouch (now Verizon) changed the ID numbers (to protect their subscribers) by using a randomly selected group of digits, others such as Sprint opted for the ease of using the cell number as the ID.

The primary privacy violation is that a Web site could collect this data and initiate an unsolicited direct marketing call to the customer on the cell phone the visitor was surfing from. Even more invasive, it could track a customer's behavior on the site and sell that data to a third party, along with the cell phone number.

Sadly, most customers remain unaware of this issue, since the number broadcasting goes on behind the scenes. Furthermore, the fix is a simple one, as proven by Verizon, which sends out a random number when a user connects to the Web.

Most of the major carriers have since vowed to patch the problem.

But I am citing this example to show that there are areas to wireless privacy that will continue to surface.

I don't believe that AT&T and Sprint decided to use subscribers' phone numbers as identifiers for any reason other than simplicity for the carrier. Had they been advised of the repercussion, they never would have deployed the technology. Can I prove this? Yes, by using basic business principles. There was no financial advantage to the carriers, and the discovery was a source of embarrassment. That's not much of a revenue strategy.

The point is that these infractions will continue because no technology deployment is without flaws. Like the wired Web, any situation that makes for a catchy headline will be well publicized (such as the occasional mishap on eBay, which may account for a minor percentage of their sales but nonetheless is featured on the nightly news).

In the beginning, the big privacy stories will be similar to the AT&T/Sprint issue just discussed. Wireless privacy's biggest challenge will be keeping the headlines in perspective.

THE PRIVACY FOR CASH TRADE-OFF

Would you be willing to let companies that supply you with services know more about you if that meant you got a discount?

Here's a hypothetical that will shortly be a reality. As you know, car insurance rates are based on your age, accident history, and where you live. Because this is a statistical assessment based on assumptions instead of real data, it is not always fair. What if your insurer said, "If you install a wireless tracking device on your car for a couple hundred dollars, we will reduce your rates based on how you actually drive"? The device in question would measure not only miles, but where you went (the risk of driving in high-crime areas), when you drove (more day than night or vice versa), how fast you drove (including speed limit infringements), and actual miles driven.

That's a lot of information; however, you're told that if you drive less than 5,000 miles a year, always obey the speed limit, rarely drive at night, and frequent only safer neighborhoods, it could mean as much as a 50 percent reduction in rates. Worth it?

It depends on the privacy trade-off ratio. For me, 50 percent would be worth it, but 10 percent would probably not. Every customer will have a different threshold, and that's the point. Businesses, like car insurance, will use wireless to reduce their risks, but in doing so, you benefit financially.

However, one of the grayer issues of wireless privacy, an example of which is also related to cars, is precisely the type you should expect to see more of. The scenario occurs when consumers are fully cognizant of the use of wireless technology, then learn the data has been used against them, it causes outrage. By definition, there has been no security breach because of an informed consent; however, when the corroborating data is used against the person, it stings.

This true story originates from New Haven, Connecticut, where James Turner rented a minivan from Acme Rent-a-Car in October 2000. Perhaps because he was a regular customer of Acme's, he failed to notice a new stipulation in bold print at the top of the rental contract. It read, "Vehicles in excess of the posted limit will be charged a $150 fee per occurrence. All our vehicles are GPS equipped."

Unfortunately, Turner didn't understand the breadth of GPS, that integrated systems like the ones you read about on page 171 that include GPS are capable of much more than global positioning. Driving habits are also recorded. In fact, the warning should have included this, so that's certainly a point in Turner's favor.

Nonetheless, Acme's speed threshold of safety is 79 miles per hour. Anything above that they consider "excessive speed" and as such charge a $150 penalty for each infraction. It wasn't until $450 was deducted from the debit card that Turner used to pay for the rental that he was made aware of Acme's notice of his behavior. Because Turner drove from Connecticut to Virginia, the car, along with his driving habits, was tracked across seven states. When Turner realized this, he said, "It felt creepy."

The larger argument is that Turner was forced to give up his privacy in exchange for the privilege of renting from Acme. Had he been more cognizant of the depth of Acme's wireless tracking process, he could have gone to at least five other New Haven car rental agencies that don't use tracking, according to a report in the *New Haven Advocate,* the folks who broke this story.

That will work fine for now, but what about five years out, when all the car rental agencies include these economically feasible and technologically reliable devices in their fleet? Consider the advantages for the car rental agencies. They will have a much better chance of seeing that their renters abide by speeding laws; they will be alerted when their vehicles cross boundaries for which they are not approved; and they will be able to account for each and every one of their vehicles in just a few minutes. For these reasons, this type of wireless tracking for the car rental agencies is inevitable. Now, they may not impose fines for breaches, as Acme does, but they'll nonetheless have an entire map of where you drove and when . . . and that is information you will have to be willing to give up in exchange for renting a car.

Here's another scenerio. As mentioned in previous chapters, radio frequency identification tags will soon be sewn into clothing as it is made. There are supply chain tracking benefits to this, as well as equal incentives on the marketing side. With RFID readers installed in dressing and fitting rooms, stores can retrieve a daily report indicating exactly which items were tried on. That can be reconciled with a daily sales report to analyze why people may be trying on an item of clothing but not buying it (for example, the design may be flawed somehow).

Now, it's important to note that at first the RFID readers would be anonymous. The store owners won't know who is trying on the items, but they will know that "at 11:10am a customer brought into the dressing room 2 large Ralph Lauren polo shirts, one large, one extra large, both turquoise, leaving the dressing room at 11:17am."

There is a corollary speculation that the companies will integrate RFID technology into their loyalty club cards so that better customers can be easily identified. Because RFID doesn't require any line of sight, readers can be stationed at strategic points in the store so that customer service employees can be made aware of their presence. No one is doing it yet, but it's relatively easy and cheap, and the RFID technology suppliers are ready the moment retail is.

Now, with the loyalty club card in the shopper's wallet this customer who just walked into the dressing room with the two polo shirts can instantly be identified by name. For fear of retribution from privacy advocates, stores will probably post (in some vague wording) that they "use radio frequency monitioring." But the genuine bottom line of such a practice will escape most.

Essentially, we can think of this practice as "mandatory compliance," even though informed. Not, by definition, a privacy invasion, though it may feel like one. That is the threat in the wireless privacy frontier.

Afterword

IF YOU FINISH this book with only one thought it should be this: Wireless is not a revolution. It is a transformation.

Let's clarify the difference by understanding that the Internet was a genuine revolution. From the time it was made available to the general public, circa 1993–94, to widespread adaptation was less than 36 months. Since revolutions are defined as a sudden, radical change, the Internet qualifies not only because of e-mail, the Web, and the ability to zap a file from one part of the planet to another but also in the way the Net has inalterably influenced how we think and communicate.

Accordingly, if the dot.com bombs of 2000 proved one aspect of business, it is this: The faster the change, the faster the failure.

The reality is that wireless has been around for over a century, when wirefree telegraphy was invented in the mid-1890s by Guglielmo Marconi. It has since influenced virtually every aspect of communications technology.

Remember when home telephones were bolted to the wall? When grocery checkers input prices manually instead of reading them wirelessly by a beam of light?

In addition to not being a revolution, it's important to note that wireless is not a technology for the sake of technology either. Wirefree extends that which already exists through giving it new functionally and enriched value. Consider that home phones now roam and cash registers can now log far more data than just a price. Wireless makes any use more useful.

On its own, wireless should be considered an additional information channel. But wireless is never alone. It always converges with existing technology, liberating whatever it is matched with.

Despite the zeal with which wirefree is being embraced, we must be careful to remember that wireless is not a culture on its own. However, it is wildly affecting the culture of business. The first way will be the sense of freedom for employer and employee, who will now have friction-free access to one other and the data that keeps their enterprises flowing. For this reason, wireless promotes a peace of mind that few technologies have ever achieved.

So when someone asks you if this book is about the wireless revolution, you can respond "no." Instead, it is about the unstrung possibilities of a technology we have embraced for over a hundred years.

Wireless is a technology evolution.

Section 4

■

TERMINOLOGY

QUICK

REFERENCE

3G: Third-generation network. 3G has data rates up to 2 Mbps, which is plenty to support high-speed Internet access, videoconferencing, and full-motion video. As of 2002, most of the United States was on 2G or 2.5G.

802.11a: The standard developed after 802.11b. I know, I know, "a" after "b." The important difference is that the data rates are up to five times faster and the standard operates in a different frequency (5 GHz) from that of 802.11b. As such, it will get around conflicts with groups of devices sharing 2.4 GHz, which is what 802.11b runs on.

802.11b: The most popular type of wireless network standard, which gained popularity starting in 2000 because it was much faster than its sibling 802.11a.

Access Point: Key component of a wireless local-area network. It is the hub that wirelessly links portable devices to the "big computer in the back." Think of it as a relay station. These hubs are placed wherever people need to access, therefore a user must be within a certain distance. Since they have a limited range, there are many in one wireless LAN installation. Also referred to as "APs."

Bluetooth: A specification that allows for short-range wireless connections (up to 30 feet because of its limited power consumption) among all different types of devices, such as printers to computers, cell phone to headsets, local-area network to a handheld device. Bluetooth is often thought of as the "cable killer" because of the idea that it will eventually eliminate all hardwired connections. Furthermore, Bluetooth devices in the same circumference constitute ad hoc networks, letting people share files easily.

Developed by Ericsson, Nokia, Intel, Toshiba, and IBM. Named after the Danish King Harald Bluetooth.

Bandwidth: The nontechnical definition, and how it is used in this book, is the amount of information that can be transmitted at one time. Low-bandwidth devices include 56K modems (standard on most PCs). High-bandwidth devices include office T1 lines and local-area networks that run at 11 Mbps, which is up to 200 times faster than a 56K modem.

Broadband: High-speed connectivity that can handle several types of data at once, such as voice and video.

GSM: Stands for Global Standard for Mobile. This is the primary network type used in Europe and Asia (except Japan) and thus is infiltrating other countries, including the United States.

iMode: A service launched by NTT DoCoMo in Japan in 1999 that has become a smashing success among the Japanese. Part of the reason it is so successful is that the entire system is proprietary and that control has been key to the fact that the system works to delivers on its promise.

Infrared/IrDA: A way of linking two devices using only a beam of light, no cables. When linked, the devices can exchange data up to 10 to 20 feet. For example, most handheld units, including PalmPilots and Handspring handhelds, have infrared options to beam data and programs from one device to another.

Landline: A traditional wired phone line. What you have in your home or office.

Local-Area Network: Also known as LAN. A computer network that covers a specific location, such as a company's offices. They are high speed and allow for file sharing and access to the Internet, printers, and storage devices. Non-wireless networks are usually connected by Ethernet cabling. Wirefree LANs use access points (see above) instead of cables. Most companies are moving toward a combination of wired and wireless. The agreed standard is the 802.11 family, of which currently there is 802.11b and 802.11a. (See each.)

ReFLEX: The first two-way paging system that allows pagers to respond to messages, initiate them, and even confirm receipt. Is alpha-numeric. Invented by Motorola. Popular with executives and for remote vending machine data collection.

RFID: Radio frequency identification. A way of transmitting information using radio waves, which eliminates any "line-of-sight" issues. For instance, an item with an RFID tag can be tucked in a box but still accounted for. Up to 50 tags can be counted per second. The tags are also extremely durable and can even have data written to them. Often compared to bar codes, which require a line of sight (think of your supermarket scanner), offer only a minimum amount of data, and are easily damaged, hence unreadable. If they become cheap enough, RFID in the far future should replace bar codes.

Short Message Service: See SMS.

Smart Device: Generic term to describe a handheld instrument that has reasonable processing power, a wireless Internet connection, mobile voice capability, and a display that is easily legible. Furthermore, features common on a PalmPilot-type device, such as scheduling and contact management, would also be included. Future version of the "dream device" will include two-way videoconferencing and a digital camera for still photos. The "perfect" smart device does not, in my opinion, yet exist. Sometimes referred to as "smart phones."

SMS: Short message service. A staple of GSM cellular service; allows users to exchange text messages up to 160 characters long that show up instantly on the device of the recipient. In other words, it's not like e-mail, which has to be opened. Also offered at very low flat rates per message. Slowly gaining U.S. popularity but plagued with the problem of different networks—in other words, Sprint and AT&T users can't exchange SMS missives. This is not the case in Europe and other countries where they use one standard, GSM, and can therefore swap messages easily.

Telematics: Term used to describe wireless communication built into vehicles. Includes tracking devices and global positioning systems. The most famous telematics service provider is OnStar.

Telemetrics: A wireless technology that remotely monitors or controls a device or exchanges information without human intervention.

Transponder: Used with RFID technology. A battery-powered device that transmits information in response to signals emanating from an RFID reader. The Mobil Speedpass "black barrels" are transponders. They are also tags attached to cars (for toll payments). Transponder is a combination of *trans*mitter and res*ponder.*

WAP: A system designed to deliver Web-based content to mobile devices with Internet connectivity. Basically scales down Web info so that it can be read on a handheld. Talked about widely but had only minimal penetration by the end of 2001.

Wirefree/Wireless: Any communication or data exchange that takes place without cables.

WLAN: Wireless local-area network. A group of computers that are "connected" using a combination of radio waves and transmitters to keep the data flowing from the hardwired main computer network "in the back" to the roaming computer and handheld devices "in the front."

WML: Is the medium by which WAP devices work. WML is to wireless what HTML (as the standard interface) is to the Web.

WPAN: Wireless personal-area network. Occurs when two or more devices connect wirefree. They are usually ad hoc. When two people beam data to each other using their PalmPilots, at that moment they have created a WPAN. Also, when Bluetooth devices communicate, that is often referred to as a WPAN.

WWAN: Wireless wide-area network. Used to describe a network with a large geographical range. The biggest are those run by the cellular phone companies. What's confusing is that some technologists refer to a network built in a city as "wide area," while others diminish the size reference considerably by referring to a wireless network installation of several offices of the same company as "wide area."

Index